Welsh Bus Handbook

British Bus Publishing

Body codes used in the Bus Handbook series:

Type:
A	Articulated vehicle
B	Bus, either single-deck or double-deck
BC	Express - high-back seating in a bus body
C	Coach - high-back seating
CN	Coach - low floor (Niederflur)
M	Minibus with design capacity of 16 seats or less
N	Low-floor bus (Niederflur), either single-deck or double-deck
O	Open-top bus (CO = convertible open-top; PO = Partial open-top)

Seating capacity is then shown. For double-decks the upper deck quantity is followed by the lower deck.

Door position:-
C	Centre entrance/exit
D	Dual doorway
F	Front entrance/exit
R	Rear entrance/exit (no distinction between doored and open)
T	Three or more access points

Equipment:-
L	Lift for wheelchair
M	Mail compartment
T	Toilet
TV	Training vehicle; RV Recovery vehicle (only former buses listed)

e.g. - B32/28F is a double-deck bus with thirty-two seats upstairs, twenty-eight down and a front entrance/exit.
N43D is a low-floor bus with two doorways.

Re-registrations:-
Where a vehicle has gained new index marks the details are listed at the end of each fleet showing the current mark, followed in sequence by those previously carried starting with the original mark.

Other books in the series:
The Scottish Bus Handbook
The Ireland & Islands Bus Handbook
The North East Bus Handbook
The Yorkshire Bus Handbook
The Lancashire, Cumbria and Manchester Bus Handbook
The Merseyside and Cheshire Bus Handbook
The North and West Midlands Bus Handbook
The East Midlands Bus Handbook
The South Midlands Bus Handbook
The Welsh Bus Handbook
The Chilterns and West Anglia Bus Handbook
The East Anglia Bus Handbook
The South East Bus Handbook
The South West Bus Handbook
The South Central Bus Handbook

Annual books are produced for the major groups:
The Stagecoach Bus Handbook
The FirstGroup Bus Handbook
The Arriva Bus Handbook
The National Express Handbook

Associated series:
The Hong Kong Bus Handbook
The Leyland Lynx Handbook
The Model Bus Handbook
The Postbus Handbook
The Toy & Model Bus Handbook - Volume 1 - Early Diecasts
The Fire Brigade Handbook (fleet list of each local authority fire brigade)
The Fire Brigade Handbook - Special Appliances Volume 1
The Fire Brigade Handbook - Special Appliances Volume 2
The Police Range Rover Handbook

The Welsh Bus Handbook

The Welsh Bus Handbook is part of The Bus Handbook series that details the fleets of selected bus and coach operators. These Bus Handbooks are published by *British Bus Publishing*. The current list is shown on page 2. Handbooks for FirstGroup, Arriva and Stagecoach are also published annually along with a books detailing the operators who provide vehicles on National Express service.

Quality photographs for inclusion in the series are welcome and a fee is payable. The publishers unfortunately cannot accept responsibility for any loss and request you show your name on each picture or slide.

To keep the fleet information up to date we recommend the Ian Allan publication, **Buses** published monthly, or for more detailed information, the PSV Circle monthly news sheets.

The writer and publisher would be glad to hear from readers should any information be available which corrects or enhances that given in this publication.

Series Editor: Bill Potter
Principal Editors for *The Welsh Bus Handbook*: David Donati & John Jones

Acknowledgments:
We are grateful to Keith Grimes, Ian Kirby, Simon Nicholas, John Mays, The Crosville Enthusiasts' Club, the PSV Circle and the operating companies for their assistance in the compilation of this book.

The cover photograph is by Tony Wilson, rear cover by John Jones

1st Edition - 1994 - 1-897990-08-1
2nd Edition - 1996 (South Wales) - 1-89700-18-9
2nd Edition - 1996 (North & West Wales) - 1-89700-19-7

ISBN 1 897990 67 7 (3rd Edition)
Published by *British Bus Publishing Ltd*
The Vyne, 16 St Margaret's Drive, Wellington,
Telford, Shropshire, TF1 3PH

Telephone: 01952 255669 - Facsimile 01952 222397 - www.britishbuspublishing.co.uk
© British Bus Publishing Ltd, May 2000

CONTENTS

Alpine	5
Arriva Cymru	8
Arthur Thomas	18
Arvonia	19
Bebb	21
Berwyn	22
Brian Isaac	23
Bridgend Bus Company	24
Browns of Builth	25
Bryn Melyn	26
Burrows	27
Bysiau Cwm Taf	28
Bysiau Ffoshelig	29
Caelloi	30
Cardiff Bus	31
Cerbydau Carreglefn Coaches	36
Cerbydau Cenarth Coaches	37
Clynnog & Trefor	38
Coastal Continental	41
Cross Gates Coaches	41
D&G Coaches	42
Diamond Glantawe	43
Eagles & Crawford	45
East End	46
Edwards Bros	46
Edwards Coaches	49
Ellis Travel	51
Express Motors	52
Ferris Holidays	54
First Cymru	55
G H A Coaches	66
G M	68
Gavenny Bus	68
George Edwards & Son	70
Goodsir	71
Glyn Williams	73
Gwyn Williams	74
Hawkes	76
Henly's	78
Howells Coaches	79
IBT - Kingfisher	80
James Brothers	82
John's Travel	82
Jones Llanfaethlu	84
Jones Login	86
D Jones & Son	86
E Jones & Sons	88
W E Jones & Son	89
K M P	91
Ken Hopkins	92
Lewis Whitland	93
Lewis y Llan	94
Llithfaen Motors	95
P & O Lloyd	96
Llynfi Coaches	97
Longs	98
M & H Travel	100
Mansel David	101
Martin	102
Merlyn's	103
Meyers	104
Mid Wales Travel	105
Midway Motors	106
Nefyn Coaches	106
Newport Transport	108
Oare's of Holywell	111
Owens Motors	112
Pencoed Travel	113
Phil Anslow Travel	114
Phillips	116
Pied Bull Coaches	117
Porthcawl Omnibus Co	118
Pullman Coaches	119
Richards Bros	120
Shamrock	123
Shuttle	128
Silcox	129
Silver Star	133
Sixty-Sixty	134
Stagecoach Red & White	135
Summerdale	144
Tanat Valley	145
Thomas Bros	147
Thomas Coaches	148
Townlynx	151
Vale of Llangollen	152
Venture Travel	123
Voel Coaches	154
Watts	155
Wilkins Travel	156
Williams Bala	158
Williams	159
Index to vehicles	161

ALPINE

Hughes Brothers (Llanrwst & Trefriw) Ltd, Builder Street West, Llandudno, Conwy, LL30 1HH

JPL105K	Leyland Atlantean PDR1A/1Spl	Park Royal	O43/24D	1972	Crosville Cymru, 1995
HEN867N	Leyland Leopard PSU4C/2R	Willowbrook Warrior (1991)	B44F	1975	Arriva Cymru, 1998
TBX713	Leyland Leopard PSU3C/4R	Willowbrook Warrior (1988)	B53F	1976	Davies Bros. Pencader, 1999
MBX447	Leyland Leopard PSU3C/4R	Willowbrook Warrior (1989)	B53F	1976	Davies Bros. Pencader, 1999
VUP850	Bedford YMT	Duple Dominant	C53F	1976	Creams, Porthmadog, 1990
SMS125P	Daimler Fleetline CRG6LXB	Alexander AD	B44/31F	1976	Highland Country, 1997
NDL654R	Bristol VRT/SL3/6LXB	Eastern Coach Works	B43/31F	1977	Solent Blue Line, 1997
OWE856R	Bristol VRT/SL3/501	Eastern Coach Works	B43/31F	1977	Empire Goldstar, Llandudno Jct, 1996
PUF586R	Bristol VRT/SL3/6LXB	Eastern Coach Works	B43/31F	1977	Caelloi, Pwllheli, 1995
RWA860R	Bristol VRT/SL3/501	Eastern Coach Works	B43/31F	1977	Empire Goldstar, Llandudno Jct, 1996
RWA861R	Bristol VRT/SL3/501	Eastern Coach Works	B43/31F	1977	Empire Goldstar, Llandudno Jct, 1996
WDM352R	Bristol VRT/SL3/501	Eastern Coach Works	B43/31F	1977	Happy Days, Woodseaves, 1995
BPT927S	Bristol VRT/SL3/6LXB	Eastern Coach Works	B43/31F	1977	Northumbria, 1994
BPT928S	Bristol VRT/SL3/6LXB	Eastern Coach Works	B43/31F	1977	Northumbria, 1994
TDT863S	Bristol VRT/SL3/501	Eastern Coach Works	B43/31F	1977	Empire Goldstar, Llandudno Jct, 1996
PJC630S	Ford R1114	Duple Dominant II	C53F	1978	Creams, Porthmadog, 1990
CPT737S	Bristol VRT/SL3/6LXB	Eastern Coach Works	B43/31F	1978	Northumbria, 1994
URF677S	Bristol VRT/SL3/501	Eastern Coach Works	B43/31F	1978	PMT, 1994
FTU376T	Bristol VRT/SL3/501	Eastern Coach Works	B43/31F	1978	Crosville Cymru, 1996
FTU386T	Bristol VRT/SL3/501	Eastern Coach Works	B43/31F	1978	North Western, 1997
HUP768T	Bristol VRT/SL3/6LXB	Eastern Coach Works	B42/31F	1978	Northumbria, 1994
WDA981T	Leyland Fleetline FE30AGR	MCW	B43/33F	1978	Stuarts, Dukinfield, 1997
XTB5T	Leyland Atlantean AN68A/1R	East Lancashire	B45/31F	1978	Warrington, 1998
XTB6T	Leyland Atlantean AN68A/1R	East Lancashire	B45/31F	1978	Warrington, 1998
XTB8T	Leyland Atlantean AN68A/1R	East Lancashire	B45/31F	1978	Warrington, 1998
XTB9T	Leyland Atlantean AN68A/1R	East Lancashire	B45/31F	1978	Warrington, 1998
XTB11T	Leyland Atlantean AN68A/1R	East Lancashire	B45/31F	1978	Warrington, 1998
GMB392T	Leyland National 11351A/1R (6HLXB)		B49F	1979	Arriva North West, 1999
KMA395T	Leyland National 11351A/1R (6HLXB)		B49F	1979	Arriva North West, 1999
KMA396T	Leyland National 11351A/1R (6HLXB)		B49F	1979	Arriva North West, 1999
KMA397T	Leyland National 11351A/1R (6HLXB)		B49F	1979	Arriva North West, 1999
TCC2T	Ford R1114	Duple Dominant II	C53F	1979	Creams, Porthmadog, 1990
BRC838T	Bristol VRT/SL3/6LXB	Eastern Coach Works	B43/31F	1979	Wall's, Northenden, 1995
BRC840T	Bristol VRT/SL3/6LXB	Eastern Coach Works	B43/31F	1979	Wall's, Northenden, 1995
DWY140T	Bristol VRT/CLO/6LXD	Eastern Coach Works	D40/01F	1979	Ieuan Williams, Deiniolen, 1999
JMB406T	Bristol VRT/SL3/501	Eastern Coach Works	B43/31F	1979	North Western, 1997
OBR771T	Bristol VRT/SL3/6LXB	Eastern Coach Works	B43/31F	1979	Tees & District, 1994

Alpine operate three open-top Leyland Atlanteans including VTD720T, an East Lancashire-bodied example formerly at Rossendale. The walls of Conwy Castle provide the impressive backdrop to this bus, which is seen on the Llandudno and Conwy tour on behalf of Guide Friday whose colours it carries. *John Jones*

Alpine is the second largest operator in north Wales after Arriva Cymru, though much of the fleet is primarily used on school contracts. Double-decks, mostly with Eastern Coach Works bodies, constitute a substantial part of the fleet. CPT737S is a 1978 Bristol VRT, one of four acquired from Northumbria in 1994. It is seen leaving Llandudno depot. *John Jones*

SAS858T	Leyland Fleetline FE30AGR	Eastern Coach Works	B43/32F	1979	Highland Scottish, 1999
UAS68T	Leyland Fleetline FE30AGR	Eastern Coach Works	B43/32F	1979	Highland Scottish, 1999
VTD720T	Leyland Atlantean AN68A/1R	East Lancashire	O43/32F	1979	Rossendale, 1994
XSJ664T	Leyland Fleetline FE30AGR	Northern Counties	B44/31F	1979	Green Buses, Bournemouth, 1995
ECS884V	Leyland Fleetline FE30AGR	Northern Counties	B44/31F	1979	Green Buses, Bournemouth, 1995
PCA419V	Bristol VRT/SL3/501	Eastern Coach Works	B43/31F	1979	Empire Goldstar, Llandudno Jct, 1996
PCA422V	Bristol VRT/SL3/501	Eastern Coach Works	B43/31F	1980	North Western, 1997
PCA425V	Bristol VRT/SL3/501	Eastern Coach Works	B43/31F	1979	North Western, 1997
GRF712V	Bristol VRT/SL3/501	Eastern Coach Works	BC39/28F	1980	PMT, 1994
RMA442V	Bristol VRT/SL3/501	Eastern Coach Works	B43/31F	1980	Crosville Cymru, 1996
KUX221W	Leyland Leopard PSU5D/4R	Duple Dominant IV	C57F	1980	Whittle Bus & Coach, 2000
-	Leyland Leopard PSU5D/5R	Duple Dominant II	C57F	1980	Empire Goldstar, Llandudno Jct, 1996
HJB460W	Bristol VRT/SL3/6LXB	Eastern Coach Works	B43/31F	1980	Wallis, Northenden, 1995
HJB463W	Bristol VRT/SL3/6LXB	Eastern Coach Works	B43/31F	1980	Wallis, Northenden, 1995
BEY7W	Bedford YMT	Duple Dominant	B53F	1981	Arriva Cymru, 1998
BMA520W	Bristol VRT/SL3/6LXB	Eastern Coach Works	B43/31F	1981	Arriva Cymru, 1998
WTU499W	Bristol VRT/SL3/501	Eastern Coach Works	B43/31F	1981	North Western, 1997
YMB501W	Bristol VRT/SL3/6LXB	Eastern Coach Works	B43/31F	1981	Arriva Cymru, 1999
YMB503W	Bristol VRT/SL3/6LXB	Eastern Coach Works	B43/31F	1981	Arriva Cymru, 1999
TKM109X	Bedford YMT	Wadham Stringer Vanguard	B61F	1982	Maidstone, 1987
TKM110X	Bedford YMT	Wadham Stringer Vanguard	B61F	1982	Maidstone, 1987
CKM137Y	Bedford YMT	Wright TT	B61F	1982	Coombs, Weston, 1998
TIB9157	Bova EL26/581	Bova Europa	C53F	1982	Tourmaster, Crowland, 1999
FIL4161	Leyland Tiger TRCTL11/2R	Plaxton Paramount 3200E	C53F	1983	Empire Goldstar, Llandudno Jct, 1996
JEY554Y	Leyland Tiger TRCTL11/3R	Plaxton Paramount 3500	C49F	1983	Arriva Cymru, 1999
A698AWB	Bedford YMT	Duple Dominant	B55F	1984	George Edwards, Bwlchgwyn, 1998
A801LEY	Volvo B10M-61	Duple Laser	C57F	1984	
A942TYA	DAF SB2300DHS585	Plaxton Paramount 3200	C53F	1984	Regina, Blaenau Ffestiniog, 1997
B567NCC	Bova EL28/581	Duple Calypso	C53F	1984	
B176WYV	Leyland Cub CU435	Wadham Stringer Vanguard	B32F	1984	Empire Goldstar, Llandudno Jct, 1996
B925HFF	DAF SB2300DHS585	Plaxton Paramount 3200	C53F	1984	Regina, Blaenau Ffestiniog, 1997
D257WEY	Bedford YNT	Duple 320	C53F	1987	
E661KCX	DAF SB2305DHS585	Duple 340	C57F	1988	Redwing, Camberwell, 1993
JAZ9864	DAF SB2305DHS585	Duple 340	C57F	1988	Redwing, Camberwell, 1993

Alpine operate a small coach fleet for tours and excursions in addition to the service fleet. Pictured with its Select index mark is Dennis Javelin T7ALP which carries a Marcopolo Explorer 2 body. The Royal Red name comes from a former Llandudno operator which was purchased some time ago. *John Jones*

F62AVV	Iveco Daily 49.10	Robin Hood City Nippy	B25F	1989	Ribble Valley Carriage Co. 1997
F42DJC	Iveco Daily 49.10	Robin Hood City Nippy	B25F	1989	
F43DJC	Iveco Daily 49.10	Robin Hood City Nippy	B25F	1989	
F916TTP	Mercedes-Benz 811D	Robin Hood	B25F	1990	
G142JCC	Iveco Daily 49.10	Phoenix	BC25F	1990	
G761HJC	Hestair Duple SDA1512	Duple 425	C57F	1990	
G762HJC	Hestair Duple SDA1512	Duple 425	C57F	1990	
M515ACC	Mercedes-Benz 709D	Marshall C19	B25F	1994	
N3ALP	Volvo B10M-62	Plaxton Première 320	C55F	1996	
N4ALP	Volvo B10M-62	Plaxton Première 320	C55F	1996	
P5ALP	Volvo B10M-62	Plaxton Première 350	C55F	1997	
R6ALP	Dennis Javelin	Marcopolo Explorer	C57F	1998	
T7ALP	Dennis Javelin	Marcopolo Explorer 2	C57F	1999	
W9ALP	MAN 18-310 HOCL-R	Marcopolo Continental 340	C57F	2000	

Special event vehicles

JC2772	Guy Wolf CFP	J Roberts	B20F	1935	preservation, 1996
CCC596	Guy Otter LL0D	Roe	FB25F	1954	preservation, 1993
WND477	Leyland Tiger Cub PSUC1/2	Duple Britannia	C41F	1958	preservation, 1996
691DDE	Leyland Atlantean PDR1A/1	Northern Counties	O43/30D	1970	Wall's, Sharston, 1993

Previous Registrations:

1862HX	XFR842V	JEY554Y	UTN956Y, HCC852
691DDE	STO534H	MBX447	MUS104P
CCC596	From new	TBX713	MFR303P
FIL4161	RNY308Y	VUP850	KJC364P
JAZ9864	E663KCX		

Depots: Builder Street West, Llandudno; Central Coach Garage, Llanrwst; Marsh Road, Rhyl and Beacon TE, Tywyn.
Livery: Green and cream (buses and contract vehicles), white (coaches).

The Welsh Bus Handbook

ARRIVA CYMRU

ARRIVA gwasanaethu Cymru / serving Wales

Arriva Cymru Ltd, Imperial Buildings, Glan-y-Mor Road,
Llandudno Junction, LL31 9RU

Single deck vehicles:

SDD24	N24FWU	DAF SB220LC550	Northern Counties Paladin	B49F	1995	West Coast Ms, Campbeltown, 1996
SDD25	N25FWU	DAF SB220LC550	Northern Counties Paladin	B49F	1995	West Coast Ms, Campbeltown, 1996
STL25	DJN25X	Leyland Tiger TRCTL11/2R	East Lancashire (1992)	B53F	1982	Arriva Midlands North, 2000
SLC27	K27EWC	Leyland Lynx LX2R11C15Z4R	Leyland Lynx 2	B49F	1992	Colchester, 1994
SLG28	H28MJN	Leyland Lynx LX2R11G15Z4R	Leyland Lynx	B49F	1991	Colchester, 1994
SLG29	H29MJN	Leyland Lynx LX2R11G15Z4R	Leyland Lynx	B49F	1991	Colchester, 1994
SLC30	H130LPU	Leyland Lynx LX2R11C15Z4R	Leyland Lynx 2	B49F	1990	Colchester, 1994
SLC37	E37EVW	Leyland Lynx LX2R11C15Z4R	Leyland Lynx	B49F	1988	Colchester, 1994
SLC38	G38YHJ	Leyland Lynx LX2R11C15Z4R	Leyland Lynx	B49F	1989	Colchester, 1994
SLC39	G39YHJ	Leyland Lynx LX2R11C15Z4R	Leyland Lynx	B49F	1989	Colchester, 1994
SLC40	G40YHJ	Leyland Lynx LX2R11C15Z4R	Leyland Lynx	B49F	1989	Colchester, 1994
SLC41	G41VME	Leyland Lynx LX2R11C15Z4S	Leyland Lynx	B49F	1989	Arriva Southern Counties (KT), 1999
STL42	A42SMA	Leyland Tiger TRCTL11/2R	East Lancashire (1992)	B53F	1984	Arriva Midlands North, 2000
SDD47	M847RCP	DAF SB220LC550	Northern Counties Paladin	B49F	1995	Citybus, Southampton, 1996
SDD49	M849RCP	DAF SB220LC550	Northern Counties Paladin	B49F	1995	Citybus, Southampton, 1996
SLC49	E49WEM	Leyland Lynx LX112L10ZR1R	Leyland Lynx	B49F	1988	Devaway, Bretton, 1998

SLC66-70 — Leyland Lynx LX112L10ZR1R — Leyland Lynx — B49F — 1989 — Chesterfield, 1995

66	F66FKW	67w	F67FKW	68	F68FKW	69	F69FKW
70	F70FKW						

CTC68	IIL9168	Leyland Tiger TRCL10/3ARZM	Plaxton Paramount 3200 III	C53F	1989	Maidstone & District, 1997
CTC69	IIL9169	Leyland Tiger TRCL10/3ARZM	Plaxton Paramount 3200 III	C53F	1989	Maidstone & District, 1997
SLC73	H733HWK	Leyland Lynx LX2R11C15Z4R	Leyland Lynx 2	B51F	1990	Clydeside (McGills), 1997
STL102	B102KPF	Leyland Tiger TRCTL11/3RH	East Lancashire (1991)	B59F	1984	Arriva Midlands North, 2000
STL207	YPJ207Y	Leyland Tiger TRCTL11/3R	East Lancashire (1992)	B59F	1982	Arriva Midlands North, 2000
SLC254	H254PAJ	Leyland Lynx LX2R11C15Z4S	Leyland Lynx 2	B49F	1991	North East (Durham County), 1999
SLG256	E256TUB	Leyland Lynx LX1126LXCTFR1S	Leyland Lynx	B49F	1987	Yorkshire, 1998
SLG258	E258TUB	Leyland Lynx LX1126LXCTFR1S	Leyland Lynx	B49F	1987	Yorkshire, 1998
SLG262	E262TUB	Leyland Lynx LX1126LXCTFR1S	Leyland Lynx	B49F	1988	Yorkshire, 1998
SLC276	F276AWW	Leyland Lynx LX112L10ZR1S	Leyland Lynx	B49F	1988	Arriva Yorkshire, 1999
SLC289	F289AWW	Leyland Lynx LX112L10ZR1S	Leyland Lynx	B49F	1988	Arriva Yorkshire, 1999
SLC290	F290AWW	Leyland Lynx LX112L10ZR1S	Leyland Lynx	B49F	1988	Arriva Yorkshire, 1999
SLC293	F293AWW	Leyland Lynx LX112L10ZR1S	Leyland Lynx	B49F	1988	Arriva Yorkshire, 1999
SSC302	F302MNK	Leyland Swift LBM6T/2RA	Wadham Stringer Vanguard II	B35F	1989	The Shires, 1997
SSC303	F303MNK	Leyland Swift LBM6T/2RA	Wadham Stringer Vanguard II	B35F	1989	The Shires, 1997
SLC304	F304AWW	Leyland Lynx LX112L10ZR1S	Leyland Lynx	B49F	1989	Arriva Yorkshire, 1999

SLG311-316 — Leyland Lynx LX2R11G15Z4S — Leyland Lynx — B49F — 1990 — Southern Counties (C&NS), 1998

311	G311DPA	313	G313DPA	314	G314DPA	315	G315DPA
312	G312DPA					316	G316DPA

SLC324	G324NNW	Leyland Lynx LX2R11C15Z4S	Leyland Lynx	B49F	1990	Arriva Yorkshire (S), 1999
SLC334	H34PAJ	Leyland Lynx LX2R11C15Z4S	Leyland Lynx 2	B49F	1991	Arriva North East (DC), 1999
SLC340	G34VME	Leyland Lynx LX2R11C15Z4S	Leyland Lynx	B49F	1989	Southern Counties (C&NS), 1998
SLC350	G35VME	Leyland Lynx LX2R11C15Z4S	Leyland Lynx	B49F	1989	Southern Counties (C&NS), 1998
SLC360	G36VME	Leyland Lynx LX2R11C15Z4S	Leyland Lynx	B49F	1989	Arriva Southern Counties (KT), 1999
SLC390	G39VME	Leyland Lynx LX2R11C15Z4S	Leyland Lynx	B49F	1989	Arriva Southern Counties (KT), 1999
CVV395	MEY395	Volvo B10M-61	Plaxton Paramount 3500 II	C53F	1986	Purple, Bethesda, 1998
SDG426	S426MCC	DAF DE02GSSN220	Plaxton Prestige	N42F	1999	
SDG427	S427MCC	DAF DE02GSSN220	Plaxton Prestige	N42F	1999	
SDG428	S428MCC	DAF DE02GSSN220	Plaxton Prestige	N42F	1999	
SDG429	S429MCC	DAF DE02GSSN220	Plaxton Prestige	N42F	1999	
STL430	UJN430Y	Leyland Tiger TRCTL11/2R	East Lancashire (1991)	B53F	1982	Arriva Midlands North, 2000
SDC521	R521UCC	Dennis Dart SLF	Plaxton Pointer	N39F	1997	
SDC522	R522UCC	Dennis Dart SLF	Plaxton Pointer	N39F	1997	
SMC553	V553ECC	Dennis Dart SLF	Plaxton Pointer MPD	N27F	2000	

Much of the Arriva Cymru's fleet has been replaced in recent times, gaining many Leyland Lynx from sister companies. One of these is SLC340, G34VME, that arrived with seven similar buses from Arriva Southern Counties where it operated for Croydon and North Surrey. It is seen arriving at Aberystwyth. The reduction in the fleet age profile continued as the Lynx make way for low floor Dennis Darts. *John Jones*

SMC554	V554ECC	Dennis Dart SLF	Plaxton Pointer MPD	N27F	2000		
SMC556	V556ECC	Dennis Dart SLF	Plaxton Pointer MPD	N27F	2000		
SMC557	V557ECC	Dennis Dart SLF	Plaxton Pointer MPD	N27F	2000		
SDC558	S558MCC	Dennis Dart SLF	Alexander ALX200	N40F	1998		
SDC559	S559MCC	Dennis Dart SLF	Alexander ALX200	N40F	1998		
SDC560	T560JJC	Dennis Dart SLF	Plaxton Pointer 2	N39F	1999		
SDC561	T561JJC	Dennis Dart SLF	Plaxton Pointer 2	N39F	1999		
SDC562	T562JJC	Dennis Dart SLF	Plaxton Pointer 2	N39F	1999		
SDC563	T563JJC	Dennis Dart SLF	Plaxton Pointer 2	N39F	1999		

SMC564-570 Dennis Dart SLF Plaxton Pointer MPD N27F 1999

564	T564JJC	566	T566JJC	568	T568JJC	569	T569JJC	570	T570JJC
565	T565JJC	567	T567JJC						

SDC571-591 Dennis Dart SLF Plaxton Pointer 2 N39F 1999-2000

571	V571DJC	576	V576DJC	580	V580DJC	584	V584DJC	588	V588DJC
572	V572DJC	577	V577DJC	581	V581DJC	585	V585DJC	589	V589DJC
573	V573DJC	578	V578DJC	582	V582DJC	586	V586DJC	590	V590DJC
574	V574DJC	579	V579DJC	583	V583DJC	587	V587DJC	591	V591DJC
575	V575DJC								

SLC642	E642VFY	Leyland Lynx LX112L10ZR1R	Leyland Lynx	B51F	1988	Devaway, Bretton, 1998
SLC654	J654UHN	Leyland Lynx LX2R11C15Z4S	Leyland Lynx 2	B49F	1991	Arriva North East (DC), 1998
SLC655	J655UHN	Leyland Lynx LX2R11C15Z4S	Leyland Lynx 2	B49F	1991	Arriva North East (DC), 1999
SDC848	S848RJC	Dennis Dart SLF	Plaxton Pointer 2	N39F	1998	Ieuan Williams, Deiniolen, 1999
CDD944	NEY819	DAF SB3000WS601	Van Hool Alizée	C49FT	1995	London North East, 1998
CDD945	M945LYR	DAF SB3000WS601	Van Hool Alizée	C49FT	1995	London North East, 1998

The Welsh Bus Handbook

Minibuses:

MMM113	G113PGT	Mercedes-Benz 811D	Alexander Sprint	B28F	1990	Arriva North West (NW), 1999	
MMM117	M943UDT	Mercedes-Benz 709D	Plaxton Beaver	B25F	1995	Mercedes-Benz demonstrator, 1996	
MMM118	P688KCC	Mercedes-Benz 709D	Plaxton Beaver	B27F	1997		
MMM119	P658KEY	Mercedes-Benz 711D	Plaxton Beaver	B27F	1997		

MMM211-228

Mercedes-Benz 709D — Robin Hood — BC25F* — 1988-89 — *212/5/7 are B25F; 219/21 are B27F

		214	F214DCC	218	F218DCC	222	F222DCC	226	F426EJC
211	F211DCC	215	F215DCC	219	F219DCC	223	F223DCC	227	F427EJC
212	F212DCC	216	F216DCC	220	F220DCC	224	F424EJC	228	F428EJC
213	F213DCC	217	F217DCC	221	F221DCC	225	F425EJC		

MMM229-240

Mercedes-Benz 709D — Robin Hood — BC25F* — 1989 — *232/7/8 are B25F; 229/33/5 are B27F

229	G229FJC	233	G233FJC	235	G235FJC	237	G237FJC	239	G239FJC
230	G230FJC	234	G234FJC	236	G236FJC	238	G238FJC	240	G240FJC
232	G232FJC								

MMM241	G241GCC	Mercedes-Benz 709D	Phoenix	BC25F	1989		
MMM242	G242GCC	Mercedes-Benz 709D	Phoenix	BC25F	1989		
MMM243	G243GCC	Mercedes-Benz 709D	Phoenix	BC25F	1989		
MMM260	G160YRE	Mercedes-Benz 709D	LHE Commuter	B29F	1989	Stevensons, 1994	
MMM261	G161YRE	Mercedes-Benz 709D	LHE Commuter	B29F	1989	Stevensons, 1994	
MMM262	G162YRE	Mercedes-Benz 709D	LHE Commuter	B29F	1989	Stevensons, 1994	
MMM263	G163YRE	Mercedes-Benz 709D	LHE Commuter	B29F	1989	Stevensons, 1994	
MMM296	J296NNB	Mercedes-Benz 709D	Reeve Burgess Beaver	B27F	1992	Arriva North West (NW), 1999	
MMM297	J297NNB	Mercedes-Benz 709D	Reeve Burgess Beaver	B27F	1992	Arriva North West (NW), 1999	
MMM335	L35OKV	Mercedes-Benz 811D	Wright NimBus	B33F	1993		
MMM336	L36OKV	Mercedes-Benz 811D	Wright NimBus	B33F	1993		
MMM337	L37OKV	Mercedes-Benz 811D	Wright NimBus	B33F	1993		
MMM338	L38OKV	Mercedes-Benz 811D	Wright NimBus	B33F	1993		

MMM351-377

Mercedes-Benz 709D — Reeve Burgess Beaver — BC25F — 1989

351	G151FJC	370	G170FJC	372	G172FJC	374	G174FJC	376	G176FJC
352	G152FJC	371	G171FJC	373	G173FJC	375	G175FJC	377	G177FJC
369	G169FJC								

MMM385	M385KVR	Mercedes-Benz 709D	Alexander Sprint	B27F	1995	North Western (Bee Line), 1996	
MMM394	M394KVR	Mercedes-Benz 709D	Alexander Sprint	B27F	1995	North Western (Bee Line), 1996	
MMM411	M411BEY	Mercedes-Benz 811D	Alexander Sprint	B33F	1995		
MMM412	M412BEY	Mercedes-Benz 811D	Alexander Sprint	B33F	1995		
MMM413	M413BEY	Mercedes-Benz 811D	Alexander Sprint	B33F	1995		
MMM455	M455HPG	Mercedes-Benz 709D	Alexander Sprint	B25F	1994	Southern Counties (G&WS), 1998	
MMM456	M456HPG	Mercedes-Benz 709D	Alexander Sprint	B25F	1994	Southern Counties (G&WS), 1998	
MMM457	M457HPG	Mercedes-Benz 709D	Alexander Sprint	B23F	1994	Southern Counties (G&WS), 1998	
MMM523	N523DCC	Mercedes-Benz 811D	Wright NimBus	B31F	1995	Ieuan Williams, Deiniolen, 1999	
MMM638	L638DNA	Mercedes-Benz 709D	Alexander Sprint	B27F	1994	AA, Ayr, 1996	
MMM645	E45UKL	Mercedes-Benz 609D	Reeve Burgess	B20F	1987	Maidstone & District, 1997	
MMM676	G76PKR	Mercedes-Benz 609D	Reeve Burgess	B20F	1988	Southern Counties (K&S), 1998	
MMM701	F701KMA	Mercedes-Benz 709D	Reeve Burgess Beaver	B27F	1989	Midland, 1995	
MMM702	F702KMA	Mercedes-Benz 709D	Reeve Burgess Beaver	B27F	1989	Midland, 1995	
MMM704	F704KMA	Mercedes-Benz 709D	Reeve Burgess Beaver	B27F	1989	Midland, 1995	
MMM711	M711YJC	Mercedes-Benz 709D	Marshall C19	B25F	1994		
MMM712	M712YJC	Mercedes-Benz 709D	Marshall C19	B25F	1994		
MMM713	M713YJC	Mercedes-Benz 709D	Marshall C19	B25F	1994		
MMM714	M714YJC	Mercedes-Benz 709D	Marshall C19	B25F	1994		
MMM715	L715WCC	Mercedes-Benz 709D	Marshall C19	B27F	1993		
MMM716	L716WCC	Mercedes-Benz 709D	Marshall C19	B27F	1993		
MMM717	L717WCC	Mercedes-Benz 709D	Marshall C19	B27F	1993		

Opposite, top: **The first Mercedes-Benz Vario for the fleet were received during 1997-98 when twenty-four arrived including MMM802, R802YJC, seen at Denbigh before departing north to Rhyl. It is reported these will be the last minibuses, replacements where needed being MPD Darts, and since the withdrawal of the MetroRiders received from Yorkshire Arriva Cymru now has an all-Mercedes minibus fleet again.** *John Jones*
Opposite, bottom: **The latest single-deck arrivals for Arriva Cymru are low-floor Dennis Darts. SDC558, S558MCC, is one of a pair with attractive Alexander ALX200 bodywork and is seen here leaving Amlwch from where it will head south across Anglesey and to the Gwynedd mainland.** *John Jones*

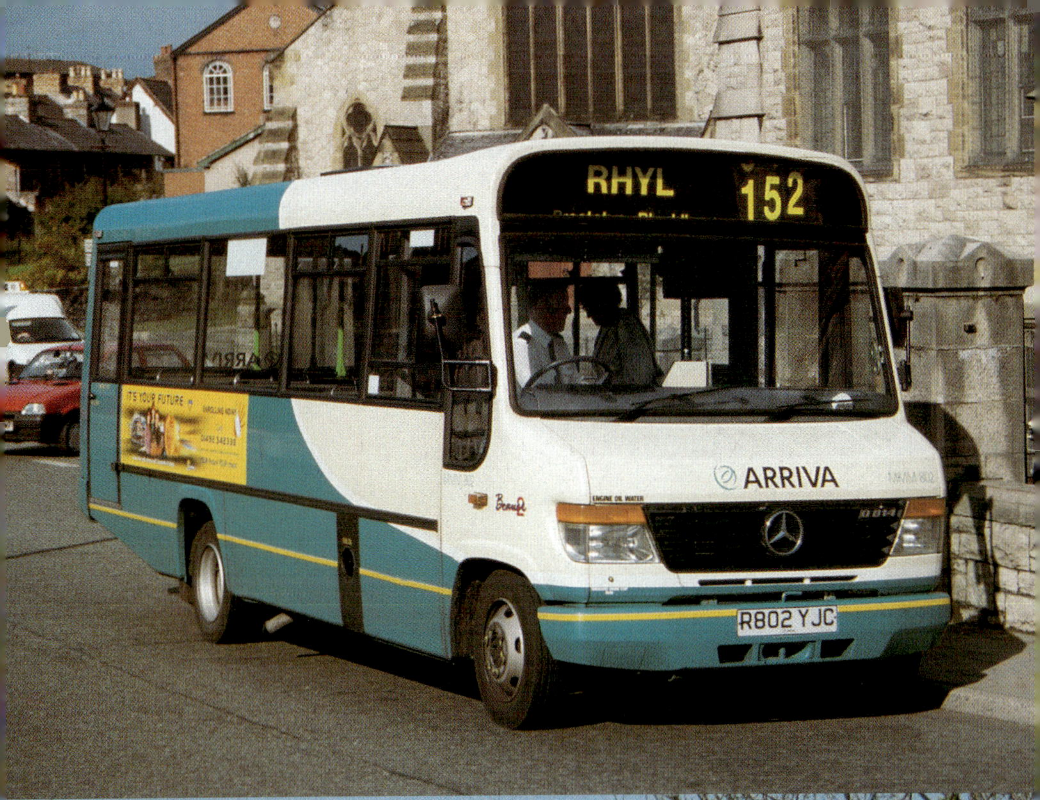
RHYL
152
ARRIVA
R802 YJC

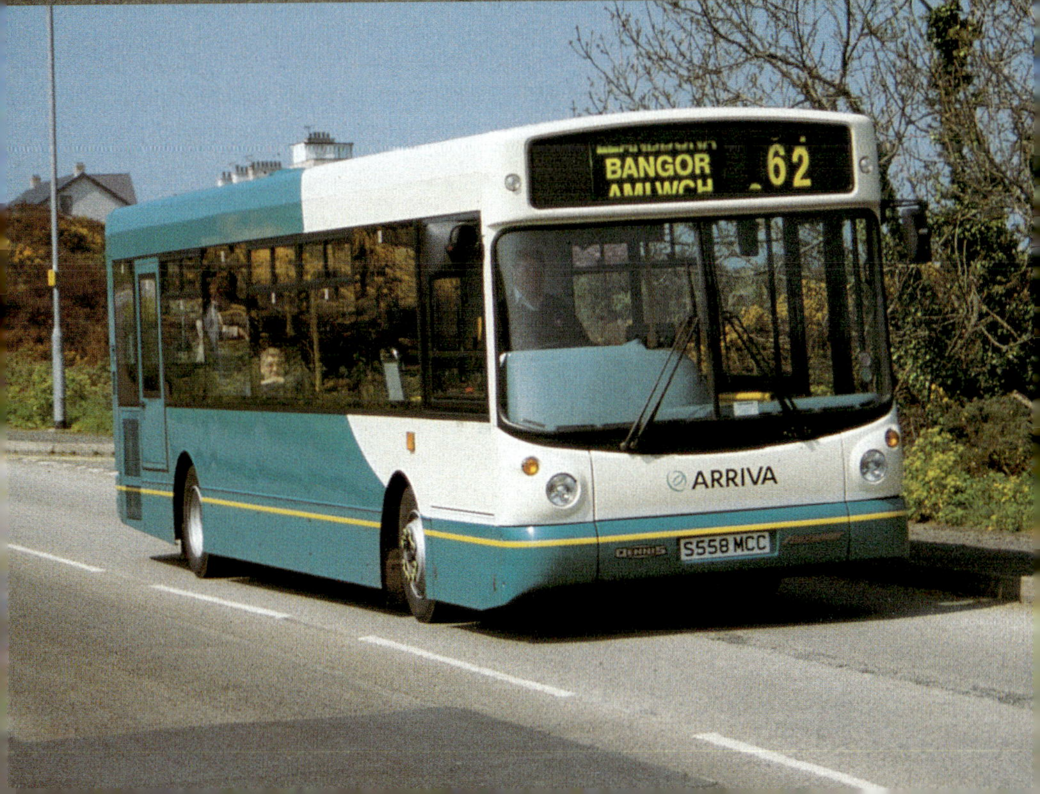
BANGOR
62
ARRIVA
S558 MCC

The first generation of minibuses have been eliminated from the Arriva Cymru fleet by later examples in the MMM class. MMM456, M456HPG, is a Mercedes-Benz 709 with Alexander Sprint bodywork latterly operating with Arriva Guildford and West Surrey. It is seen at Aberystwyth preparing for the next run on a route for many years previously operated by Evans of Penrhyncoch. *John Jones*

MMM718	N718DJC	Mercedes-Benz 811D	Alexander Sprint	B31F	1995		
MMM719	N719DJC	Mercedes-Benz 811D	Alexander Sprint	B31F	1995		
MMM721	L421CPB	Mercedes-Benz 709D	Dormobile Routemaker	B25F	1993	London & Country(G&WS), 1997	
MMM722	L422CPB	Mercedes-Benz 709D	Dormobile Routemaker	B25F	1993	Arriva Southern Counties, 1999	
MMM723	L423CPB	Mercedes-Benz 709D	Dormobile Routemaker	B25F	1993	Arriva Southern Counties, 1999	
MMM725	L425CPB	Mercedes-Benz 709D	Dormobile Routemaker	B25F	1993	Arriva Southern Counties, 1999	
MMM727	L427CPB	Mercedes-Benz 709D	Dormobile Routemaker	B27F	1994	Arriva Southern Counties, 1999	
MMM728	L428CPC	Mercedes-Benz 709D	Danescroft	B27F	1994	Arriva Southern Counties, 1999	
MMM738	L438FPA	Mercedes-Benz 709D	Plaxton Beaver	B23F	1994	Southern Counties(G&WS), 1998	
MMM739	L439FPA	Mercedes-Benz 709D	Plaxton Beaver	B23F	1994	Southern Counties(G&WS), 1998	
MMM746	L646DNA	Mercedes-Benz 709D	Dormobile Routemaker	B27F	1994	Arriva North West (NW), 1999	
MMM749	H149NOJ	Mercedes-Benz 709D	Carlyle	B29F	1991	Kentish Bus, 1997	
MMM751	L151FRJ	Mercedes-Benz 709D	Alexander Sprint	B23F	1993	Arriva North West (M), 1999	
MMM752	L152FRJ	Mercedes-Benz 709D	Alexander Sprint	B23F	1993	Arriva North West (M), 1999	
MMM753	L153FRJ	Mercedes-Benz 709D	Alexander Sprint	B23F	1993	Arriva North West (M), 1999	
MMM754	L154FRJ	Mercedes-Benz 709D	Alexander Sprint	B23F	1993	Arriva North West (M), 1999	
MMM755	K155CRE	Mercedes-Benz 709D	Dormobile Routemaker	B27F	1993	London & Country (HB), 1997	
MMM756	K156BRF	Mercedes-Benz 709D	Dormobile Routemaker	B27F	1993	London & Country (HB), 1997	
MMM757	K157BRF	Mercedes-Benz 709D	Dormobile Routemaker	B27F	1993	London & Country (HB), 1997	
MMM758	M458JPA	Mercedes-Benz 709D	Alexander Sprint	B23F	1994	Southern Counties(G&WS), 1998	
MMM766	M466MPM	Mercedes-Benz 709D	Plaxton Beaver	B21F	1995	Arriva Southern Counties, 2000	
MMM767	M467MPM	Mercedes-Benz 709D	Plaxton Beaver	B21F	1995	Arriva Southern Counties, 2000	
MMM768	N468SPA	Mercedes-Benz 709D	Alexander Sprint	B27F	1995	Southern Counties(G&WS), 1998	
MMM770	N470SPA	Mercedes-Benz 709D	Alexander Sprint	B27F	1995	Southern Counties(G&WS), 1998	
MMM771	N671TPF	Mercedes-Benz 709D	Plaxton Beaver	B23F	1995	Southern Counties(G&WS), 1998	

MMM793-797		Mercedes-Benz 709D	Alexander Sprint	B27F	1996		
793	N993CCC	794	N994CCC	795	N995CCC	796	N996CCC	797	N997CCC

1998 saw the arrival of seven new Northern-Counties bodied Leyland Olympians for route 1, the busy service between Wrexham and Chester, although one has since been reallocated. DVV233, R233AEY, illustrates the route branding applied to these buses as it arrives at Wrexham bus station. *John Jones*

MMM801-819		Mercedes-Benz Vario O814	Plaxton Beaver 2	B27F	1998		
801	R801YJC	805	R805YJC	810	R810YJC	814	R814YJC	817	R817YJC
802	R802YJC	807	R807YJC	811	R811YJC	815	R815YJC	818	R818YJC
803	R803YJC	808	R808YJC	812	R812YJC	816	R816YJC	819	R819YJC
804	R804YJC	809	R809YJC	813	R813YJC				

MMM820	G120TJA	Mercedes-Benz 811D	Carlyle	B31F	1990	London & Country (GWS), 1997
MMM821	R821YJC	Mercedes-Benz Vario O814	Plaxton Beaver 2	B27F	1998	
MMM822	S822MCC	Mercedes-Benz Vario O814	Plaxton Beaver 2	B27F	1998	
MMM823	S823MCC	Mercedes-Benz Vario O814	Plaxton Beaver 2	B27F	1998	
MMM824	S824MCC	Mercedes-Benz Vario O814	Plaxton Beaver 2	BC29F	1998	
MMM825	S825MCC	Mercedes-Benz Vario O814	Plaxton Beaver 2	BC29F	1998	
MMM842	K542OGA	Mercedes-Benz 811D	Dormobile Routemaker	B33F	1982	Ieuan Williams, Deiniolen, 1999
MMM886	R486UCC	Mercedes-Benz Vario O814	Plaxton Beaver 2	B27F	1997	
MMM887	R487UCC	Mercedes-Benz Vario O814	Plaxton Beaver 2	B27F	1997	

MMM892-899		Mercedes-Benz Vario O810	Plaxton Beaver 2	B31F	1997	Arriva Yorkshire (Y), 2000
892	R792DUB	894	R794DUB	896	R796DUB	898	R798DUB	899	R799DUB
893	R793DUB	895	R795DUB	897	R797DUB				

MMM981	K981KGY	Mercedes-Benz 709D	Dormobile Routemaker	B29F	1993	Kentish Bus, 1997
MMM982	K982KGY	Mercedes-Benz 709D	Dormobile Routemaker	B29F	1993	Kentish Bus, 1997
MMM983	K983KGY	Mercedes-Benz 709D	Dormobile Routemaker	B29F	1993	Kentish Bus, 1997
MMM996	N996KUS	Mercedes-Benz 709D	UVG Citistar	B29F	1995	Redline, Penwortham, 1996

The Welsh Bus Handbook

With the exception of a few Bristol VRs at Aberystwyth and the open-top fleet the double-deck fleet is all Olympian. The earliest of these date from 1987, originating in Yorkshire. Seen here is Eastern Coach Works-bodied DOG507, CWR507Y, arriving at Porthmadog having crossed The Cob, the causeway crossing the Glaslyn estuary. *John Jones*

Double Deck Vehicles:

DOL103	A103OUG	Leyland Olympian ONTL11/1R	Northern Counties	B43/28F	1984	Yorkshire Bus (WR), 1997	
DOL104	A104OUG	Leyland Olympian ONTL11/1R	Northern Counties	B43/28F	1984	Yorkshire Bus (SY), 1997	
DOL114	TPD114X	Leyland Olympian ONTL11/1R	Roe	B43/29F	1982	Arriva Southern Counties (WS), 2000	
DOL119	TPD119X	Leyland Olympian ONTL11/1R	Roe	B43/29F	1982	Londonlinks, 1997	
DOL122	TPD122X	Leyland Olympian ONTL11/1R	Roe	B43/29F	1982	Londonlinks, 1997	
DOL126	TPD126X	Leyland Olympian ONTL11/1R	Roe	B43/29F	1982	Londonlinks, 1997	
DOG186	B186BLG	Leyland Olympian ONLXB/1R	Eastern Coach Works	B45/32F	1984	Yorkshire, 1998	
ODL190	JTD390P	Daimler Fleetline CRL6-33	Northern Counties	O49/29F	1975	Southend, 1993	
DOG191	B191BLG	Leyland Olympian ONLXB/1R	Eastern Coach Works	B45/32F	1985	Crosville, 1986	
DOG192	B192BLG	Leyland Olympian ONLXB/1R	Eastern Coach Works	B45/32F	1985	Crosville, 1986	
DOG193	B193BLG	Leyland Olympian ONLXB/1R	Eastern Coach Works	B45/32F	1985	Crosville, 1986	
DOG194	B194BLG	Leyland Olympian ONLXB/1R	Eastern Coach Works	B45/32F	1985	Crosville, 1986	
ODL195	JTD395P	Daimler Fleetline CRL6-33	Northern Counties	O49/29F	1976	Southend, 1993	
DOG196	B196BLG	Leyland Olympian ONLXB/1R	Eastern Coach Works	B42/27F	1985	Crosville, 1986	
DOG208	C208GTU	Leyland Olympian ONLXB/1R	Eastern Coach Works	B45/32F	1985	Crosville, 1986	
EOG209	C209GTU	Leyland Olympian ONLXB/1R	Eastern Coach Works	BC42/27F	1985	Crosville, 1986	
DOG210	C210GTU	Leyland Olympian ONLXB/1R	Eastern Coach Works	B42/27F	1985	Crosville, 1986	
DOG211	C211GTU	Leyland Olympian ONLXB/1R	Eastern Coach Works	B42/27F	1985	Crosville, 1986	
EOG212	C212GTU	Leyland Olympian ONLXB/1R	Eastern Coach Works	BC42/27F	1985	Crosville, 1986	

DOG219-232

Leyland Olympian ONLXB/1R Eastern Coach Works B45/32F* 1983 Kentish Bus, 1995*
*219/20 are B44/32F; 219 Southern Counties (KT), 1999

219	WDC219Y	221	AEF221Y	224	AEF224Y	230	CEF230Y	232	CEF232Y
220	WDC220Y	222	AEF222Y	229	AEF229Y				

DVV233-239

Volvo Olympian Northen Counties Palatine I B47/29F 1998

233	R233AEY	235	R235AEY	237	R237AEY	238	R238AEY	239	R239AEY
234	R234AEY	236	R236AEY						

DOG257	C257UAJ	Leyland Olympian ONLXB/1R	Eastern Coach Works	B45/32F	1985	Arriva Southern Counties, 1999	
DOG258	C258UAJ	Leyland Olympian ONLXB/1R	Eastern Coach Works	B45/32F	1985	Kentish Bus, 1995	
DOG413	B513LFP	Leyland Olympian ONLXB/1R	Eastern Coach Works	B45/32F	1984	Fox County, 1998	
OVL429	RLG429V	Bristol VRT/SL3/501	Eastern Coach Works	O43/31F	1980	Crosville, 1991	
OVG467	WTU467W	Bristol VRT/SL3/6LXB	Eastern Coach Works	O43/31F	1981	Midland, 1994	
OVG478	WTU478W	Bristol VRT/SL3/6LXB (6LXC)	Eastern Coach Works	O43/31F	1981	Midland, 1994	

D(O)VG512-530

Bristol VRT/SL3/6LXB   Eastern Coach Works   B43/31F*   1981   Crosville, 1986
*512/9/28 are O43/31F (prefix OVG); 519 Midland, 1994

512	YMB512W	517	YMB517W	519	YMB519W	522	BMA522W	528	DCA528X
516w	YMB516W	518	YMB518W						

DOG506	CWR506Y	Leyland Olympian ONLXB/1R	Eastern Coach Works	B45/32F	1982	Yorkshire Bus (SY), 1997
DOG507	CWR507Y	Leyland Olympian ONLXB/1R	Eastern Coach Works	B45/32F	1982	Yorkshire Bus (WR), 1997
DOG508	CWR508Y	Leyland Olympian ONLXB/1R	Eastern Coach Works	B45/32F	1982	Yorkshire (South), 1998
DOG509	CWR509Y	Leyland Olympian ONLXB/1R	Eastern Coach Works	B45/32F	1982	Yorkshire Bus (SY), 1997
DOG510	CWR510Y	Leyland Olympian ONLXB/1R	Eastern Coach Works	B45/32F	1982	Yorkshire (South), 1998
DOG512	CWR512Y	Leyland Olympian ONLXB/1R	Eastern Coach Works	B45/32F	1983	Yorkshire (North), 1998
DOG513	CWR513Y	Leyland Olympian ONLXB/1R	Eastern Coach Works	B45/32F	1982	Yorkshire Bus (SY), 1997
DOG522	CWR522Y	Leyland Olympian ONLXB/1R	Eastern Coach Works	B45/32F	1983	Yorkshire Bus (WR), 1997
DOG523	CWR523Y	Leyland Olympian ONLXB/1R	Eastern Coach Works	B45/32F	1983	Yorkshire Bus (WR), 1997
DOG527	CWR527Y	Leyland Olympian ONLXB/1R	Eastern Coach Works	B45/32F	1983	Yorkshire Bus (Y), 1997
DOG531	EWX531Y	Leyland Olympian ONLXB/1R	Eastern Coach Works	B45/32F	1983	Yorkshire, 1998
DOG576	A576NWX	Leyland Olympian ONLXB/1R	Eastern Coach Works	B45/32F	1984	Yorkshire, 1998
OVG961	YCU961T	Bristol VRT/SL3/6LXB	Eastern Coach Works	O43/31F	1979	Northumbria, 1994
DOG991	F991UME	Leyland Olympian ONLXB/1RH	Optare	B47/29F	1989	Arriva Southern Counties (KT), 1999

Ancilliary:

TB1	JTL804V	Bedford YLQ	Plaxton Supreme IV Exp	TV	1979	Lewis, Llanrhystud, 1995
TB5	TPD106X	Leyland Olympian ONTL11/1R	Roe	TV	1982	Arriva Southern Counties (WS), 2000
REC3	C221EKJ	Mercedes-Benz L608D	Rootes	RV	1986	Maidstone & District, 1997
REC4	D28KKP	Mercedes-Benz L608D	Rootes	RV	1986	Maidstone & District, 1997
REC5	C220EKJ	Mercedes-Benz L608D	Rootes	RV	1986	Maidstone & District, 1997
REC6	TXA114K	Leyland Leopard PSU3/3R	Alexander Y	RV	1972	Clydeside (McGills), 1997
REC8	AJA144B	Leyland Leopard PSU3/3RT	Alexander Y	RV	1964	Midland, 1993
MMM43	D443UHC	Mercedes-Benz L608D	Reeve Burgess	TV	1986	Hastings & District, 1987
TB82	D82VCC	Mercedes-Benz L608D	Reeve Burgess	TV	1986	
MMM154	D154VRP	Mercedes-Benz L608D	Alexander AM	TV	1986	
SBB389	GEY389Y	Bedford YNT	Duple Dominant IV	TV	1982	Purple, Bethesda, 1998
SBB812	TNR812X	Bedford YMQ	Duple Dominant IV	TV	1981	Purple, Bethesda, 1998

Previous Registrations:

DJN25X	PPC106X, OIB3510

MEY395	C120DWR
NEY819	M944LYR
UJN430Y	WPH124Y, FBZ2514
YCU961T	OBR774T, WSV571

IIL9168	F714ENE
IIL9169	F710ENE

Allocations:-

Aberystwyth (Park Avenue)

Outstations - Abermule, Llanrhystud, New Quay and Tregaron

Mercedes-Benz	MMM211	MMM212	MMM411	MMM455	MMM456	MMM725	MMM758	MMM796
	MMM797	MMM812	MMM813	MMM899				
Swift	SSC302	SSC303						
Dart	SMC553	SMC554	SMC556					
Lynx	SLG311	SLG312	SLC340	SLC350				
Coach	CVV592	CDD945						
Tiger	STL24	STL42	STL102	STL207	STL430			
VR	DVG518	DVG522						
Olympian	DOL114	DOL119	DOL122	DOL126	DOG229	DOG232	DOG991	

Bangor (Beach Road)

Outstations - Amlwch, Caernarfon and Holyhead

Mercedes-Benz	MMM213	MMM217	MMM239	MMM240	MMM241	MMM243	MMM260	MMM261
	MMM262	MMM263	MMM335	MMM336	MMM337	MMM412	MMM413	MMM457
	MMM523	MMM746	MMM808	MMM809	MMM810	MMM811	MMM996	
Dart	SDC560	SDC561	SMC566	SMC567	SMC568	SMC569	SDC848	
Coach	CVV593	CVV395	CDD944					
Lynx	SLG28	SLG29	SLC37	SLC66	SLC68	SLC70	SLC116	SLG256
	SLG258	SLG276	SLC293	SLC360				
Olympian	DOL104	DOG221	DOG 413	DOG506	DOG508	DOG512	DOG513	DOG527

Chester (Manor Lane, Hawarden)

Mercedes-Benz	MMM113	MMM242	MMM676	MMM721	MMM722	MMM723	MMM727	MMM728
	MMM807	MMM817	MMM818	MMM819	MMM821	MMM823	MMM824	MMM825
	MMM981	MMM982	MMM983					
Dart	SDG426	SDG427	SDG428	SDG429	SDC571	SDC572	SDC585	SDC586
	SDC587	SDC588	SDC589	SDC590	SDC591			
Lynx	SLC27	SLC49	SLC254	SLG262	SLC289	SLC290	SLC642	SLG313
	SLG314	SLG315	SLG316	SLC654	SLC655			
Olympian	DOG191	DOG192	DOG193	DOG194	DOG196	DOG208	DOG230	DVV239

Dolgellau (Arran Road)

Outstation - Machynlleth

Mercedes-Benz	MMM715	MMM716	MMM717	MMM749	MMM771	MMM820
Coach	CTC68	CTC69				
Dart	SDC562	SDC563	SMC570			
Lynx	SLC30	SLC38	SLC39	SLC40	SMC553	SMC554	SMC556
Bristol VR	DVG517					
Olympian	DOL103	DOG257	DOG510			

Llandudno Junction (Glan-y-mor Road)

Mercedes-Benz	MMM117	MMM210	MMM211	MMM212	MMM296	MMM297	MMM351	MMM352
	MMM385	MMM394	MMM638	MMM718	MMM719	MMM751	MMM752	MMM753
	MMM754	MMM766	MMM767	MMM842	MMM886	MMM887	MMM892	MMM893
	MMM894							
Dart	SDC558	SDC559	SDC573	SDC574	SDC575	SDC576	SDC577	SDC578
Lynx	SLC73	SLC304	SLC324	SLC390				
Olympian	DOG222							

Llanrwst (London Road)

Mercedes-Benz	MMM118	MMM119	MMM711	MMM712	MMM713	MMM714
Dart	SMC564	SMC565				

Pwllheli (West End Garage)

Mercedes-Benz	MMM215	MMM238
Dart	SDC521	SDC522
Lynx	SLC69	
Olympian	DOG507	DOG509

In contrast to its Tilling days as Crosville, Arriva Cymru operate just seven coaches. The latest are a pair of DAF SB3000s with Van Hool Alizèe bodies used on the Traws-Cambria joint service with Stagecoach Red & White that runs between Holyhead and Cardiff. An early morning journey starts at Aberystwyth and extends beyond Cardiff to Bristol. CDD945, M945LYR is seen heading for Bristol as it passes through Swansea in March 2000. *John Jones*

Rhyl (Ffynnongroew Road)

Outstation - Denbigh

Mercedes-Benz	MMM338	MMM369	MMM370	MMM371	MMM372	MMM373	MMM374	MMM375
	MMM376	MMM377	MMM738	MMM739	MMM755	MMM756	MMM757	MMM793
	MMM801	MMM802	MMM803	MMM804	MMM805	MMM822		
Dart	SMC557	SDC579	SDC580	SDC581	SDC582	SDC583	SDC584	
DAF	SDD24	SDD25	SDD47	SDD48				
Lynx	SLC334							
Open-top	ODL190	ODL195	OVL429	OVG467	OVG478	OVG512	OVG519	OVG528
	OVG961							
Olympian	EOG209	DOG210	DOG211	EOG212	DOG219	DOG531	DOG576	

Wrexham (Berse Road, Caego)

Mercedes-Benz	MMM214	MMM218	MMM219	MMM220	MMM221	MMM222	MMM223	MMM224
	MMM225	MMM226	MMM227	MMM228	MMM229	MMM230	MMM232	MMM233
	MMM234	MMM235	MMM236	MMM768	MMM770	MMM794	MMM795	MMM814
	MMM815	MMM816	MMM895	MMM896	MMM897	MMM898		
Olympian	DOG196	DOG220	DOG224	DVV233	DVV234	DVV235	DVV236	DVV237
	DVV238	DOG258	DOG522	DOG523				

Unallocated

Mercedes-Benz	MMM216	MMM237	MMM645	MMM701	MMM702	MMM704	MMM727
Lynx	SLC67	SLC254					
Bristol VR	DVG516						

The Welsh Bus Handbook

ARTHUR THOMAS

**AA, JT, BE & GA Thomas, Brynteg Garage, 91 Pontardulais Road,
Gorseinon, Swansea, SA4 4FQ**

ERU390V	Leyland Leopard PSU3E/4R	Plaxton Supreme IV Exp	C53F	1979	Jones, Llandeilo, 1999
AVK172V	Leyland Atlantean AN68A/2R	Alexander AL	B49/37F	1980	Stagecoach Midland Red, 1999
KAD353V	Leyland Leopard PSU5C/4R	Plaxton Supreme IV	C57F	1980	Cyril Evans, Senghenydd, 1994
LFR862X	Leyland National 2 NL106AL11/1R		B44F	1981	Stagecoach United Counties, 1999
LFR864X	Leyland National 2 NL106AL11/1R		B44F	1981	Stagecoach United Counties, 1999
PSX180Y	Leyland Leopard PSU3G/4R	Alexander AYS	B53F	1982	Stagecoach Fife Scottish, 1999
PSX184Y	Leyland Leopard PSU3G/4R	Alexander AYS	B53F	1982	Stagecoach Fife Scottish, 1999

Livery: Cream, red and blue or white

The latest arrivals for Arthur Thomas' service are a pair of Leyland National 2s from Stagecoach United Counties. LFR864X, which had still to be painted into livery, is seen loading passengers in Kingsway in Swansea. *John Jones*

ARVONIA

R Morris, Arvonia Garage, The Square, Llanrug, Gwynedd, LL55 4AA

E103JNH	Renault-Dodge S56	Alexander AM	BC23F	1987	City of Nottingham, 1997
367ARV	Ford Transit VE6	Chassis Developments	BC16F	1988	Rose, Walderslade, 1999
J221HDS	Mercedes-Benz 811D	Carlyle	C19F	1992	Patterson, Birmingham, 1995
L2ARV	Van Hool T815H	Van Hool Alicron	C49FT	1994	
M2ARV	EOS E180Z	EOS 90	C49FT	1995	
N2ARV	EOS E180Z	EOS 90	C49FT	1996	
P2ARV	EOS E180Z	EOS 90	C48FT	1997	
R2ARV	MAN 18.310	Noge Catalan 350	C48FT	1998	
W2ARV	Setra S315 GT HD	Setra	C44FT	2000	

Previous Registrations:
367ARV   E821EVS, NMC528, E274CGJ

Livery: Individual

The small, Llanrug-based, Arvonia fleet comprises two contrasting vehicle types - high specification coaches for tours and minibuses for local services and contracts. Pictured at Stryd Bangor in Caernarfon is J221HDS, a Carlyle-bodied Mercedes-Benz 811D. *John Jones*

BEBB

Bebb Travel plc, The Coach Station, Llantwit Fardre, Rhondda Cynon Taff, CF38 2HB

V32HAX	Setra S315GT-HD	Setra	C44FT	1999
V34HAX	Setra S315GT-HD	Setra	C44FT	1999
V35HAX	Setra S315GT-HD	Setra	C44FT	1999
S36UBO	Volvo B10M-62	Plaxton Expressliner 2	C49FT	1998
V37KWO	Volvo B10M-62	Plaxton Première 320	C53F	2000
S45UBO	Volvo B10M-62	Plaxton Expressliner 2	C44FT	1998
S46UBO	Volvo B10M-62	Plaxton Expressliner 2	C44FT	1998
S47UBO	Volvo B10M-62	Plaxton Expressliner 2	C44FT	1998
S48UBO	Volvo B10M-62	Plaxton Expressliner 2	C44FT	1998
S49UBO	Volvo B10M-62	Plaxton Expressliner 2	C44FT	1998
S51UBO	Volvo B10M-62	Plaxton Expressliner 2	C46FT	1998
S52UBO	Volvo B10M-62	Plaxton Expressliner 2	C46FT	1998
S53UBO	Volvo B10M-62	Plaxton Expressliner 2	C46FT	1998
V54HAX	Volvo B10M-62	Plaxton Première 320	C57F	1999
V56KWO	Volvo B10M-62	Plaxton Première 320	C53F	2000
V57KWO	Volvo B10M-62	Plaxton Première 320	C53F	2000
V58KWO	Volvo B10M-62	Plaxton Première 320	C53F	2000
V59KWO	Volvo B10M-62	Plaxton Première 320	C53F	2000
S62UBO	Volvo B12T	Jonckheere Mistral 70	C46FT	1998
S63UBO	Volvo B12T	Jonckheere Mistral 70	C46FT	1998
S64UBO	Volvo B12T	Jonckheere Mistral 70	C46FT	1998
S65UBO	Volvo B12T	Jonckheere Mistral 70	C46FT	1998
S69UBO	Volvo B10M-62	Jonckheere Mistral 50	C49FT	1998
S71UBO	Volvo B10M-62	Jonckheere Mistral 50	C49FT	1998
S72UBO	Volvo B10M-62	Jonckheere Mistral 50	C49FT	1998
T73JBO	Mercedes-Benz Vario O814D	Autobus Nouvelle 2	BC33F	1999
T74JBO	Mercedes-Benz Vario O814D	Autobus Nouvelle 2	BC33F	1999
T75JBO	Mercedes-Benz Vario O814D	Autobus Nouvelle 2	BC33F	1999
T76JBO	Mercedes-Benz Vario O814D	Autobus Nouvelle 2	BC33F	1999
V78JKG	Optare L1070	Optare Excel	B38F	1999
V79JKG	Optare L1070	Optare Excel	B38F	1999
V81JKG	Optare L1070	Optare Excel	B38F	1999
W82NDW	Optare M850	Optare Solo	B29F	2000
W83NDW	Optare M850	Optare Solo	B29F	2000
W84NDW	Optare M850	Optare Solo	B29F	2000
W86NDW	Optare M850	Optare Solo	B29F	2000
W87NDW	Optare M850	Optare Solo	B29F	2000
R89GWO	Mercedes-Benz Vario O814D	Autobus Nouvelle 2	C29F	1998
R91GWO	Mercedes-Benz Vario O814D	Autobus Nouvelle 2	C29F	1998
S92UBO	Mercedes-Benz Vario O814D	Autobus Nouvelle 2	C25F	1998

Livery: White, blue, turquoise and pink; National Express; Rapide

Opposite, top: **October 1999 marked the return of full-size buses to the Bebb fleet after several years absence. The Optare Excels provide additional capacity and low floor accessibility on the Cardiff Express route that links Beddau with the Welsh capital. V78JKG is pictured on Main Road in Church Village early in 2000.**
Opposite, bottom: **Bebb operate one of the most modern fleets in the UK and have recently replaced two-year-old Mercedes-Benz with Optare Solo products. W83NDW is seen turning into Taff Street in Pontypridd on its first day in service, March 1st.** *John Jones*

BERWYN

Cerbydau Berwyn Coaches

B Japheth, Berwyn, Trefor, Gwynedd, LL54 5LY

OWW905P	Bristol VRT/SL3/6LX	Eastern Coach Works	B43/31F	1976	Ieuan Williams, Deiniolen, 1997
WBD876S	Bristol VRT/SL3/6LXB	Eastern Coach Works	B43/31F	1977	GHA, Bettws Gwerfil Goch, 1997
XNV885S	Bristol VRT/SL3/6LXB	Eastern Coach Works	B43/31F	1978	GHA, Bettws Gwerfil Goch, 1997
YBF681S	Bristol VRT/SL3/501	Eastern Coach Works	B43/31F	1978	Silver Star, Caernarfon, 1997
SGR778V	Bristol VRT/SL3/6LXB	Eastern Coach Works	B43/31F	1979	GHA, Bettws Gwerfil Goch, 1995
KYU88X	Bedford YMQ	Wadham Stringer Vanguard	B41F	1982	E Stott & Sons, Milnsbridge, 1995
EWV515	Leyland Tiger TRCTL11/3RZ	Duple 320	C50FT	1987	Lewis, Llanrhystud, 1997
D272MDB	Freight-Rover Sherpa	Freight-Rover	M8L	1987	Griffiths, Hyde, 1992
D68VDV	Volvo B10M-61	Plaxton Paramount 3200 III	C49FT	1988	Dartline Coaches, Exter, 1999
E151AGG	Dennis Javelin 11SDA1906	Plaxton Paramount 3200 III	C51F	1988	Evans, Tregaron, 1998
NIW6519	Volvo B10M-61	Van Hool Alizèe H	C51FT	1988	Rossendale (Ellen Smith), 1999
F62XRP	Mercedes-Benz 609D	Reeve Burgess Beaver	BC23F	1988	Hulleyis of Baslow, 1998
F114YVP	MCW MetroRider MF158/16	MCW	B28F	1988	Stagecoach Western Buses, 1997
F242OFP	Dennis Javelin 11SDA1906	Duple 320	C55F	1989	Lewis, Llanrhystud, 1998
F723TLW	Iveco Daily 49.10	Robin Hood City Nippy	B25F	1989	Brook, Werneth, 1997
G112JBO	Leyland Tiger TRCL10/2ARZM	Plaxton Paramount 3500 III	C49F	1990	George Edwards, Bwlchgwyn, 2000
G116JBO	Leyland Tiger TRCL10/2ARZM	Plaxton Paramount 3500 III	C49FT	1990	George Edwards, Bwlchgwyn, 2000
G490RVR	Ford Transit VE6	Ford	M8	1990	Evans, Tregaron, 1993
G554RVR	Ford Transit VE6	Ford	M8	1990	Evans, Tregaron, 1993
H544KSG	Iveco Daily 49.10	Carlyle Dailybus 2	B25F	1990	William Hamilton, Maybole, 1994
J248SOC	Iveco Daily 49.10	Carlyle Dailybus 2	B25F	1991	Llynfi Coaches, 1993
L849MWX	Leyland-DAF 400	Leyland-DAF	M8L	1993	Leeds Community Transport, 1997
TIB5002	Ford Transit VE6	Pearl	M14	1993	Evans, Tregaron, 1998
M378BJC	Volvo B10M-62	Plaxton Periere 350	C49FT	1995	Caelloi, Pwllheli, 2000
N737NDD	Toyota Coaster HZB50R	Caetano Optimo III	C21F	1995	
R12CBC	Dennis Dart SLF	Plaxton Pointer 2	N39F	1997	
S12CBC	Mercedes-Benz Vario O814D	Plaxton Beaver 2	B31F	1998	

Previous Registrations:

AAZ9102	E91NVH	F723TLW	F205HGN, RIB5085
D68VDV	D710MWX, LIL6536	NIW6519	E329OMG
EWV515	D137HML, TXI8755, USV330	TIB5002	From new

Livery: White, yellow and brown or yellow, green and red

Route 12 links Caernarfon with Pwllheli on which alternative journeys are operated by Berwyn who usually uses this low-floor Dennis Dart on the duty. R12CBC is seen arriving at Pwllheli when a similar Clynnog & Trefor vehicle would be approaching Caernarfon at the northern end of the route. *John Jones*

BRIAN ISAAC

Brian Isaac Coaches Ltd, Coach Hire Centre, Kemys Way, Swansea Enterprise Park, Morriston, Swansea, SA6 8QF

JWE247W	Leyland Leopard PSU5D/4R	Plaxton Supreme IV	C50F	1981	Brewers, 1996
JWE248W	Leyland Leopard PSU5D/4R	Plaxton Supreme IV	C50F	1981	Brewers, 1996
ANA608Y	Leyland Atlantean AN68D/1R	Northern Counties	B43/32F	1983	Stagecoach Manchester, 1998
ANA651Y	Leyland Atlantean AN68D/1R	Northern Counties	B43/32F	1983	Stagecoach Manchester, 1998
ANA653Y	Leyland Atlantean AN68D/1R	Northern Counties	B43/32F	1983	Stagecoach Manchester, 1998
HIL2859	Volvo B10M-61	Plaxton Paramount 3500 II	C49FT	1986	Marchant, Cheltenham, 1998
540CCY	Volvo B10M-61	Plaxton Paramount 3500 II	C49FT	1986	Marchant, Cheltenham, 1998
LBZ2577	Volvo B10M-61	Plaxton Paramount 3500 III	C48FT	1987	Embling, Guyhirn, 1998
WOI3003	Dennis Javelin 12SDA1907	Duple 320	C53FT	1988	Ipswich, 1993
WOI3004	Dennis Javelin 12SDA1907	Duple 320	C53FT	1988	Ipswich, 1993
HJI548	Volvo B10M-61	Plaxton Paramount 3500 III	C48FT	1988	Silver Star, Caernarfon, 1998
F531NRD	Mercedes-Benz 811D	Optare StarRider	B26F	1988	Reading (Newbury Buses), 1999
F535NRD	Mercedes-Benz 811D	Optare StarRider	B26F	1988	Reading (Newbury Buses), 1999
F360SPD	Mercedes-Benz 811D	Optare StarRider	B26F	1989	Reading (Newbury Buses), 2000
F361SPD	Mercedes-Benz 811D	Optare StarRider	B26F	1989	Reading (Newbury Buses), 2000
G233EOA	Iveco Daily 49.10	Carlyle Dailybus 2	B25F	1989	Midland Fox, 1997
G237EOA	Iveco Daily 49.10	Carlyle Dailybus 2	B25F	1989	Midland Fox, 1997
G98SKR	Iveco Daily 49.10	Phoenix	B25F	1990	Stagecoach South (EK), 1996
H859NOC	Iveco Daily 49.10	Carlyle Dailybus 2	B25F	1991	RoadRunner, Motherwell, 1994
431DWN	Dennis Javelin 12SDA1907	Duple 320	C53FT	1991	
J113LKO	Iveco Daily 49.10	Carlyle Dailybus 2	B23F	1991	Hawksworth, Upton, 1997
J114LKO	Iveco Daily 49.10	Carlyle Dailybus 2	B23F	1991	Hawksworth, Upton, 1997
J886PNC	Iveco Daily 49.10	Carlyle Dailybus 2	B25F	1991	Stagecoach South (EK), 1997
K75TBX	Renault Master	Pearl	M15	1993	Arrow, Llansamlet, 1998
L500BWN	Dennis Javelin 12SDA2117	Plaxton Première 320	C51FT	1993	
M36LHP	Volvo B10M-62	Plaxton Première 350	C49FT	1995	Harry Shaw, 2000
M38LHP	Volvo B10M-62	Plaxton Première 350	C49FT	1995	Harry Shaw, 2000
N313VWN	Dennis Javelin 12SDA2155	Berkhof Excellence 1000LD	C51FT	1996	
T687BWN	Volvo B10M-62	Berkhof Axial 50	C51FT	1999	

Previous Registrations:

431DWN	H510RCY	HJI548	E911UNW
540CCY	C455CWR	WOI3003	E340KBJ
LBZ2577	D770NYC, BIW8106, BVA300, D877FFH	WOI3004	E341KDX
HIJ2859	C452CWR		

Livery: White, blue and magenta

ANA651Y is one of a trio of Northern Counties-bodied Leyland Atlanteans acquired from Stagecoach Manchester in 1998 for use on school contracts. It is seen on Valley Way in the Swansea Enterprise Park, a short distance from its base.
John Jones

BRIDGEND BUS COMPANY

PJ John, 34 Salisbury Road, Maesteg, Bridgend, CF34 9EG

UFT919T	Bedford YMT	Plaxton Supreme IV	C53F	1978	Carver, Ellesmere Port, 1999	
AEF819A	Leyland Leopard PSU3E/4R	Duple Dominant IIE	C49F	1979	Shamrock, Pontypridd, 2000	
CTX382X	Bristol VRT/SL3/6LXB	Alexander AL	B44/31F	1980	Shamrock, Pontypridd, 2000	
CTX392X	Bristol VRT/SL3/6LXB	Alexander AL	B44/31F	1980	Shamrock, Pontypridd, 2000	
CTX393X	Bristol VRT/SL3/6LXB	Alexander AL	B44/31F	1980	Shamrock, Pontypridd, 2000	
CTX395X	Bristol VRT/SL3/6LXB	Alexander AL	B44/31F	1980	Shamrock, Pontypridd, 2000	
MIL6783	Leyland Tiger TRCTL11/2R	Plaxton Viewmaster IV Exp	C53F	1981	Shamrock, Pontypridd, 2000	
MIL6784	Leyland Tiger TRCTL11/2R	Plaxton Viewmaster IV Exp	C53F	1981	Shamrock, Pontypridd, 2000	
PIL2489	Ford R1014	Plaxton Supreme V	C33F	1982	Shamrock, Pontypridd, 2000	
A447PFO	Bedford YNT	Plaxton Paramount 3200	C53F	1983	Shamrock, Pontypridd, 1999	
C469BHY	Ford Transit 190	Dormobile	B16F	1986	Alister's, Barry, 1999	
D879UFJ	Mercedes-Benz 609D	Reeve Burgess	B20F	1987	Shamrock, Pontypridd, 1999	
D640NOE	MCW Metrorider MF150/4	MCW	B23F	1987	Brownis of Builth, 2000	
E129RDW	MCW Metrorider MF150/31	MCW	BC23F	1987	Shamrock, Pontypridd, 2000	
E192UKG	Freight-Rover Sherpa	Carlyle Citybus 2	B20F	1988	Alister's, Barry, 1999	
E226VOH	Freight-Rover Sherpa	Carlyle Citybus 2	BC20F	1988	Gwyn Williams, Lower Tumble, 1999	
F112AHB	Mercedes-Benz 709D	Reeve Burgess Beaver	B25F	1988	Shamrock, Pontypridd, 1999	
F113AHB	Mercedes-Benz 709D	Reeve Burgess Beaver	B25F	1988	Shamrock, Pontypridd, 1999	
F428EMB	Mercedes-Benz 609D	PMT	B20F	1988	Shamrock, Pontypridd, 1999	
F961XWM	Mercedes-Benz 609D	North West Coach Sales	B20F	1988	Shamrock, Pontypridd, 1999	
F962XWM	Mercedes-Benz 609D	North West Coach Sales	B20F	1988	Shamrock, Pontypridd, 1999	
F963XWM	Mercedes-Benz 609D	Robin Hood	B24F	1988	Shamrock, Pontypridd, 1999	
F964XWM	Mercedes-Benz 609D	North West Coach Sales	B24F	1988	Shamrock, Pontypridd, 1999	
G841CLV	Mercedes-Benz 609D	North West Coach Sales	B20F	1989	Shamrock, Pontypridd, 1999	
PIL2488	DAF SB2305DHS585	Van Hool Alizée	C51FT	1989	Shamrock, Pontypridd, 2000	
H690UHH	Mercedes-Benz 709D	Made-to-Measure	B28F	1991	Shamrock, Pontypridd, 2000	
PIL3563	Ford Transit VE6	Ford	M14	1992	Alister's, Barry, 1999	

Previous Registrations:

A447PFO	A411OFO	PIL2488	F643OHD
AEF819A	OMA508V	PIL2489	YHA344X, PDN644
MIL6783	VOY181X	PIL3563	J36OOD
MIL6784	VOY183X		

Depot: Plot 106, Village Farm Industrial Estate, Pyle
Livery: Light blue

A new-comer to the South Wales bus service scene is Bridgend Bus Company which commenced operations during 1999. The principal services run from Bridgend to Blaengarw and Nantymoel competing with First Cymru. The fleet is dominated by Mercedes-Benz minibuses acquired from Shamrock, which include F113AHB seen near Sarn. *John Jones*

BROWNS of BUILTH

N W Brown, 15 High Street, Builth Wells, Powys, LD1 5RY.

FYA201T	Bedford YLQ	Duple Dominant II Express	C45F	1979	Coombs, Weston-super-Mare, 1995	
JVJ511Y	Bedford YNT	Duple Dominant IV	C53F	1982	Central Coachways, 1992	
A511LPP	Bedford YMP	Plaxton Paramount 3200	C35F	1983	Whites Coaches, Berinsfield, 1992	
A945MDH	Bedford YNT	Plaxton Paramount 3200	C49F	1984	Central Coachways, 1992	
A946MDH	Bedford YNT	Plaxton Paramount 3200	C49F	1984	Central Coachways, 1992	
D441BCJ	Bedford CF	Steedrive Parflo	M12	1987		
D914BFO	Bedford CF	Steedrive Parflo	M12	1987	Sargeants, Llanfaredd, 1988	
D683NCV	Freight-Rover Sherpa	Made-to-Measure	M16	1987	Prosser, Mountain Ash, 1998	
D858FCJ	Freight-Rover Sherpa	Freight-Rover	M16	1988	Humphreys, Rhayader, 1998	
E737EVJ	Bedford YMP	Plaxton Paramount 3200 III	C35F	1987		
E329EVH	DAF MB230LT615	Plaxton Paramount 3500 III	C53F	1988	Smiths, Alcester, 1989	
E262REP	MCW MetroRider MF150/16	MCW	B25F	1987	Cardiff Bus, 1996	
E147TBO	MCW MetroRider MF150/78	MCW	B23F	1988	Cardiff Bus, 1996	
E149TBO	MCW MetroRider MF150/79	MCW	BC23F	1988	Cardiff Bus, 1996	
E133YUD	DAF MB230LT615	Plaxton Paramount 3500 III	C53F	1988	Oxford Bus Company, 1998	
E134YUD	DAF MB230LT615	Plaxton Paramount 3500 III	C53F	1988	Oxford Bus Company, 1998	
F428JRJ	Ford Transit VE6	Deansgate	M14	1989	Bayley's, Malvern, 1999	
G767RVJ	Freight Rover Sherpa	Crystals	C16F	1989		
G307VNB	Ford Transit VE6	Deansgate	M14	1990	Bayley's, Malvern, 1999	
G777WFC	Optare MetroRider MR09	Optare	B25F	1990	Oxford Bus Company, 1999	
H169OTG	Optare MetroRider MR01	Optare	B31F	1990	Cardiff Bus, 2000	
H399CJF	DAF SB2305DHS585	Caetano Algarve	C53F	1990	Brittain's, Northampton, 1993	
H920OOJ	Leyland-DAF 400	Brown	M16	1991	ex van, 1999	
J100OMP	DAF SB2305DHTD585	Plaxton Paramount 3200 III	C57F	1991	Hardings, Redditch, 1997	
W214UFO	Mercedes-Benz Vario O814	Plaxton Cheetah	C25F	2000		

Depot: Tynrheol, Hundred House
Livery: White and maroon

E147TBO is from a trio of MCW MetroRiders acquired by Brown's of Builth from Cardiff Bus in 1996. It is seen entering Llandrindod Wells on a wet day last spring having returned from an early morning journey to Brecon. *John Jones*

BRYN MELYN

Bryn Melyn Motor Services Ltd, Abbey Road Garage, Llangollen, Denbighshire, LL20 8SN

BNT667T	Ford R1114	Plaxton Supreme IV	C53F	1979	Britannia, Telford, 1992
UDM451V	Bristol VRT/SL3/6LXB	Eastern Coach Works	B43/31F	1980	Crosville Wales, 1996
XGR445V	Ford R1114	Plaxton Supreme IV	C53F	1980	Pearce, Yatton, 1992
GNT435V	Ford R1114	Plaxton Supreme IV	C53F	1980	Britannia, Telford, 1994
GGM110W	Bristol VRT/SL3/6LXB	Eastern Coach Works	B43/31F	1980	Gwyn Williams, Lower Tumble, 1998
YMB502W	Bristol VRT/SL3/6LXB	Eastern Coach Works	B43/31F	1981	Arriva Cymru, 1998
D92VCC	Mercedes-Benz L608D	Reeve Burgess	B20F	1987	Arriva Cymru, 1999
F201OPD	Dennis Dominator DDA1020	East Lancashire	B51/33F	1988	London & Country, 1998
J912PEY	Mercedes-Benz 410D	North West Coach Sales	M15	1992	
L495XNR	Mercedes-Benz 814D	Dormobile Routemaker	BC33F	1993	
R669UCC	Mercedes-Benz Vario O814D	Marshall C16	B33F	1997	
S908JCC	Mercedes-Benz Vario O814D	Marshall Master	B33F	1998	

Livery: White, blue, yellow and red

Since the last edition of this handbook, Bryn Melyn has enhanced the fleet with a pair of Mercedes-Benz Varios and four double-deck buses. Of note from the latter is F201OPD, a Dennis Dominator with a high-capacity East Lancashire body that arrived from London & Country in 1998. *John Jones*

BURROWS

R & D Burrows Ltd, Water Street, Ogmore Vale, Bridgend, CF32 7AN

PPH473R	Bristol VRT/SL3/501	Eastern Coach Works	B43/31F	1977	Brewers, 1993
WKO125S	Bristol VRT/SL3/6LXB	Eaetern Coach Works	B43/31F	1978	Arriva Southern Counties (K), 2000
GTX744W	Bristol VRT/SL3/6LXB	Eastern Coach Works	B43/31F	1978	Turner, Bristol, 2000
TIB5912	Bova EL26/581	Bova Europa	C46FT	1983	International Cs, Dundee, 1993
PIW4792	Leyland Tiger TRCTL11/3R	Plaxton Supreme IV	C57F	1983	Timis Travel, Sheerness, 2000
TIB5909	DAF SB2300DHS585	Berkhof Esprite 350	C49FT	1983	Travelfar, Henfield, 1990
A	MCW Metrobus DR102/42	MCW	B45/31F	1984	Arriva Southern Counties (K), 2000
NIL3945	DAF MB230DKVL615	Plaxton Paramount 3500 II	C53F	1986	Austin, Earlston, 1996
D509OTA	Iveco Daily 49.10	Robin Hood City Nippy	BC21F	1986	Red Bus, 1999
NIL3946	Leyland Tiger TRCL10/3ARZM	Plaxton Paramount 3500 III	C49FT	1988	Classic, Annfield Plain, 1996
K777GSM	Dennis Javelin 12SDA2117	Plaxton Paramount 3200 III	C57F	1993	Mayne, Buckie, 1997

Previous Registrations:

NIL3945	C704LMA, 1810VT, C863NCA, BAZ4773, C684WKS		
NIL3946	F304JFT	TIB5912	YGY642Y
PIW4792	DNK577Y, LXI9367	TIB5909	A647NOO, 9195PU, A330NJK

Depot: Penllwyngwent Industrial Estate, Aber Road, Ogmore Vale
Livery: Blue and white

Although Burrows ceased its commercial routes some time ago, four double-deck buses are retained for school contracts. PPH473R is one of the full-height Bristol VRs purchased by National Bus for London Country and is seen leaving the depot at Penllwyngwent for school duty in September 1999. *John Jones*

BYSIAU CWM TAF

DC Edwards, Penrheol, Cyffig, Whitland, Carmarthenshire, SA34 0HG

LPJ323P	Bedford YRQ	Duple Dominant	C45F	1976	Mevrig Morgan, Lampeter, 2000
A233GNR	Volvo B10M-61	Duple Dominant IV	C53F	1984	Lewis, Whitland, 1999
279NDE	Volvo B10M-61	Plaxton Paramount 3500 III	C53F	1987	Nefyn Coaches, 1998
E716BDM	Mercedes-Benz 709D	Advanced Vehicle Builders	M12	1988	Lewis, Whitland, 1999
E302BWL	Mercedes-Benz 709D	Reeve Burgess Beaver	BC25F	1988	Nefyn Coaches, 1998
KUI1371	Volvo B10M-60	Plaxton Paramount 3500 III	C50F	1991	Silver Star, Caernarfon, 1999
M298XSF	Mercedes-Benz 711D	Onyx	BC24F	1995	Graham, Kilkeel, 1998
M647UCT	Mercedes-Benz 711D	Autobus Classique	BC24F	1995	Collins, Roch, 2000
P743RDE	Dennis Javelin 12SDA2136	Plaxton Première 320	C53F	1996	
P688HND	Mercedes-Benz 709D	Plaxton Beaver	B27F	1996	Davies Bros, Pencader, 1999
P680LWA	LDV Convoy	Crystals	M16	1997	Evans, Tregaron, 1998
T5TAF	Dennis Javelin	Berkhof Axial 50	C51FT	1999	

Previous Registrations:-

279NDE	E559UHS	KUI1371	H606UWR

Livery: White, blue and grey

A recent newcomer to tendered bus work for Carmarthenshire Council is Bysia Cwm Taf whose principal service is the 224 between Whitland and Carmarthen. Mercedes-Benz E302BWL is seen approaching Carmarthen bus station on a journey that commenced at the town's Glan Gwili Hospital. *John Jones*

BYSIAU FFOSHELIG

Bysiau Ffoshelig - Ffoshelig Coaches - Teithiau Moethus Ffoshelig.

P R Evans, Ffoshelig Garage, Blaen-y-coed Road, Newchurch, Carmarthenshire SA33 6EG

JUH229W	Leyland Leopard PSU4F/2R	Duple Dominant	B45F	1981	Porthcawl Omnibus Co, 1996
KUY442X	Volvo B58-56	Plaxton Supreme IV Exp	C53F	1982	Ffoshelig Motors, 1996
LIL9924	Leyland Leopard PSU3G/4R	Plaxton Supreme V Express	C53F	1982	Mayne, Clayton, 1998
JUI1720	Leyland Tiger TRCTL11/3R	Plaxton Supreme V	C57F	1982	Dysiau cwm Taf, 1999
JIL2433	Volvo B10M-61	Plaxton Paramount 3500	C49FT	1983	White Lion, Tredegar, 1997
RAZ9859	Volvo B10M-61	Plaxton Paramount 3200 II	C57F	1985	White Lion, Tredegar, 1997
KUI1372	Volvo B10M-61	Plaxton Paramount 3500 III	C53F	1987	Dysiau cwm Taf, 2000
V2FOS	Dennis Javelin	Berkhof Axial 50	C51FT	1999	

Previous Registrations:

JIL2433	NGT1Y, KXI366	LIL9924	VRC610Y
JUI1720	UPG349X	RAZ9859	B908SPR, DSU772
KUI1372	D290WDM, VLT290, VLT151, D327UTU, 526NDE, D185KDE		

Livery: Cream, and two-tone brown.

It is pleasing to note that, since the retirement of the Jones family in 1996, the Ffoshelig business has been maintained in the same excellent condition. Evidence of this is seen in JUH229W, a Leyland Leopard with Duple Dominant bodywork and one of five new to Merthyr Tydfil in 1981. It has recently been re-seated with high-back seating. *John Jones*

CAELLOI

T H, E, EB & N Jones, West End Garage, Pwllheli, Gwynedd, LL53 5PH

M10CAE	Volvo B10M-62	Plaxton Première 320	C53F	1995	Paul S Winson, Loughborough, 1998
N418EJC	Volvo B10M-62	Plaxton Première 350	C49FT	1996	
P9CAE	Volvo B9M	Van Hool Alizée	C38FT	1996	Ellison, St Helens, 1999
P10CAE	Volvo B10M-62	Van Hool Alizée HE	C49FT	1997	
S490MCC	Dennis Dart SLF	Plaxton Pointer 2	N39F	1998	
T10CAE	Volvo B10M(T)	Van Hool Alizée II	C49FT	1999	
W10CAE	Volvo B10M(T)	Van Hool Alizée II	C49FT	2000	

Previous Registrations:
M10CAE   M749LDU   P9CAE   P465JWB

Livery: White, red orange and yellow.

Arriva Cymru and Caelloi each provide one bus to run Route 5 between Pwllheli and Porthmadog. Caelloi usually allocate S490MCC, a low floor Dennis Dart with Pointer bodywork, seen here approaching Star Coast World (formerly Butlins Holiday Camp) near Penychain. During the journey of some forty-minutes between termini passengers will see picturesque Llanystumdwy, the birthplace of David Lloyd George, and Criccieth.
John Jones

CARDIFF BUS

Cardiff City Transport Services Ltd, Sloper Road, Leckwith, Cardiff, CF11 9TB

010	E830ATT		Mercedes-Benz 709D		Reeve Burgess Beaver	BC25F	1988		Stagecoach Devon, 1998
011	F714FDV		Mercedes-Benz 709D		Reeve Burgess Beaver	BC25F	1988		Stagecoach Devon, 1998
012	F405KOD		Mercedes-Benz 709D		Reeve Burgess Beaver	BC25F	1989		Stagecoach Devon, 1998
013	F408KOD		Mercedes-Benz 709D		Reeve Burgess Beaver	BC25F	1989		Stagecoach Devon, 1998

023-029						B40F	1995		
			Dennis Dart 9.8SDL3054		Alexander Dash				
023	N23OBO	025	N25OBO	027	N27OBO	028	N28OBO	029	N29OBO
024	N24OBO	026	N26OBO						

101-109			Optare MetroRider MR15		Optare	B31F	1994		*101-3/7-9 are BC31F
101	L101GBO	103	L103GBO	105	L105GBO	107	M107JHB	109	M109JHB
102	L102GBO	104	L104GBO	106	L106GBO	108	M108JHB		

110-133			Optare MetroRider MR15		Optare	B31F	1994-95		
110	M110KBO	116	M116KBO	121	M121KBO	126	M126KBO	130	M130KBO
112	M112KBO	117	M117KBO	122	M122KBO	127	M127KBO	131	M131KBO
113	M113KBO	118	M118KBO	123	M123KBO	128	M128KBO	132	M132KBO
114	M114KBO	119	M119KBO	124	M124KBO	129	M129KBO	133	M133KBO
115	M115KBO	120	M120KBO	125	M125KBO				

134-143			Optare MetroRider MR15		Optare	B31F	1996		
134	N134PTG	136	N136PTG	138	N138PTG	140	N140PTG	142	N142PTG
135	N135PTG	137	N137PTG	139	N139PTG	141	N141PTG	143	N143PTG

144-158			Dennis Dart SLF		Plaxton Pointer MPD	N30F	1999		
144	T144DAX	147	T147DAX	150	T150DAX	153	V153JKG	156	V156JKG
145	T145DAX	148	T148DAX	151	V151JKG	154	V154JKG	157	V157JKG
146	T146DAX	149	T149DAX	152	V152JKG	155	V155JKG	158	V158JKG

167-175			Optare MetroRider MR01		Optare	B31F	1990-91		
167	G167HWO	172	H172RBO	173	H173RD	174	H174NDO	175	H175RBO
171	H171OTGO								

In reply to competition on the Ely routes, Cardiff Bus acquired four secondhand Mercedes-Benz minibuses in 1998. One of a pair from Stagecoach Devon is 011, F714FDV, which, like the others, carry labels for Ely Value Bus on a white vehicle. These buses now only operate in addition to the normal service with which it now competes.
John Jones

Almost all of the thirty-six Northern Counties-bodied Volvo Ailsa buses new to Cardiff have been refurbished during the last few years. Following the changes, 405, NDW405X, displays its electronic destination and revised livery that uses more white. It is seen in Westgate Street and, after calling at the bus station, will head east to St Mellons. *John Jones*

176-187		Optare MetroRider MR01		Optare		B31F	1992		
176	J176WAX	179	J179WAX	182	J182WAX	184	K184YDW	186	K186YDW
177	J177WAX	180	J180WAX	183	K183YDW	185	K185YDW	187	K187YDW
178	J178WAX	181	J181WAX						

188-197		Optare MetroRider MR15		Optare		B31F	1994		
188	L188DDW	190	L190DDW	192	L192DDW	194	L194DDW	196	L196DDW
189	L189DDW	191	L191DDW	193	L193DDW	195	L195DDW	197	L197DDW

231-240		Leyland Lynx LX112L10ZR1R		Leyland		B49F*	1989	*237-240 are BC47F	
231	F231CNY	233	F233CNY	235	F235CNY	237	F237CNY	239	F239CNY
232	F232CNY	234	F234CNY	236	F236CNY	238	F238CNY	240	F240CNY

241-259		Leyland Lynx LX2R11C15Z4R		Leyland		B49F	1989-90		
241	F241CNY	245	F245CNY	249	G249HUH	253	G253HUH	257	G257HUH
242	F242CNY	246	F246CNY	250	G250HUH	254	G254HUH	258	G258HUH
243	F243CNY	247	F247CNY	251	G251HUH	255	G255HUH	259	G259HUH
244	F244CNY	248	F248CNY	252	G252HUH	256	G256HUH		

Opposite, top: During 1999 a new livery was introduced to a few low-floor buses. One of fifteen Mini Pointer Darts is 146, T146DAX, which carries the Cardiff Bay blue colour relieved with cream and orange. It was pictured descending Penylan Hill while operating route 100, a service that links St Mellons with Ely on the opposite side of the city. Another 25 Plaxton MPDs are expected during 2000 to increase the frequency on the St Mellon services. *John Jones*

Opposite, bottom: Eight Alexander-bodied Volvo buses purchased from Fife Scottish may be the last double-decks to arrive in the fleet. These brought the number of the Ailsa type to 56 and displaced the last Bristol VRTs leaving just a few Olympians for driver training. Pictured on Penylan Hill is 451, A971YSX. *John Jones*

Twenty Plaxton Super Pointer Darts received during 1998-99 formed the largest single delivery for Cardiff for nearly twenty years. Seen carrying Easyrider livery is 313, S313SHB, pictured as it turns into Wood Street. It is expected that Cardiff Bay Blue livery will be applied to these vehicle in due course.   *John Jones*

260-271			Leyland Lynx LX2R11C15Z4S		Leyland Lynx 2		B49F	1991	260 Volvo Bus, 1991	
260	H49NDU	263	J263UDW	266	J266UDW	268	J268UDW		270	J270UDW
261	J261UDW	264	J264UDW	267	J267UDW	269	J269UDW		271	J271UDW
262	J262UDW	265	J265UDW							

272-286			Scania N113CRB		Plaxton Verde		B51F	1992		
272	J272UWO	275	J275UWO	278	J278UWO	282	J282UWO		285	J285UWO
273	J273UWO	276	J276UWO	279	J279UWO	284	J284UWO		286	J286UWO
274	J274UWO	277	J277UWO	281	J281UWO					

287-293			Scania N113CRB		Alexander Strider		B50F	1994		
287	L287ETG	289	L289ETG	291	L291ETG	292	L292ETG		293	L293ETG
288	L288ETG	290	L290ETG							

301-320			Dennis Dart SLF		Plaxton Pointer SPD		N41F	1998-99		
301	S301SHB	305	S305SHB	309	S309SHB	313	S313SHB		317	S317SHB
302	S302SHB	306	S306SHB	310	S310SHB	314	S314SHB		318	S318SHB
303	S303SHB	307	S307SHB	311	S311SHB	315	S315SHB		319	S319SHB
304	S304SHB	308	S308SHB	312	S312SHB	316	S316SHB		320	S320SHB

361-371			Dennis Dart SLF		Plaxton Pointer SPD		N41F	2000		
361	W361VHB	363	W363VHB	365	W365VHB	367	W367VHB		369	W369VHB
362	W362VHB	364	W364VHB	366	W366VHB	368	W368VHB		371	W371VHB

401-436			Volvo-Ailsa B55-10 MkIII		Northern Counties		B39/35F	1982-84		
401	NDW401X	409	NDW409X	416	NDW416X	423	RKG423Y		430	A430VNY
402	NDW402X	410	NDW410X	417	NDW417X	424	RKG424Y		431	A431VNY
403	NDW403X	411	NDW411X	418	NDW418X	425	RKG425Y		432	A432VNY
404	NDW404X	412	NDW412X	419	RKG419Y	426	RKG426Y		433	A433VNY
405	NDW405X	413	NDW413X	420	RKG420Y	427	RKG427Y		434	A434VNY
406	NDW406X	414	NDW414X	421	RKG421Y	428	A428VNY		435	A435VNY
407	NDW407X	415	NDW415X	422	RKG422Y	429	A429VNY		436	A436VNY
408	NDW408X									

Leyland Lynx repaints have, since late 1999, received orange roofs as shown in this picture of 253, G253HUH taken in February 2000. The vehicle was crossing from Dumfries Place into Station Terrace on a diversion following the closure of the city centre for a Wales-Italy rugby match. *John Jones*

437-446		Volvo-Ailsa B55-10 MkIII		Alexander RV		B45/37F	1984	MTL (Merseybus), 1996	
437	A151HLV	439	A154HLV	441	A158HLV	443	A160HLV	445	A162HLV
438	A152HLV	440	A156HLV	442	A159HLV	444	A161HLV	446	A163HLV
447	DEM821Y		Volvo-Ailsa B55-10 MkIII		Alexander RV	B45/31F	1982	MTL (Merseybus), 1996	
448	DEM822Y		Volvo-Ailsa B55-10 MkIII		Alexander RV	B45/31F	1982	MTL (Merseybus), 1996	
449-456		Volvo-Ailsa B55-10		Alexander AV		B44/37F	1984	Fife Scottish, 1997-99	
449	A969YSX	451	A971YSX	453	A973YSX	455	A967YSX	456	A968YSX
450	A970YSX	452	A972YSX	454	A974YSX				
601-607		Scania N113DRB		Alexander RH		B47/33F	1990		
601	G601KTX	603	G603KTX	605	G605KTX	606	G606KTX	607	G607KTX
602	G602KTX	604	G604KTX						
608	J608VDW		Scania N113DRB		Alexander RH	B47/31F	1992		
609	J609VDW		Scania N113DRB		Alexander RH	B47/31F	1992		
610	J610VDW		Scania N113DRB		Alexander RH	B47/31F	1992		

Ancilliary vehicles

509	RBO509Y	Leyland Olympian ONLXB/1R	East Lancashire	TV	1983
512	A512VKG	Leyland Olympian ONLXB/1R	East Lancashire	TV	1984
566	C566GWO	Leyland Olympian ONLXB/1R	East Lancashire	TV	1985

Liveries: Orange and white (double decks); orange, white and brown (single decks); Cardiff Bay blue, cream and orange (low-floor buses)

CERBYDAU CARREGLEFN COACHES

A W Lewis, Carreglefn Garage, Carreglefn, Anglesey LL68 OPR

GCC572	Commer Avenger TS3	Duple Corinthian	C41F	1959	preservation, 1995
MVC12P	Bedford YRT	Plaxton Supreme III Express	C53F	1976	Fallon, Dunbar, 1982
UEY441T	Bedford YMT	Duple Dominant	B61F	1978	Cerbydan Berwyn Coaches, 1992
MCH351W	Bedford YMT	Duple Dominant	B55F	1980	Cerbydau Berwyn Coaches, 1999
997EAY	Volvo B10M-61	Plaxton Viewmaster IV	C51F	1981	Caelloi, Pwllheli, 1990
GEY371	Volvo B10M-61	Duple Dominant	C51F	1982	Evans, Tregaron, 1994
FJC239	Volvo B10M-61	Caetano Algarve	C49FT	1983	Watson, Staindrop, 1997
NJC393	Volvo B10M-61	Plaxton Paramount 3200 II	C53F	1986	Brittain's, Northampton, 1991
E304BWL	Mercedes-Benz 709D	Reeve Burgess Beaver	BC25F	1988	Nefyn Coaches, 1999
H604UWR	Volvo B10M-60	Plaxton Paramount 3500 III	C50F	1991	Nefyn Coaches, 1999
S135UEY	Mercedes-Benz Vario O814D	Plaxton Beaver 2	B31F	1998	

Previous Registrations:

997EAY	JSJ434W	H604UWR	H604UWR, 521WDE
FJC239	ODS463Y, PRV288, C701KDS, OCV726, C117MGA, PGE88Y, PJI3044	NJC393	C124PNH
GEY124	A279GFF	UEY441T	AKK172T, PJI3044
GEY371	WUD322X		

Livery: Blue and cream/white

The Carreglefn fleet includes several vehicles that carry cherished index marks originally issued before 1974 by local County Council offices. GEY371, currently carried by this Duple Dominant, was a former Anglesey mark most appropriate to this operation which is based in the north of the island.
John Jones

CERBYDAU CENARTH COACHES

WG James and DCR & AWL James, Falls Garage, Cenarth, Newcastle Emlyn,
Cardiganshire SA38 9JP

Reg	Chassis	Body	Seating	Year	History
NWO731	DAF MB200DKL600	Plaxton Supreme IV	C55F	1978	Wealden, Five Oak Green, 1992
WWL532T	AEC Reliance 6U2R	Duple Dominant II Express	C49F	1979	Heyfordian, Upper Heyford, 1994
MNM26V	Bedford YLQ	Plaxton Supreme IV	C33F	1980	Walker, New Greencroft, 1990
SND297X	Leyland Leopard PSU5D/4R	Plaxton Supreme V	C49FT	1981	Wilkins, Cymmer, 1989
GKE441Y	Leyland Olympian ONTL11/2RSp	Eastern Coach Works	C44/28F	1983	Stephenson, Rochford, 1998
A260VWN	Renault Master T35D	Holdsworth	M8	1984	private owner, 1989
WJI8931	Leyland Tiger TRCTL11/3RH	Duple 320	C51F	1986	Stephenson, Rochford, 1998
WJI8932	Leyland Tiger TRCTL11/3RH	Duple 320	C51F	1986	Stephenson, Rochford, 1998
C944LOJ	Dodge S56	Dormobile	B27F	1986	untraced operator, 1998
JBZ4492	DAF SB2305DHTD585	Plaxton Paramount 3200 III	C57F	1986	Smith, High Wycombe, 1998
OJI6403	Bedford YMP	Plaxton Paramount 3200 III	C31F	19??	Crosskeys, Newingreen, 1996
G869YBX	Renault Trafic	Holdsworth	M14	1989	
WJI1414	DAF SB3000DKV585	Van Hool Alizée	C53F	1990	North Kent Express, 1999
G732ETX	Ford Transit VE6	Ford	M8	1990	J&S Taxi, Nantyglo, 1996
J918HGD	Mercedes-Benz 609D	Made-to-Measure	BC24F	1991	Springhall, Kempsey, 1998
K355NWM	Nissan Vanette	Nissan	M8	1992	West Glamorgan CC, 1998
S865AEJ	Renault Master	Cymric	M8L	1999	
T310SEJ	Renault Master	Cymric	M14	1999	
V630EEJ	Renault Master	Cymric	M14	2000	

Previous Registrations:

JBZ4492	D295XCX	WJI1414	G965KJX
NWO731	YDG500S	WJI8931	C263SPC
OJI6403	D602TMR, FTG567, FTG9, D267RDA	WJI8932	C253SPC
		WWL532T	YPL103T, 9945NE

Livery: White, red, orange and yellow

Since the last edition Cerbydau Cenarth Coaches has replaced its Daimler Fleetline with GKE441Y, a Leyland Olympian with the ECW coach body designed for interurban duties. New to Maidstone and District, the vehicle allows more flexibility than the bus-seated Fleetline, by having high-back coach seating.
John Jones

CLYNNOG & TREFOR

Clynnog & Trefor Motor Co Ltd, The Garage, Trefor, Gwynedd, LL54 5HP.

Reg	Chassis	Body	Config	Year	Previous owner
URF660S	Bristol VRT/SL3/501	Eastern Coach Works	B43/31F	1977	GHA, Bettws Gwerfil Goch, 1996
XDV604S	Bristol VRT/SL3/6LXB	Eastern Coach Works	B43/31F	1978	Tally Ho!, Kingsbridge, 1997
TDE701S	Bedford YMT	Duple Dominant II	C53F	1978	Evans, Tregaron, 1994
XSU653	Volvo B58-56	Plaxton Supreme III	C53F	1978	Evans, Tregaron, 1997
BAU178T	Bristol VRT/SL3/6LXB	Eastern Coach Works	B43/31F	1978	Stagecoach United Counties, 1998
CNH602T	Bedford YMT	Duple Dominant	B63F	1978	Geoff Amos, Eydon, 1997
BKE850T	Bristol VRT/SL3/6LXB	Eastern Coach Works	B43/31F	1979	Stagecoach South (SCB), 1997
FRP909T	Bristol VRT/SL3/6LXB	Eastern Coach Works	B43/31F	1979	Stagecoach United Counties, 1998
JMB404T	Bristol VRT/SL3/501	Eastern Coach Works	B43/31F	1979	Primrose Coaches, Hayle, 1994
BFJ209T	Bedford YMT	Plaxton Supreme IV	C53F	1979	Evans, Tregaron, 1996
USU192	Volvo B58-56	Plaxton Supreme IV	C53F	1979	Godson, Crossgates, 1995
34BCG	Volvo B58-56	Plaxton Supreme IV	C53F	1980	Tappins, Didcot, 1994
TMA254V	Bedford YMT	Duple Dominant II	C53F	1980	Bowman, Craignure, 1997
CJH117V	Bristol VRT/SL3/6LXB	Eastern Coach Works	B43/31F	1980	Stagecoach South, 1999
XJJ660V	Bristol VRT/SL3/6LXC	Eastern Coach Works	B43/31F	1980	Stagecoach South (EK), 1999
FAA356W	Volvo B58-61	Plaxton Supreme IV	C53F	1981	Evans, Tregaron, 1999
LFJ874W	Bristol VRT/SL3/6LXC	Eastern Coach Works	B43/31F	1981	Stagecoach South, 1999
CJJ679W	Bristol VRT/SL3/6LXB	Eastern Coach Works	B43/31F	1981	Stagecoach South (EK), 1999
ESU294	Bedford YNT	Plaxton Supreme V Express	C53F	1982	Clarkes of London, 1986
151WYB	Volvo B10M-61	Plaxton Paramount 3500	C48FT	1983	M&H, Denbigh, 1998
RJE40S	Volvo B10M-61	Jonckheere Jubilee P50	C49FT	1983	Griffiths, Y Felin Heli, 1996
D114DRV	Iveco Daily 49.10	Robin Hood City Nippy	B21F	1986	North Devon, 1999
D228VCD	Iveco Daily 49.10	Robin Hood City Nippy	B21F	1986	Southern National, 1999
E278HDL	Iveco Daily 49.10	Robin Hood City Nippy	B23F	1987	Solent Blue Line, 1997
E280HDL	Iveco Daily 49.10	Robin Hood City Nippy	B23F	1987	Solent Blue Line, 1997

The Clynnog & Trefor Bristol VR fleet now totals ten. An arrival from South Coast Buses is BKE850T. It is seen here along side YBF681S of Berwyn that still bears evidence of its Silver Star livery. *Ralph Stevens*

In common with a number of north Wales operators, Clynnog & Trefor has chosen the low-floor Dennis Dart for its service duties. New in 1997, this 39-seat Plaxton received registration TRM15S from a 1977 Ford R1114 before it entered service. It is seen climbing out of Trefor on a journey south to Pwllheli. *John Jones*

SSU632	Volvo B10M-61	Jonckheere Jubilee P599	C53FT	1988	KMP, Llanberis, 1995
HSU548	Volvo B10M-61	Jonckheere Jubilee P599	C53FT	1988	KMP, Llanberis, 1996
F866PAC	Iveco Daily 49.10	Robin Hood City Nippy	B19F	1988	Stagecoach Midland Red, 1996
G913KWF	Iveco Daily 49.10	Reeve Burgess Beaver	B25F	1989	Lionspeed, West Bromwich, 1998
H446YKH	Iveco Daily 49.10	Reeve Burgess Beaver	B25F	1990	East Yorkshire, 1997
H448YKH	Iveco Daily 49.10	Reeve Burgess Beaver	B25F	1990	East Yorkshire, 1997
KSV361	Volvo B10M-60	Jonckheere Deauville	C51FT	1993	Staffordian, Stafford, 1996
YSU446	Volvo B10M-62	Jonckheere Mistral 50	C53F	1995	Evans, Tregaron, 1997
TRM15S	Dennis Dart SLF	Plaxton Pointer 2	N39F	1997	
S810MCC	Volvo B10M-62	Van Hool Alizée II	C49FT	1999	
W247OCC	Volvo B10M-62	Jonckheere Mistral 50	C49FT	2000	

Previous Registrations:

151WYB	RME974Y	RJE40S	NVV550Y
34BCG	DJB866V	SSU632	E77AEY, 7CCH, E246AJC
ESU294	BGS299X	TDE701S	BUS964S
FSU106	?	USU192	OVH624T
HSU548	E773YJC, A7KMP, E264AJC	XSU653	XWX172S, BYD90B, 668VDE, TDE705S
KSV361	L300BVA	YSU446	KSK983, M988HHS, OFA590, M93HSU

Livery: Cream, red and orange; yellow, green and red (Dart). White and blue (Leger Travel)
Depot: The Garage, Trefor. Outstations: Y Felin Heli; Menai Bridge and Pentraeth.

Coastal Continental's seven double-decks make up sixty per cent of this operators fleet. The latest arrivals are a pair of Alexander-bodied Bristol VRTs from Cardiff Bus. One of these, WTG376T, is seen along side LMS151W, a Leyland Fleetline new to Alexander Midland also bodied in Falkirk. *John Jones*

The Cross Gates Coaches fleet contains a variety of chassis and body makes including a pair of Scanias with Van Hool Alizèe L bodywork. E217FLD was the first to be acquired and is seen while parking after returning from a school run. *John Jones*

COASTAL CONTINENTAL

Coastal Continental Coachline Ltd, Hinds Garage, 15 Dock View Road, Barry,
Vale of Glamorgan CF63 4JP

ROK452M	Daimler Fleetline CRG6LX	East Lancashire	B44/30F	1974	West Midlands Travel, 1988
ROK459M	Daimler Fleetline CRG6LX	East Lancashire	B44/30F	1974	Blackhorse Coaches, 1989
LHT729P	Bristol VRT/SL3/6LXB	Eastern Coach Works	B43/27D	1976	City Line, Bristol, 1990
OKG292R	Ford R1114	Plaxton Supreme III	C53F	1976	
OCU420R	Leyland Leopard PSU3C/4R	Plaxton Supreme III	C51F	1977	Hunter, Seaton Delaval, 1981
WDA966T	Leyland Fleetline FE30AGR	MCW	B43/33F	1978	Travel West Midlands, 1997
WTG376T	Bristol VRT/SL3/6LXB	Alexander AL	B44/31F	1979	Cardiff Bus, 1999
CTX391V	Bristol VRT/SL3/6LXB	Alexander AL	B44/31F	1980	Cardiff Bus, 1999
DFB680W	Leyland Leopard PSU3E/4R	Duple Dominant II Express	C53F	1980	Thomas of Barry, 1989
CUP759W	Bedford VAS5	Duple Dominant	C29F	1980	Parkin, Saham Toney, 1993
LMS151W	Leyland Fleetline FE30AGR	Alexander AD	B44/31F	1980	Brentwood Coaches, 1999

Livery: Dark blue and silver (buses); brown and cream (coaches)

CROSS GATES COACHES

Cross Gates Coaches Ltd, Cross Gates, Llandrindod Wells, Powys   LD1 6RE

JUX65V	Mercedes-Benz 0303	Plaxton Supreme IV	C49FT	1980	Williams, Brecon, 1995
SIB7356	DAF MB200DKTL600	Plaxton Supreme V	C57F	1982	Evans, Tregaron, 1996
7074DK	Leyland Tiger TRCTL11/2R	Plaxton Supreme VI Exp	C53F	1982	Hills of Tredegar, 1991
WAO646Y	Leyland Tiger TRCTL11/2R	Alexander TE	C49F	1983	Evans, Tregaron, 1997
529FN	Scania K112CRS	Van Hool Alizée SH	C49FT	1984	British Airways, 1985
RYX492	Scania K112CRS	Van Hool Alizée SH	C49FT	1984	Hills Services, Stibb Cross, 1990
D76HRU	DAF MB200DKTL600	Plaxton Paramount 3200 III	C57F	1987	Evans, Tregaron, 2000
D90ALX	Scania K112CRB	East Lancashire	BC37F	1987	British Airways, Heathrow, 2000
E215FLD	Scania N112DRB	Van Hool Alizée L	C47F	1987	Gatwick Airport, 1998
E217FLD	Scania N112DRB	Van Hool Alizée L	C47F	1987	Speedlink, 1997
SBZ1621	Freight Rover Sherpa	Carlyle	B18F	1987	Evans, Tregaron, 1999
E185UKG	Freight Rover Sherpa	Carlyle Citybus 2	B20F	1988	Henley, Abertillery, 1998
PPT910	Scania K113CRB	Van Hool Alizée H	C55F	1991	Boon's, Boreham, 1995
K902PLM	Mercedes-Benz 609D		B16FL	1993	B&G, Milton Keynes, 1998
K106UFP	Toyota Coaster HDB30R	Caetano Optimo II	C21F	1993	Owen, Oswestry, 1997
M794MTH	Mercedes-Benz 709D	Mellor	B27F	1994	Castle, Llandovery, 1998
N10CGC	Scania K113CRB	Irizar Century 12.35	C49FT	1996	
N681YAV	Iveco TurboDaily 59.12	Marshall C31	B27F	1996	Pete's Travel, West Bromwich, 1999

Previous Registrations:

529FN	B187VPP		RYX492	B188VPP
7074DK	NDW142X		SBZ1621	D152NON
JUX65V	NMJ297V, 8914RU, PPT910		SIB7356	TND428X
PPT910	H825RWJ			

Livery: White and turquoise

D & G COACHES

D O Brotherton, 3 Llwyn Bleddyn Road, Rachub, Llanllechid, Gwynedd, LL57 3EF

UKG474S	Leyland Leopard PSU4E/2R	Willowbrook	B43F	1978	Davies Bros, Pencader, 1999
MFV30T	Leyland Leopard PSU4E/4R	East Lancashire	B47F	1978	Arthur Thomas, Gorseinon, 1996
MFV32T	Leyland Leopard PSU4E/4R	East Lancashire	B47F	1978	Burnley & Pendle, 1996
C324LDT	Volvo B9M	Plaxton Paramount 3200 II	C43F	1986	Airport Parking, Copthorne, 1995
D219SKD	Mercedes-Benz L608D	Alexander AM	B20F	1986	North Western (Bee Line), 1996
RBZ3428	Mercedes-Benz L608D	Reeve Burgess	B20F	1986	WEC, Wemyss Bay, 1999
F808TMD	Volvo B10M-60	Van Hool Alizée	C52F	1989	Tellings-Golden Miller, 1997
BAZ7052	Volvo B10M-60	Van Hool Alizée	C53F	1990	Shearings, 1997
R962FYS	Mercedes-Benz Vario O810	Mellor	C33F	1998	

Previous Registrations:
BAZ7052   G852RNC   RBZ3428   D39UAO

Livery: White and blue

D&G Coaches finds the shorter PSU4 version of the Leopard ideal for working the Bangor to Gerlan service due to the narrow twisting route that parallels the A5 trunk road from Ogwen Valley towards Bethesda. MFV30T joined the fleet, which already contained another similar bus from Burnley & Pendle, in 1996 and is seen passing Bangor Post Office when heading for y Clot terminus. *John Jones*

DIAMOND GLANTAWE

D Coaches Ltd, 98 Woodfield Street, Morriston, Swansea, SA6 6HE

MUT253V	Dennis Dominator DD120	East Lancashire	B46/33F	1981	Leicester Citybus, 1996
MUT254V	Dennis Dominator DD120	East Lancashire	B46/33F	1981	Leicester Citybus, 1996
MUT255V	Dennis Dominator DD120	East Lancashire	B46/33F	1981	Leicester Citybus, 1996
MUT261V	Dennis Dominator DD120	East Lancashire	B46/33F	1980	Leicester Citybus, 1996
MUT262V	Dennis Dominator DD120	East Lancashire	B46/33F	1981	Leicester Citybus, 1996
MUT263V	Dennis Dominator DD120	East Lancashire	B46/33F	1980	Leicester Citybus, 1996
MCY839X	Leyland Tiger TRCTL11/2R	Plaxton Supreme V Express	C53F	1982	Rees & Williams, Tycroes, 1988
SND429X	Leyland Atlantean AN68A/1R	Northern Counties	B43/32F	1981	Stagecoach Manchester, 1997
SND462X	Leyland Atlantean AN68A/1R	Northern Counties	B43/32F	1982	Stagecoach Manchester, 1997
SND487X	Leyland Atlantean AN68A/1R	Northern Counties	B43/32F	1982	Stagecoach Manchester, 1997
SND505X	Leyland Atlantean AN68B/1R	Northern Counties	B43/32F	1982	Stagecoach Manchester, 1997
SND513X	Leyland Atlantean AN68B/1R	Northern Counties	B43/32F	1982	Stagecoach Manchester, 1997
SND519X	Leyland Atlantean AN68B/1R	Northern Counties	B43/32F	1982	Stagecoach Manchester, 1997
ANA582Y	Leyland Atlantean AN68B/1R	Northern Counties	B43/32F	1982	Stagecoach Manchester, 1997
ANA589Y	Leyland Atlantean AN68D/1R	Northern Counties	B43/32F	1982	Stagecoach Manchester, 1997
ANA596Y	Leyland Atlantean AN68D/1R	Northern Counties	B43/32F	1982	Stagecoach Manchester, 1997
ANA604Y	Leyland Atlantean AN68D/1R	Northern Counties	B43/32F	1982	Stagecoach Manchester, 1997
WAO644Y	Leyland Tiger TRCTL11/2R	Alexander TE	C49F	1983	Lancaster, 1993
A708LNC	Leyland Atlantean AN68D/1R	Northern Counties	B43/32F	1984	Stagecoach Manchester, 1997

In recent years, D Coaches Ltd has replaced early Atlanteans and Fleetlines with a dozen late Atlanteans from Stagecoach Manchester. ANA589Y retains the orange livery and is seen while operating Swansea's only Park and Ride service. *John Jones*

Diamond Holidays took an early example of the Iveco Eurorider which features bodywork by Beulas EuroRider. This modern styling is illustrated here as P724JYA passes a famous toy store in Cardiff's Hayes Bridge Road. The competitive exchange rate of the Euro during 2000 has allowed the products of Spanish coachbuilders such as Beulas, Irizar and Ayats in their exports to customers using British Pounds.
John Jones

HIL8914	Leyland Tiger TRCTL11/3RH	Duple 340	C49FT	1985	Lancaster, 1993
J400CCH	Volvo B10M-60	Berkhof Excellence 2000HL	C50FT	1992	Cantabrica, Watford, 1998
J500CCH	Volvo B10M-60	Berkhof Excellence 2000HL	C50FT	1992	Cantabrica, Watford, 1998
M392MWN	Ford Transit VE6	Ford	M14	1994	Days, Swansea, 1997
M105OCY	Ford Transit VE6	Ford	M14	1995	Days, Swansea, 1997
N620TTH	Ford Transit VE6	Ford	M14	1995	Days, Swansea, 1998
N714CYC	Volvo B10M-62	Van Hool Alizèe	C48FT	1996	
N715CYC	Volvo B10M-62	Van Hool Alizèe	C48FT	1996	
N716CYC	Volvo B10M-62	Van Hool Alizèe	C48FT	1996	
N717CYC	Volvo B10M-62	Van Hool Alizèe	C48FT	1996	
P337CEP	Volvo B10M-62	Caetano Algarve II	C48F	1997	
P338CEP	Volvo B10M-62	Caetano Algarve II	C48F	1997	
P339CEP	Volvo B10M-62	Caetano Algarve II	C48F	1997	
P721JYA	Volvo B10M-62	Van Hool Alizèe HE	C48FT	1997	
P722JYA	Volvo B10M-62	Van Hool Alizèe HE	C48FT	1997	
P723JYA	Volvo B10M-62	Van Hool Alizèe HE	C48FT	1997	
P724JYA	Iveco EuroRider 391.12.35	Beulas Stergo E	C49FT	1997	
S752XYA	Volvo B10M-62	Van Hool Alizèe II	C48FT	1998	

Previous Registrations:
HIL8914   C76KLG

Depot: Plot 15, Duffryn Close, Swansea Enterprise Park, Morriston
Livery: Cream and maroon (buses); cream, maroon, red and gold (coaches)

EAGLES & CRAWFORD

J F, J K & W P Eagles, 53 New Street, Mold, Flintshire, CH7 1NY

JIL2037	Volvo B58-56	Duple Dominant II	C53F	1979	Caelloi, Pwllheli, 1998
UTU691V	Leyland Leopard PSU3E/4R	Plaxton Supreme IV	C53F	1979	
AHU512V	Bristol VRT/SL3/6LXB	Eastern Coach Works	B43/31F	1980	City Line, 1994
RMA435V	Bristol VRT/SL3/501	Eastern Coach Works	B43/31F	1980	Crosville Cymru, 1991
BMA521W	Bristol VRT/SL3/6LXB	Eastern Coach Works	B43/31F	1981	Arriva Cymru, 1998
YMB509W	Bristol VRT/SL3/6LXB	Eastern Coach Works	B43/31F	1981	Crosville Cymru, 1991
DCA525X	Bristol VRT/SL3/6LXB	Eastern Coach Works	B43/31F	1981	Crosville Cymru, 1997
E756HJF	Dennis Javelin 12SDA1907	Duple 320	C57F	1988	Astley, Bury, 1991
E118MHN	Mercedes-Benz L307D	Devon Conversions	M12	1988	Botterill et al, Thornton le Dale, 1997
E246RBE	Mercedes-Benz L307D	Coachcraft	M12	1988	ERB Services, Newcastle, 1999
560DFM	Volvo B10M-61	Plaxton Paramount 3500 III	C53F	1988	Dodsworth, Boroughbridge, 1996
E700YNS	Dennis Javelin 8.5SDL1903	Plaxton Paramount 3200 III	C35F	1988	J Leask & Son, Lerwick, 1998
G258EHD	DAF SB2305DHS585	Duple 340	C57F	1989	BAA, Gatwick, 1993
H168DJU	Toyota Coaster HB31R	Caetano Optimo	C21F	1990	
RJI5712	Van Hool T815H	Van Hool Alizèe H	C49FT	1991	Hargreaves, Hebden, 1999

Previous Registrations:

560DFM	E598UHS
JIL2037	JGB611T, LSU939, TCW782T
RJI5712	H628TKU

Livery: White, blue and orange

Double-deck buses are operated by Eagles & Crawford to fulfil school contracts. Currently, these are all Eastern Coach Works-bodied Bristol VRTs and, all bar one, originate from Crosville. Pictured at Queensferry is **BMA521W**. *John Jones*

EAST END

R J Jones & Sons Ltd, East End Garage, 5 Pontardawe Road, Clydach,
Swansea SA6 5NT

STJ847L	Seddon RU	Seddon	B51F	1972	Fylde, 1982
WHN468M	Seddon RU	Pennine	B47D	1974	Darlington, 1991
HBD166N	Bristol VRT/SL2/6LX	Eastern Coach Works	B43/31F	1975	United Counties, 1989
HDL410N	Bristol VRT/SL2/6LX	Eastern Coach Works	B39/31F	1975	Southern Vectis, 1990
OVV847R	Bristol VRT/SL3/6LXB	Eastern Coach Works	B43/31F	1976	United Counties, 1991
RRP861R	Bristol VRT/SL3/6LXB	Eastern Coach Works	B43/31F	1977	United Counties, 1991
RPR715R	Bristol VRT/SL3/6LXB	Eastern Coach Works	B43/31F	1977	Solent Blue Line, 1995
HUP763T	Bristol VRT/SL3/6LXB	Eastern Coach Works	B43/31F	1978	Carlton Cs, Carlton-le-Moorside, 1999
JAK211W	Bristol VRT/SL3/6LXB	Eastern Coach Works	B43/31F	1980	Stagecoach East Midland, 1999
WTU473W	Bristol VRT/SL3/6LXB	Eastern Coach Works	B43/31F	1980	London & Country, 1997
TWR465W	Bristol VRT/SL3/6LXB	Eastern Coach Works	B43/31F	1981	Carlton Cs, Carlton-le-Moorside, 1999
VNH156W	Leyland Leopard PSU3F/4R	Duple Dominant IV	C49F	1981	United Counties, 1991
VEX296X	Bristol VRT/SL3/6LXB	Eastern Coach Works	B43/31F	1981	Oareis of Holywell, 2000
HUI8123	Leyland Tiger TRCTL11/3R	Duple Laser	C49F	1982	Oareis of Holywell, 1997
B27PAJ	Dennis Falcon SDA417	Northern Counties	B47D	1985	Stagecoach Transit, 1999
B29PAJ	Dennis Falcon SDA417	Northern Counties	B47D	1985	Stagecoach Transit, 1999
C135SPB	Leyland Tiger TRCTL11/3RH	Berkhof Everest 370	C53F	1986	Ferlin, Bedfont, 2000
E41MMT	Mercedes-Benz 609D	Reeve Burgess	C24F	1987	Highfield, Wigan, 1999

Previous Registration
HUI8123   BCK314Y, OIW5804, GBG606Y

Livery: Green and cream (buses); white and blue (coaches)

EDWARDS BROS

R W Edwards, The Garage, Broad Haven Road, Tiers Cross, Haverfordwest, Pembrokeshire,
SA62 3DA

NIL7708	Volvo B58-56	Plaxton Supreme IV	C53F	1981	Smith, High Wycombe, 2000
RCW649X	Leyland Leopard PSU3F/5R	Plaxton Supreme IV	C53F	1982	Smith, Carlton, 1999
A734JAY	Volvo B10M-56	Plaxton Paramount 3200 E	C53F	1984	Rover, Bromsgrove, 1991
526NDE	Volvo B10M-61	Plaxton Paramount 3200 II	C57F	1985	Go Goodwin, Eccles, 1999
668VDE	Leyland Tiger TRCTL11/3RZ	Plaxton Paramount 3500 II	C53F	1985	Eagle, Bristol, 1997
E885MYP	Freight Rover Sherpa	Freight Rover	M16	1988	private owner, 1992
E333MDE	Dennis Javelin 11SDL1905	Duple 320	C53F	1988	
F383MUT	Mercedes-Benz 609D	Yeates	C24F	1988	
F567ABV	Freight Rover Sherpa	Elme Orion	B21F	1989	Evans, Tregaron, 1992
G684AAD	Mercedes-Benz 709D	PMT	B25F	1989	Serveverse, Tamworth, 1999
3432RE	Volvo B10M-60	Jonckheere Deauville P599	C51FT	1990	Vale of Llangollen, 1998
M940CDE	LDV 400	LDV	M16	1995	
N682AOJ	LDV 400	Lonsdale	M16	1996	private owner, 1998
N50RDE	Dennis Javelin 12SDA2155	Plaxton Première 320	C53F	1996	
P971SDE	MAN 11.220HOCL-R	Caetano Algarve II	C35F	1997	
R607USP	Dennis Javelin	Caetano Porto	C57F	1997	Docherty's Midland, Auchterarder, ë00
S499CDE	Mercedes-Benz Sprinter 614D	Onyx	BC24F	1998	
W200ODE	Bova FHD12.370	Bova Futura	C49FT	2000	

Previous Registrations:

3432RE	G382RNH, VLT288, G563JJC	891VDE	D403HEU
526NDE	B533BML, 8214VC, B201PEY, WSV552, B229PEY	NIL7708	SFP812X
668VDE	B510UNB	WJB490	-

Livery: Cream, tan and brown

The East End double-deck fleet has now grown to eleven buses, all being Bristol VRTs. First to arrive was HBD166N, shown here in its home base, which has been with the fleet for eleven years. This fleet was known for its operation of several Seddon buses though it now comprises just two. *John Jones*

Currently the longest serving vehicle with Edwards Bros is E333MDE, a Dennis Javelin with Duple 320 bodywork, seen here at the new depot yard in the south Pembrokeshire village of Tiers Cross. *Byron Gage*

EDWARDS COACHES

M C Edwards; Grays Coaches Ltd, Newtown Ind Est, Llantwit Fardre,
Rhondda Cynon Taff, CF38 2EE

Reg	Chassis	Body	Seating	Year	History
FRJ243D	Leyland Titan PD2/40	Metro Cammell	B36/28F	1966	Powell, Church Village, 1990
ORU236G	Leyland Atlantean PDR1A/1	Alexander A	B43/31F	1969	Mainline, Tonyrefail, 1984
WTN647H	Leyland Atlantean PDR2/1	Alexander J	B48/30D	1969	Mainline, Tonyrefail, 1984
PDW99H	Leyland Atlantean PDR1A/1	Alexander A	B43/31F	1970	K&P John, Llanharry, 1985
TDW315J	Leyland Atlantean PDR1A/1	Alexander J	B43/31F	1971	Taff-Ely, 1987
ULJ252J	Leyland Atlantean PDR1A/1	Alexander J	B43/31F	1971	Cyril Evans, Senghenydd, 1990
ULJ253J	Leyland Atlantean PDR1A/1	Alexander J	B43/31F	1971	Cyril Evans, Senghenydd, 1994
ULJ260J	Leyland Atlantean PDR1A/1	Alexander J	B43/31F	1971	Thomas, Clydach Vale, 1989
ULJ264J	Leyland Atlantean PDR1A/1	Alexander J	B43/31F	1971	Thomas, Clydach Vale, 1992
BPA342K	Leyland Atlantean PDR2/1	Alexander L	B49/31D	1971	Thomas, West Ewell, 1994
XRU281K	Leyland Atlantean PDR1A/1	Alexander J	B43/31F	1972	Cyril Evans, Senghenydd, 1994
VNB173L	Leyland Atlantean AN68/1R	Northern Counties	B43/32F	1972	Finglands, 1995
XJA515L	Leyland Atlantean AN68/1R	Park Royal	B43/32F	1972	Finglands, 1995
WBN981L	Leyland Atlantean AN68/1R	Park Royal	B43/32F	1973	Yorkshire Rider, 1991
VNB157L	Leyland Atlantean AN68/1R	Park Royal	B43/32F	1973	Finglands, 1995
STD179L	Leyland Atlantean AN68/1R	East Lancashire	B43/31F	1973	Rennies, Dunfermline, 1986
NRG170M	Leyland Atlantean AN68/1R	Alexander AL	B45/36F	1973	Catteralls, Southam, 1996
TRT95M	Leyland Atlantean AN68/1R	Roe	B43/33F	1974	Dining Bus, Bramford, 1994
GHC521N	Leyland Atlantean AN68/1R	East Lancashire	B43/32F	1975	Harris Bus, West Thurrock, 1991
LJA611P	Leyland Atlantean AN68/1R	Northern Counties	B43/32F	1976	Finglands, 1997
NRN397P	Leyland Atlantean AN68/1R	Park Royal	B43/30F	1976	Finglands, 1997
SCN283S	Leyland Atlantean AN68A/2R	Alexander AL	B49/37F	1978	Stagecoach Busways, 1999
XPG166T	Leyland Atlantean AN68A/1R	Park Royal	B43/30F	1978	North Western (Liverline), 1997
JIL7167	Leyland Leopard PSU5C/4R	Plaxton Supreme IV	C55F	1978	AB Coaches, Paignton, 2000
STK131T	Leyland Atlantean AN68A/1R	Roe	B43/31F	1979	North Birmingham Busways, 2000
BTV651T	Leyland Atlantean AN68A/1R	East Lancashire	B47/33D	1979	Bluebird of Neath, 1997
LFR129T	Leyland Atlantean AN68A/1R	East Lancashire	B45/31F	1979	Phil Anslow, Pontypool, 1999

Opposite: **The Edwards Coaches fleet provides considerable interest for Leyland Atlantean enthusiasts with over thirty now operated and bodied with a variety of makes and styles, BPA342K, shown here at Upper Boat, was originally XKC816K with Merseyside PTE before spending some time on the Isle of Man. The lower picture illustrates NRN397P which arrived from Finglands in 1997. This was one of a large order placed by National Bus to meet high-bridge requirements and the Park Royal body styling was allocated to fleets such as Southdown, Northern General and East Yorkshire. This example was one of seventy new to Ribble and is seen in Pontypridd working to Coed-y-Lan comprehensive school at Cilfynydd.** *John Jones*

Used on contract duties, R631VYB is one of six Dutch-built Bova Futura coaches in the fleet, which can be seen at work as far away as Bargoed, Bridgend and Cardiff.
John Jones

Reg	Chassis	Body	Seats	Year	History
YKG53	DAF MB200DKL600	Plaxton Supreme IV	C57F	1979	Mayfayre, Pontypridd, 1986
FEL11V	Leyland Leopard PSU3E/4R	Plaxton Supreme IV Exp	C53F	1979	Eagle, Bristol, 1994
FUJ900V	Ford R1114	Duple Dominant II	C53F	1980	Bebb, Llantwit Fardre, 1987
NRO266V	Ford R1014	Duple Dominant II	C35F	1980	Gray's, Pontypridd, 1995
WRN134V	Leyland Atlantean AN68A/1R	East Lancashire	B45/31F	1980	Phil Anslow, Pontypool, 1999
WRN137V	Leyland Atlantean AN68A/1R	East Lancashire	B43/31F	1980	Kingsley, Birtley, 1999
TRN476V	Leyland Atlantean AN68A/1R	Eastern Coach Works	B45/31F	1980	Kingsley, Birtley, 1999
FBV490W	Leyland Atlantean AN68B/1R	Eastern Coach Works	B45/31F	1980	Crown, Bristol, 2000
FBV499W	Leyland Atlantean AN68B/1R	Eastern Coach Works	B45/31F	1980	Crown, Bristol, 2000
PWL939W	Leyland Leopard PSU3F/5R	Plaxton Supreme IV Exp	C53F	1981	Gray's, Pontypridd, 1995
NJX206W	Leyland Leopard PSU3/3R	Duple Dominant IV (1980)	C53F	1981	Byron's, Skewen, 2000
MRJ102W	Leyland Leopard PSU5D/5R	Plaxton Supreme IV	C49F	1981	SUT, Dinnington, 1991
XHR104	Volvo B10M-61	Van Hool Alizée	C40FT	1981	Byron's, Skewen, 1992
AFY180X	Leyland Atlantean AN68B/1R	Willowbrook	B45/33F	1981	Maun, Mansfield, 1999
SND293X	Leyland Leopard PSU5C/4R	Plaxton Supreme V	C57F	1981	Wessex, 1989
SND295X	Leyland Leopard PSU5C/4R	Plaxton Supreme V	C53F	1981	Wessex, 1989
SND435X	Leyland Atlantean AN68B/1R	Northern Counties	B43/32F	1981	Kingsley, Birtley, 1999
MCY111X	Leyland Leopard PSU5E/4R	Duple Dominant IV	C57F	1982	Brewers, 1994
MKH824A	Leyland Leopard PSU5E/4R	Duple Dominant IV	C53FT	1982	Brewers, 1994
MKH730A	Leyland Leopard PSU5E/4R	Duple Dominant IV	C57F	1982	Brewers, 1994
MKH678A	Leyland Leopard PSU5E/4R	Duple Dominant IV	C57F	1982	Brewers, 1994
MKH690A	Leyland Leopard PSU5E/4R	Duple Dominant IV	C57F	1982	Brewers, 1994
JBD972Y	DAF MB200DKTL600	Plaxton Supreme V	C57F	1982	West Sussex CC, Chichester, 1997
XBZ4111	DAF MB200 DKTL600	Van Hool Alizée	C49FT	1982	King, Portrush, 2000
SOI196	DAF MB200DKFL600	Jonckheere Jubilee P50	C53FT	1983	Martin, Spean Bridge, 1992
AEF32Y	Bova EL26/581	Bova Europa	C53F	1983	Grayis, Pontypridd, 1995
A228LRU	DAF MB200DKFL600	Duple Caribbean	C51FT	1984	Cled Williams, Bargoed, 1997
978HHT	DAF MB200DKFL600	Plaxton Paramount 3200	C50FT	1984	Cambrian, Trebanog, 1988
B221OJU	Bedford YNT	Duple Laser	C57F	1983	Gray's, Pontypridd, 1995
GIL3127	Bova FHD12.280	Bova Futura	C44FT	1985	Ashall, Heaton Norris, 1997
B890AJX	DAF MB200DKFL600	Duple Caribbean	C53F	1985	Hall, High Harrington, 1999
YAP104	DAF MB200DKVL600	Jonckheere Jubilee P50	C53F	1985	Roman City, Bath, 1986
SJI2449	Leyland Tiger TRCTL11/3RH(Vo)	Plaxton Paramount 3500 II	C51FT	1986	Rhondda, 1992
210HKT	Leyland Tiger TRCTL11/3RH(Vo)	Van Hool Alizée	C48FT	1986	Thomas, Clydach Vale, 1988
C598HTX	DAF MB200DKFL600	Plaxton Paramount 3200 II	C57F	1986	Humphreys, Pontypridd, 1993
E321TTX	DAF MB230LB615	Plaxton Paramount 3200 III	C55F	1988	Humphreys, Pontypridd, 1994
F208EWN	DAF SB2305DHS585	Caetano Algarve	C53F	1989	Ashell, Clayton, 2000
LIL9407	Bova FHD12.290	Bova Futura	C49FT	1989	Transcity, Crockenhill, 1996
MIL2407	Bova FHD12.290	Bova Futura	C49FT	1989	Transcity, Crockenhill, 1996
G416WFP	Bova FHD12.290	Bova Futura	C48FT	1990	Boyden, Castle Donington, 1991
J292TTX	Ford Transit VE6	Ford	M14	1991	
M542JHB	Bova FHD12.340	Bova Futura	C53FT	1994	
M720LTG	Toyota Coaster HZB50R	Caetano Optimo III	C21F	1995	
R630VYB	Bova FHD12.340	Bova Futura	C49FT	1997	
R631VYB	Bova FHD12.340	Bova Futura	C48FT	1997	

Previous Registrations:

210HKT	C334HHB	MKH824A	MCY113X
978HHT	A546XUH	NJX206W	BNW612C, FCW311W, WRC751
BPA342K	XKC816K, V649MAN	PWL939W	LWL745W, VWL817
GIL3127	B220AGK	SJI2449	C262GUH
JIL7167	XDG211S	SOI196	NNV608Y
LIL9407	F261NUT	XBZ4111	FRP832X, TZA2699, YJO755X, GIL2942, ADU233X, MIW5005
MIL2407	F262NUT	XHR104	TGD765W
MKH678A	MCY115X	YAP104	B495CBD
MKH690A	MCY116X	YKG53	HRO445V
MKH730A	MCY114X	F208EWN	F208EWN, KAZ4133

Livery: Cream and blue

ELLIS TRAVEL

F B Ellis, Church Street, Llangefni, Anglesey, LL77 7DU

	ATA556L	Bristol VRT/SL2/6LX	Eastern Coach Works	B43/32F	1973	Western National, 1986
w	HRP674N	Bristol VRT/SL2/6LX	Eastern Coach Works	B43/31F	1975	Pat's Coaches, New Broughton, 1990
	JWW226N	Bristol VRT/SL2/6LX	Eastern Coach Works	B43/31F	1975	Ieuan Williams, Deiniolen, 1999
	SNJ684R	Bristol VRT/SL3/6LXB	Eastern Coach Works	B43/31F	1977	Brighton & Hove, 1993
	VIA8311	Volvo B58-61	Plaxton Supreme III	C53F	1978	Smith, High Wycombe, 1989
	XDL304	Volvo B58-61	Plaxton Supreme IV	C51F	1979	Regency, Portsmouth, 1986
	241KRO	Volvo B10M-61	Van Hool Alizée	C48FT	1981	Reed, Kinsley, 1994
	TIB4587	Leyland Tiger TRCTL11/3R	Plaxton Paramount 3500	C49F	1984	Trumans, Pontypool, 1992
	B440VOW	Mercedes-Benz L608D	Robin Hood	C25F	1985	Aron, Northolt, 1988
	PIB2734	Iveco Daily 49.10	Robin Hood City Nippy	B21F	1986	Pickford, Grittleton, 1993
	UBZ3360	Dennis Javelin 12SDA1912	Duple 320	C57F	1988	Llynfi Coaches, Maesteg, 1999
	F368RPO	Iveco Daily 49.10	Robin Hood City Nippy	B23F	1989	Robin Hood demonstrator, 1991
	G121GOJ	Leyland DAF 400	Beadles	M16	1990	Autoservices, Pontypool, 1993
	P869GEY	Iveco TurboDaily 59.12	Mellor	B27F	1996	

Previous Registrations:

241KRO	NFJ380W	TIB4587	B488TYG	VIA8311	ADF669T
PIB2734	C516DYM	UBZ3360	E761JAY	XDL304	EWW236T

Livery: White, mauve and red (single-decks); yellow, mushroom and red (double-decks)

Llangefni is the administrative centre of Anglesey and is able to support a network of local services using the Llangefni Clipa name. Most journeys are operated by Ellis Travel. P869GEY, an Iveco TurboDaily model converted for passenger use by Mellor of Rochdale, is shown here. *John Jones*

EXPRESS MOTORS

E W & J A Jones, Gerallt, Bontnewydd, Caernarfon, Gwynedd, LL54 7VN

MDS691P	Leyland Atlantean AN68A/1R	Alexander AL	B45/31F	1976	R&M Coaches, Par, 1995
VRP39S	Bristol VRT/SL3/6LXB	Alexander AL	B45/27D	1977	Harris Bus, West Thurrock, 1996
EXI1726	Leyland Leopard PSU3E/4R	Willowbrook Warrior (1991)	B49F	1978	RoadCar, 1991
AYG849S	Bristol VRT/SL3/6LXB	Eastern Coach Works	B43/31F	1978	Keighley & District, 1990
GMB382T	Leyland National 11351A/1R		B49F	1978	Crosville Cymru, 1990
GMB649T	Leyland National 10351B/1R		B44F	1978	Crosville Cymru, 1990
KUB550V	Leyland Leopard PSU3E/4R	Plaxton Supreme IV Exp	C49F	1979	K Line, Leeds, 1996
EXI790	DAF MB200DKTL550	Plaxton Supreme IV	C44F	1980	Harris Coach, W Thurrock, 1991
FBV509W	Leyland Atlantean AN68B/1R	Eastern Coach Works	B43/31F	1981	North Western, 1997
FBV511W	Leyland Atlantean AN68B/1R	Eastern Coach Works	B43/31F	1981	North Western, 1997
RXO828	Van Hool TD815	Van Hool Alicron	C49FT	1982	Ball, Birmingham, 1997
TSO20X	Leyland Olympian ONLXB/1R	Eastern Coach Works	B45/32F	1982	Stagecoach Bluebird, 1999
EKA228Y	Dennis Lancet SDA510	Duple Dominant	BC31F	1983	Green Triangle, Lostock, 1999
TWJ340Y	Dennis Falcon HC SDA410	East Lancashire	B52F	1983	Hunt's, Alford, 1999
TWJ342Y	Dennis Falcon HC SDA410	East Lancashire	B52F	1983	Hunt's, Alford, 1999
A80RGE	Mercedes-Benz L307D	Reeve Burgess	M12	1983	Ross, Edinburgh, 1987
8443PH	Van Hool T824	Van Hool Astromega	C50/10DT	1983	Martindale, Shildon, 1992
C327PEW	Mercedes-Benz L307D	Reeve Burgess	M12	1986	Premier Travel, 1990
OJC496	Van Hool T815	Van Hool Acron	C53F	1987	Burton, Felbeck, 1998
WDZ4138	Mercedes-Benz L608D	Alexander AM	B21F	1986	Stagecoach Western Buses, 1999
E566JFR	Leyland Swift LBM6T/2RS	Wadham Stringer Vanguard	B37F	1987	Aintree Coachline, 1992
E657RVP	MCW Metrorider MF150/17	MCW	B23F	1987	Travel West Midlands, 1996
F356TSX	Mercedes-Benz 609D	Alexander Sprint	B25F	1988	Brown, East Kilbride, 1992
G609JET	Mercedes-Benz 609D	Whittaker Europa	B20F	1989	Formby Coaches, 1992
G222EOA	Mercedes-Benz 811D	Carlyle	B31F	1989	Jones, Blaenau Ffestiniog, 1992
DAY1T	DAF MB200DTL615	Van Hool Alizèe	C53F	1989	North Kent Express, 1996

Express Motors, like many bus operators in the area, invested in new vehicles for use on tendered contracts. R1EMS is an Optare Vecta-bodied MAN 11.190 which entered service in 1997. It had just completed the climb out of Penmorfa, between Porthmadoc and Caernarfon, when photographed during 1999. *John Jones*

The latest arrival in the fleet is the second of a pair of Mercedes-Benz Vario buses bodied by Plaxton. It carries a new livery of yellow and white with lettering for *Blaenau Clipa 37*, a series of routes linking villages and hamlets in the area surrounding Blaenau Ffestiniog. This livery has also been applied to other minibuses including G222EOA, G609JET and S496MCC. *John Jones*

G117OGA	Mercedes-Benz 811D	Optare StarRider	BC29F	1990	Leons, Stafford, 1998
R1EMS	MAN 11.190HOCL-R	Optare Vecta	B42F	1997	
S1EMS	Dennis Dart SLF	Plaxton Pointer SPD	N40F	1998	
S496MCC	Mercedes-Benz Vario O814D	Plaxton Beaver 2	B31F	1998	
T601JCC	Mercedes-Benz Vario O814D	Plaxton Beaver 2	B27F	1999	

Heritage fleet:

604JPU	Bristol SC4LK	Eastern Coach Works	B35F	1957	preservation, 1989
OVL494	Bristol SC4LK	Eastern Coach Works	B35F	1960	preservation, 1989
TBD278G	Bristol RELH6G	Eastern Coach Works	BC49F	1969	United Counties, 1987
TBD284G	Bristol RELH6G	Eastern Coach Works	BC49F	1969	United Counties, 1986

Previous Registrations:

8443PH	TOA747Y	OJC496	D305HMT, BIL736, D347OUA
DAY1T	F622HGO	RXO828	From new
EXI790	NEV774V	WDZ4138	D118NUS
EXI1726	YVL564S		

Livery: Turquoise and white; turquoise and black or yellow and white.
Depot: Llyfni Road, Penygroes with outstations at Blaenau Ffestiniog and Bontnewydd.

FERRIS HOLIDAYS

K Ferris and S G Owen; R Ferris, The Coach Yard, Cardiff Road, Nantgarw, Cardiff CF4 7SR

SSN250S	Ailsa B55-10	Alexander AV	B43/35F	1977	Black Prince, Morley, 1997
UCS186S	Ailsa B55-10	Alexander AV	B44/35F	1978	Black Prince, Morley, 1997
LHG445T	Bristol VRT/SL3/501	Eastern Coach Works	B43/31F	1979	APT, Rayleigh, 1999
BVR87T	Leyland Fleetline FE30AGR	Northern Counties	B43/32F	1979	KMP, Llanberis, 1997
KSD108W	Volvo Ailsa B55-10 Mk II	Alexander AV	B44/35F	1980	Black Prince, Morley, 1997
KSD113W	Volvo Ailsa B55-10 Mk II	Alexander AV	B44/35F	1980	Black Prince, Morley, 1997
L92GAX	Volvo B10M-62	Jonckheere Deauville 45	C51FT	1994	
M303KRY	Volvo B10M-62	Jonckheere Deauville 45	C51FT	1995	
M662UCT	Mercedes-Benz 711D	Autobus Classique	C25F	1995	
N595DWY	DAF DE33WSSB3000	Van Hool Alizée HE	C51FT	1995	
N615BCF	DAF DE33WSSB3000	Berkhof Excellence 1000LD	C51FT	1996	
P292UNY	DAF DE33WSSB3000	Berkhof Excellence 1000LD	C51FT	1996	
P26TTX	Volvo B12T	Jonckheere Mistral 70	C49FT	1996	Bebb, Llantwit Fardre, 1999
P27TTX	Volvo B12T	Jonckheere Mistral 70	C49FT	1996	Bebb, Llantwit Fardre, 1999
P808WWO	Volvo B10M-62	Berkhof Axial 50	C51FT	1997	
P669KRD	Volvo B10M-62	Berkhof Axial 50	C51FT	1997	
R870MRD	Volvo B10M-62	Berkhof Axial 50	C51FT	1997	
R871MRD	Volvo B10M-62	Berkhof Axial 50	C51FT	1997	
R113PMO	Volvo B12T	Berkhof Excellence 3000HD	C57/16CT	1998	
R925PTF	Volvo B12T	Berkhof Excellence 3000HD	C57/16CT	1998	
R519RGM	Volvo B12T	Berkhof Excellence 3000HD	C57/16CT	1998	
R157RJH	Volvo B12T	Berkhof Excellence 3000HD	C57/16CT	1998	
T73JKG	Volvo B10M-62	Berkhof Axial 50	C49FT	1999	
T74JKG	Volvo B10M-62	Berkhof Axial 50	C49FT	1999	
T75JKG	Volvo B10M-62	Berkhof Axial 50	C49FT	1999	
T76JKG	Volvo B10M-62	Berkhof Axial 50	C49FT	1999	
W891MDT	Neoplan N122/3	Neoplan Skyliner	C57/20DT	2000	
W892MDT	Neoplan N122/3	Neoplan Skyliner	C57/20DT	2000	

Livery: White, orange, yellow and red.

Ferris Holidays operate a fleet of luxury coaches, several of which are double-deck, to the Spanish resorts. The fleet also provides buses for local school duties. Pictured here is UCS186S, one of four Alexander-bodied buses acquired from Black Prince. The Ailsa B55 was built from Volvo parts at Irvine in Scotland. Later, Volvo acquired the company and produced the vehicles under the Volvo name.
John Jones

FIRST CYMRU

SWT - Brewers - United Welsh Coaches

First Cymru Ltd, Heol Gwyrosydd, Penlan, Swansea, SA5 7BN

101	T101XDE	Dennis Javelin GX	Plaxton Expressliner 2	C44FT	1999	
102	T102XDE	Dennis Javelin GX	Plaxton Expressliner 2	C44FT	1999	
103	T103XDE	Dennis Javelin GX	Plaxton Expressliner 2	C44FT	1999	
106	L506GEP	Volvo B10M-60	Plaxton Expressliner 2	C46FT	1993	
107	M107NEP	Dennis Javelin GX 12SDA2132	Plaxton Expressliner 2	C44FT	1994	
108	M108NEP	Dennis Javelin GX 12SDA2132	Plaxton Expressliner 2	C44FT	1994	
109	M109PWN	Dennis Javelin GX 12SDA2133	Plaxton Expressliner 2	C44FT	1995	
110	M110PWN	Dennis Javelin GX 12SDA2133	Plaxton Expressliner 2	C44FT	1995	
111	M111PWN	Dennis Javelin GX 12SDA2133	Plaxton Expressliner 2	C44FT	1995	
112	N112EWJ	Dennis Javelin GX 12SDA2153	Plaxton Expressliner 2	C44FT	1996	
113	N113VWN	Dennis Javelin GX 12SDA2153	Plaxton Expressliner 2	C44FT	1996	
114	N114VWN	Dennis Javelin GX 12SDA2153	Plaxton Expressliner 2	C44FT	1996	
115	N115VWN	Dennis Javelin GX 12SDA2153	Plaxton Expressliner 2	C44FT	1996	
116	S116RKG	Dennis Javelin GX	Plaxton Expressliner 2	C44FT	1999	
125	NIL2456	Leyland Tiger TRCTL11/3R	Plaxton Paramount 3500	C48FT	1983	Midland Red West, 1996
126	NIL2454	Leyland Tiger TRCTL11/3R	Plaxton Paramount 3500	C48FT	1983	Midland Red West, 1996
131	C312KTH	Hestair-Duple SDA1510	Duple 425	C53FT	1986	
132	ACY178A	Hestair-Duple SDA1510	Duple 425	C48FT	1986	
133	MKH487A	Hestair-Duple SDA1510	Duple 425	C48FT	1986	
134	F134DEP	Hestair-Duple SDA1510	Duple 425	C48FT	1989	
135	F135DEP	Hestair-Duple SDA1510	Duple 425	C48FT	1989	
136	F99CEP	Hestair-Duple SDA1510	Duple 425	C46FT	1989	
137	F100CEP	Hestair-Duple SDA1512	Duple 425	C46FT	1989	
139	E206BOD	Hestair-Duple SDA1510	Duple 425	C53FT	1988	Western National, 1995
140	2358DD	Leyland Tiger TRCTL11/3ARZ	Plaxton P3200 III (1992)	C57F	1992	Davies Bros, Pencader, 1999
141	FIL7131	Leyland Tiger TRCTL11/3RZM	Plaxton Paramount 3500 III	C57F	1989	Davies Bros, Pencader, 1999
142	5519DD	Leyland Tiger TRCTL11/3ARZ	Duple 340	C53FT	1989	Davies Bros, Pencader, 1999
143	5210DD	Leyland Tiger TRCL10/3ARZM	Plaxton Paramount 3500 III	C51FT	1988	Davies Bros, Pencader, 1999
144	9616DD	Leyland Tiger TRCL10/3ARZM	Duple 340	C53FT	1988	Davies Bros, Pencader, 1999
145	F612RBX	Leyland Tiger TRCTL11/3RZ	Duple 340	C55F	1988	Davies Bros, Pencader, 1999
146	8853DD	Leyland Tiger TRCL10/3RZM	Duple 340	C53FT	1988	Davies Bros, Pencader, 1999
147	8098DD	Leyland Tiger TRCTL11/3R	Duple 340	C53FT	1987	Davies Bros, Pencader, 1999
148	2405DD	Leyland Tiger TRCTL11/3RZ	Plaxton Paramount 3500 II	C53F	1987	Davies Bros, Pencader, 1999
149	7660DD	Leyland Tiger TRCTL11/3RZ	Plaxton Paramount 3500 II	C51FT	1987	Davies Bros, Pencader, 1999
150	L538XUT	Toyota Coaster HDB30R	Caetano Optimo II	C18F	1994	Grampian, 1997
151	6690DD	Leyland Tiger TRCL10/3ARZM	Plaxton Paramount 3200 III	C53F	1988	Davies Bros, Pencader, 1999
152	MIB657	Leyland Tiger TRCL10/3ARZM	Plaxton Paramount 3200 III	C53F	1988	Davies Bros, Pencader, 1999
153	WSV410	Leyland Tiger TRCTL11/2RH	Plaxton Paramount 3200	C49F	1984	Yorkshire Rider (York), 1997
156	8124DD	Leyland Tiger TRCTL11/2R	Plaxton Supreme VI Exp	C49F	1981	Davies Bros, Pencader, 1999
159	UOI4323	Volvo B10M-61	East Lancashire (1993)	B51F	1982	Yorkshire Rider (York), 1997
160	F229FSU	Leyland Tiger TRBTL11/2RP	Plaxton Derwent II	B54F	1988	Yorkshire Rider (York), 1997
162	EWW945Y	Leyland Tiger TRCTL11/3R	Plaxton Paramount 3200 E	C53F	1983	Yorkshire Rider (York), 1996
166	HUA606Y	Leyland Tiger TRCTL11/3R	Plaxton Paramount 3200 E	C49F	1984	Yorkshire Rider (York), 1997
172	L6BMS	Dennis Javelin 12SDA2131	Plaxton Première 320	C50FT	1993	
173	L8BMS	Dennis Javelin 12SDA2131	Plaxton Première 320	C53F	1993	
174	L14BMS	Dennis Javelin 12SDA2135	Plaxton Première 350	C53F	1993	
175	R175VWN	Dennis Javelin GX	Plaxton Première 350	C53F	1998	
176	R176VWN	Dennis Javelin GX	Plaxton Première 350	C53F	1998	
177	R177VWN	Dennis Javelin GX	Plaxton Première 350	C53F	1998	
178	R178VWN	Dennis Javelin GX	Plaxton Première 350	C53F	1998	
180	NIL2450	Leyland Tiger TRCTL11/3ARZA	Plaxton Paramount 3200 III	C53F	1988	Yorkshire Rider (York), 1996
188	F921FCY	DAF MB230LT615	Plaxton Paramount 3500 III	C49FT	1989	
189	LIL5069	DAF MB200DKFL600	Plaxton Paramount 3500 II	C53FT	1986	Western National, 1995
192	948RJO	DAF MB230LB615	Plaxton Paramount 3500 III	C49FT	1989	
195	H202CRH	Volvo B10M-60	Plaxton Expressliner	C46FT	1991	York Pullman, 1998
196	H326DTR	Volvo B10M-60	Plaxton Expressliner	C49FT	1991	Priory Coaches, Gosport, 1998

Apart from vehicles painted in contract livery, such as Flightlink and National Express; the First Cymru coach fleet uses the United Welsh Coaches name. Plaxton Expressliner 196, H326DTR, was acquired from Priory of Gosport in 1996 and is seen in Wood Street in Cardiff. *John Jones*

201-216 — Iveco TurboDaily 59-12 — Mellor Duet — B28F — 1992-93 — Hampshire, 1999

201	K701UTT	205	K705UTT	207	K707UTT	209	K709UTT	215	K715UTT
204	K704UTT	206	K706UTT	208	K708UTT	212	K712UTT	216	K716UTT

261	E279TTH	Mercedes-Benz 709D	Robin Hood	B20F	1987	Davies Bros, Pencader, 1999
262	E280TTH	Mercedes-Benz 709D	Robin Hood	B20F	1987	Davies Bros, Pencader, 1999
264	E282TTH	Mercedes-Benz 709D	Robin Hood	B20F	1987	Davies Bros, Pencader, 1999
271	H880EBX	Mercedes-Benz 709D	Dormobile Routemaker	B27F	1990	Davies Bros, Pencader, 1999
273	H61WNN	Mercedes-Benz 709D	Scott	BC29F	1990	Davies Bros, Pencader, 1999
274	G63SNN	Mercedes-Benz 709D	Carlyle	BC29F	1990	Davies Bros, Pencader, 1999

287-322 — Mercedes-Benz 709D — Reeve Burgess Beaver — B23F — 1988 — 294 rebodied 1997

287	E287UCY	295	E295VEP	302	E302VEP	309	F309AWN	316	F316AWN
289	E289VEP	296	E296VEP	303	E303VEP	310	F310AWN	317	F317AWN
290	E290VEP	297	E297VEP	304	E304VEP	311	F311AWN	319	F319AWN
291	E291VEP	298	E298VEP	305	E305VEP	312	F312AWN	320	F320AWN
292	E292VEP	299	E299VEP	306	E306VEP	313	F313AWN	321	F321AWN
293	E293VEP	300	E300VEP	307	F307AWN	314	F314AWN	322	F322AWN
294	E294VEP	301	E301VEP	308	F308AWN	315	F315AWN		

323-327 — Mercedes-Benz 811D — Reeve Burgess Beaver — B23F — 1989

323	F323DCY	324	F324DCY	325	F325DCY	326	F326DCY	327	F327DCY

Opposite, top:

329-347

		Mercedes-Benz 814D		Robin Hood		B31F	1989		
329	F329FCY	333	F333FCY	337	F337FCY	341	F341FCY	345	G345GEP
330	F330FCY	334	F334FCY	338	F338FCY	342	F342FCY	346	G346GEP
331	F331FCY	335	F335FCY	339	F339FCY	343	F343FCY	347	G347GEP
332	F332FCY	336	F336FCY	340	F340FCY	344	G344GEP		

348-361

		Mercedes-Benz 814D		Phoenix		B31F	1989		
348	G348JTH	351	G351JTH	354	G354JTH	357	G357JTH	360	G360JTH
349	G349JTH	352	G352JTH	355	G355JTH	358	G358JTH	361	G361JTH
350	G350JTH	353	G353JTH	356	G356JTH	359	G359JTH		

365-371

		Mercedes-Benz 814D		Phoenix		B31F	1990		
365	G365JTH	367	G367MEP	369	G369MEP	370	G370MEP	371	G371MEP
366	G366JTH	368	G368MEP						

372	G372MEP	Mercedes-Benz 814D	Plaxton Beaver (1992)	B31F	1990	

373-381

		Mercedes-Benz 814D		Phoenix		B31F	1990		
373	G373MEP	375	H375OTH	377	H377OTH	379	H379OTH	381	H381OTH
374	H374OTH	376	H376OTH	378	H378OTH	380	H380OTH		

382	H382TTH	Mercedes-Benz 814D	Reeve Burgess Beaver	B31F	1991	
383	M997CYS	Mercedes-Benz 811D	WS Wessex II	B31F	1994	Pullman, Crofty, 1995
384	L364GTH	Mercedes-Benz 609D	Cymric	B22F	1993	Rees & Williams, 1996
385	H852OWN	Mercedes-Benz 811D	Reeve Burgess Beaver	B31F	1990	Rees & Williams, 1996
386	H853OWN	Mercedes-Benz 811D	Reeve Burgess Beaver	B31F	1990	Rees & Williams, 1996
387	M257CDE	Mercedes-Benz 811D	Mellor	B31F	1994	Davies Bros, Pencader, 1999
388	M258CDE	Mercedes-Benz 811D	Mellor	BC31F	1994	Davies Bros, Pencader, 1999
389	M252CDE	Mercedes-Benz 709D	Mellor	B27F	1994	Davies Bros, Pencader, 1999
390	M253CDE	Mercedes-Benz 811D	Mellor	B31F	1994	Davies Bros, Pencader, 1999
391	M254CDE	Mercedes-Benz 811D	Mellor	B31F	1994	Davies Bros, Pencader, 1999
392	M255CDE	Mercedes-Benz 811D	Mellor	B31F	1994	Davies Bros, Pencader, 1999
393	M256CDE	Mercedes-Benz 811D	Mellor	B31F	1994	Davies Bros, Pencader, 1999
394	F607AWN	Mercedes-Benz 709D	Reeve Burgess Beaver	BC25F	1988	
395	J580VTH	Dennis Dart 9.8SDL3012	Plaxton Pointer	B40F	1992	Rees & Williams, 1996
396	J581VTH	Dennis Dart 9.8SDL3012	Plaxton Pointer	B40F	1992	Rees & Williams, 1996
397	J582VTH	Dennis Dart 9.8SDL3012	Plaxton Pointer	B40F	1992	Rees & Williams, 1996
398	K82BWN	Dennis Dart 9.8SDL3017	Alexander Dash	B40F	1993	Rees & Williams, 1996
399	L844JCY	Dennis Dart 9.8SDL3035	Plaxton Pointer	B40F	1994	Rees & Williams, 1996

401-410

		Mercedes-Benz 811D		Plaxton Beaver		B31F	1993		
401	K401BAX	403	K403BAX	405	K405BAX	407	K407BAX	409	K409BAX
402	K402BAX	404	K404BAX	406	K406BAX	408	K408BAX	410	K410BAX

411	F601AWN	Mercedes-Benz 709D	Reeve Burgess Beaver	B25F	1988	
413	F603AWN	Mercedes-Benz 709D	Reeve Burgess Beaver	B25F	1988	
418	F608AWN	Mercedes-Benz 709D	Reeve Burgess Beaver	B25F	1988	
419	F546EJA	Mercedes-Benz 709D	PMT	BC25F	1988	Yorkshire Rider, 1996
429	J901MAF	Mercedes-Benz 709D	Wadham Stringer Wessex	B21F	1991	Western National, 1996

431-437

		Mercedes-Benz 709D		Reeve Burgess Beaver		BC25F	1988	Provincial, 1996	
431	F713FDV	432	F721FDV	434	F727FDV	435	F749FDV	437	F712FDV

440-450

		Mercedes-Benz 811D		Carlyle		BC29F	1991	Ex Provincial, 1997	
440	H172GTA	443	H178GTA	445	H990FTT	447	H993FTT	449	H995FTT
441	H174GTA	444	H782GTA	446	H992FTT	448	H994FTT	450	H996FTT
442	H177GTA								

451	H173GTA	Mercedes-Benz 811D	Carlyle	B29F	1991	Hampshire, 1999
452	H175GTA	Mercedes-Benz 811D	Carlyle	B29F	1991	Hampshire, 1999
453	H179GTA	Mercedes-Benz 811D	Carlyle	B29F	1991	Hampshire, 1999
454	H788GTA	Mercedes-Benz 811D	Carlyle	B29F	1991	Hampshire, 1999

Eleven Carlyle-bodied Mercedes-Benz minibuses transferred from First Provincial in 1997. From the batch, 447, H993FTT is seen passing the McArthur Glen shopping centre at Sarn, near Bridgend. *John Jones*

481-490		Mercedes-Benz Vario O810		Plaxton Beaver 2		B27F	1998		
481	R481EDW	483	R483EDW	485	R485EDW	487	R487EDW	489	R489EDW
482	R482EDW	484	R484EDW	486	R486EDW	488	R488EDW	490	R490EDW

501-524		Dennis Dart 9SDL3034		Plaxton Pointer		B31F	1993		
501	L501HCY	506	L506HCY	511	L511HCY	516	L516HCY	521	L521HCY
502	L502HCY	507	L507HCY	512	L512HCY	517	L517HCY	522	L522HCY
503	L503HCY	508	L508HCY	513	L513HCY	518	L518HCY	523	L523HCY
504	L504HCY	509	L509HCY	514	L514HCY	519	L519HCY	524	L524HCY
505	L505HCY	510	L510HCY	515	L515HCY	520	L520HCY		

525-550		Dennis Dart 9SDL3034		Plaxton Pointer		B31F	1994		
525	L525JEP	531	L531JEP	536	L536JEP	541	L541JEP	546	L546JEP
526	L526JEP	532	L532JEP	537	L537JEP	542	L542JEP	547	L547JEP
527	L527JEP	533	L533JEP	538	L538JEP	543	L543JEP	548	L548JEP
528	L528JEP	534	L534JEP	539	L539JEP	544	L544JEP	549	L549JEP
529	L529JEP	535	L535JEP	540	L540JEP	545	L545JEP	550	L550JEP
530	L530JEP								

551-568		Dennis Dart 9SDL3034		Plaxton Pointer		B31F	1995		
551	N551UCY	555	N555UCY	559	N559UCY	563	N563UCY	566	N566UCY
552	N552UCY	556	N556UCY	561	N561UCY	564	N564UCY	567	N567UCY
553	N553UCY	557	N557UCY	562	N562UCY	565	N565UCY	568	N568UCY
554	N554UCY	558	N558UCY						

569-580		Dennis Dart SLF		Plaxton Pointer		N31F	1996		
569	P569BTH	572	P572BTH	575	P575BTH	577	P577BTH	579	P579BTH
570	P570BTH	573	P573BTH	576	P576BTH	578	P578BTH	580	P580BTH
571	P571BTH	574	P574BTH						

The Welsh Bus Handbook

FirstGroup orders have included a large number of Alexander-bodied Dennis Darts, several of which have been allocated to First Cymru. However, the first of this body type joined the fleet along with the services of Rees & Williams. Of the sixteen delivered in 1999, 629, T629SEJ, is seen in Swansea on a service which, for many years, required specially adapted buses because of the steep gradients. *John Jones*

581-599		Dennis Dart SLF		Plaxton Pointer 2		N26F	1998		
581	R581SWN	585	R585SWN	589	R589SWN	593	R593SWN	597	R597SWN
582	R582SWN	586	R586SWN	590	R590SWN	594	R594SWN	598	R598SWN
583	R583SWN	587	R587SWN	591	R591SWN	595	R595SWN	599	R599SWN
584	R584SWN	588	R588SWN	592	R592SWN	596	R596SWN		

601-608		Dennis Dart 9.8SDL3035		Plaxton Pointer		B40F	1994		
601	L601FKG	603	L603FKG	605	L605FKG	607	L607FKG	608	L608FKG
602	L602FKG	604	L604FKG	606	L606FKG				

609-618		Dennis Dart 9.8SDL3054		Plaxton Pointer		BC40F*	1995	*616 is BC36F	
609	N609MHB	611	N611MHB	613	N613MHB	615	N615MHB	617	N617MHB
610	N610MHB	612	N612MHB	614w	N614MHB	616	N616MHB	618	N618MHB
619	P619VDW		Dennis Dart		Plaxton Pointer	B40F	1997		
620	P620VDW		Dennis Dart		Plaxton Pointer	B40F	1997		
621	P621VDW		Dennis Dart		Plaxton Pointer	B40F	1997		

622-637		Dennis Dart SLF		Alexander ALX200		N37F	1999		
622	T622SEJ	626	T626SEJ	629	T629SEJ	632	T632SEJ	635	T635SEJ
623	T623SEJ	627	T627SEJ	630	T630SEJ	633	T633SEJ	636	T636SEJ
624	T624SEJ	628	T628SEJ	631	T631SEJ	634	T634SEJ	637	T637SEJ
625	T625SEJ								

702	LOI6690	Leyland Leopard PSU3D/4R	Plaxton Derwent (1987)	B51F	1977	Yorkshire Rider (Y), 1996
703	VDH244S	Leyland Leopard PSU3E/4R	Duple Dominant (1985)	B51F	1977	Yorkshire Rider (Y), 1996
707	C658KEP	Leyland Tiger TRCTL11/3RZ	Duple Laser 2	C57F	1986	Davies Bros, Pencader, 1999
709	GDE371W	Leyland Leopard PSU5D/4R (TL11)	Plaxton Supreme IV	C57F	1981	Davies Bros, Pencader, 1999
710	OUT11W	Leyland Leopard PSU3E/4R	Plaxton Supreme IV Exp	C53F	1981	Davies Bros, Pencader, 1999
711	GCY124W	Leyland Leopard PSU3E/4R	Plaxton Supreme IV Exp	C53F	1980	Davies Bros, Pencader, 1999
712	A115UDE	Leyland Tiger TRCTL11/3L	Willowbrook Warrior (1990)	B51F	1984	Davies Bros, Pencader, 1999

797	AAE654V	Leyland National 2 NL116L11/1R			B49F	1980	Bristol (City Line), 1998		
813	AWN813V	Leyland National 11351A/1R			B49F	1979			

816-825 Dennis Lance 11SDA3112 Plaxton Verde BC45F 1993

816	L816HCY	818	L818HCY	820	L820HCY	822	L822HCY	824	L824HCY
817	L817HCY	819	L819HCY	821	L821HCY	823	L823HCY	825	L825HCY

826	L218AAB	Dennis Lance 11SDA3107	Plaxton Verde	B49F	1994	Midland Red West, 1998
827	L219AAB	Dennis Lance 11SDA3107	Plaxton Verde	B49F	1994	Midland Red West, 1998
828	L220AAB	Dennis Lance 11SDA3107	Plaxton Verde	B49F	1994	Midland Red West, 1998
836	G841PNW	Van Hool A600	Van Hool	B52F	1990	Yorkshire Rider (Q), 1994
838	J916WVC	Leyland Lynx LX2R11V18245	Leyland Lynx	B51F	1992	Volvo demonstrator, 1992
839	J375WWK	Leyland Lynx LX2R11V18245	Leyland Lynx	B47F	1992	Volvo demonstrator, 1992
840	K10BMS	Leyland Lynx LX2R11C15Z4A	Leyland Lynx	B47F	1992	
841	K11BMS	Leyland Lynx LX2R11C15Z4A	Leyland Lynx	B47F	1992	
842	K12BMS	Leyland Lynx LX2R11C15Z4A	Leyland Lynx	B47F	1992	
851	AAL516A	Leyland Tiger TRCTL11/3R	Plaxton Paramount 3200	C53F	1983	Stagecoach Red & White, ē98
852	AAX529A	Leyland Tiger TRCTL11/3R	Plaxton Paramount 3200	C53F	1983	Stagecoach Red & White, ē97
853	AAX450A	Leyland Tiger TRCTL11/3R	Plaxton Paramount 3200E	C53F	1983	Stagecoach Red & White, ē97
854	AAX466A	Leyland Tiger TRCTL11/3R	Plaxton Paramount 3200E	C53F	1983	Stagecoach Red & White, ē97
855	AAX515A	Leyland Tiger TRCTL11/3R	Plaxton Paramount 3200	C53F	1983	Stagecoach Red & White, ē97
856	OIL3796	Leyland Tiger TRCTL11/3R	Plaxton Paramount 3200E	C53F	1984	The Shires, 1998

901-907 Leyland Olympian ONCL10/1RV Eastern Coach Works B45/30F 1985

901	C901FCY	903	C903FCY	905	C905FCY	906	C906FCY	907	C907FCY
902	C902FCY	904	C904FCY						

920	ANA189Y	MCW Metrobus DR102/23	MCW	B43/30F	1983	Manchester, 1998
921	ANA182Y	MCW Metrobus DR102/23	MCW	B43/30F	1983	Manchester, 1998
922	SND135X	MCW Metrobus DR102/23	MCW	B43/30F	1983	Manchester, 1998
946	XHK234X	Bristol VRT/SL3/6LXB	Eastern Coach Works	B43/31F	1981	
947	UAR587W	Bristol VRT/SL3/6LXB	Eastern Coach Works	B43/31F	1981	
949w	UAR598W	Bristol VRT/SL3/6LXB	Eastern Coach Works	B43/31F	1981	
950	ANA630Y	Leyland Atlantean AN68D/1R	Northern Counties	B43/32F	1983	Greater Manchester, 1997
951	ANA624Y	Leyland Atlantean AN68D/1R	Northern Counties	B43/32F	1983	Greater Manchester, 1997
952w	TGG739R	Leyland Atlantean AN68A/1R	Alexander AL	B45/31F	1977	Greater Glasgow, 1997
956	A748NNA	Leyland Atlantean AN68D/1R	Northern Counties	B43/32F	1984	Greater Manchester, 1997
957	A675HNB	Leyland Atlantean AN68D/1R	Northern Counties	B43/32F	1984	Greater Manchester, 1997
958	A688HNB	Leyland Atlantean AN68D/1R	Northern Counties	B43/32F	1984	Greater Manchester, 1997
960	EWS744W	Bristol VRT/SL3/680	Eastern Coach Works	B43/31F	1981	Badgerline, 1997
962w	LSU379V	Leyland Atlantean AN68A/1R	Alexander AL	B45/33F	1979	Greater Glasgow, 1997
963	A694HNB	Leyland Atlantean AN68D/1R	Northern Counties	D40/02F	1984	Greater Manchester, 1997

The first bus to be painted into the latest First Cymru livery was former First Midland Red's Dennis Lance L220AAB, now numbered 828. This vehicle was one of three to join the fleet in 1998, joining ten similar buses purchased for suburban use.
John Jones

61

976-994 Bristol VRT/SL3/501   Eastern Coach Works   B43/31F   1979-80

976w	BEP976V	**980**	BEP980V	**984**w	BEP984V	**990**	ECY990V	**994** EWN994W
978	BEP978V	**981**w	BEP981V	**989**	ECY989V	**992**	EWN992W	**995**w EWN995W

Special event vehicle:

1114	AKG219A	Leyland Leopard L1	Weymann	B44F	1961	Llynfi, Maesteg, 1988

Ancilliary vehicles:

2	G51OUB	Mercedes-Benz 709D	Dormobile Routemaker	Publicity	1990	Davies Bros, Pencader, 1999
38	LJN648P	Bristol VRT/SL3/501	Eastern Coach Works	TV	1976	Skillplace, Port Talbot, 1997
45	SHO628P	Bedford SB5	Plaxton Panorama	C41F	1976	
56	B124PEL	Bedford YNT	Plaxton Paramount 3200 E	TV	1976	Skillplace, Port Talbot, 1997
207	C207HTH	Mercedes-Benz L608D	Robin Hood	B20F	1986	Publicity
414	F604AWN	Mercedes-Benz 709D	Reeve Burges Beaver	B25F	1988	
416	F606AWN	Mercedes-Benz 709D	Reeve Burges Beaver	B25F	1988	
430	H825ERV	Mercedes-Benz 709D	Wadham Stringer Wessex	B25F	1991	Western National, 1996

Previous Registrations:

948RJO	G500JEP	C658KEP	3338DD
2358DD	A171UDE	FIL7131	F113UBX
2405DD	From new	F921FCY	F200EEP, 278TNY
5210DD	F614RBX	G841PNW	G680TKE, A6RLR
5519DD	F114UBX	GCY124W	GCY124W, FEK1F
6690DD	F721ENE	GDE371W	LHE256W, 2358DD
7660DD	From new	J901MAF	J6EDE
8098DD	D615HBX	L538XUT	L538XUT, WCY701
8124DD	KBX78X	LIL5069	C792MVH
8853DD	E237MBX	LOI6690	REL400R
A115UDE	First UK Reg	MIB657	F726ENE
AAL516A	SDW927Y	MKH487A	from new
AAX450A	SDW914Y	NIL2450	F618XWY
AAX466A	SDW917Y	NIL2454	A678KDV
AAX515A	SDW929Y	NIL2456	A657VDA
AAX529A	SDW931Y	OIL3796	A151EPA
ACY178A	From new	UOI4323	BKH129X, VOI4323
AKG219A	YBK132	WSV410	A608KYG
C312KTH	999BCY		

Allocations:

Coaching unit (Acacia Avenue, Sandfields Estate, Port Talbot) - United Welsh Coaches

DAF coach	188	192		
Duple 425	132	136		
Javelin coach	172	173	174	175
Volvo coach	195	196		
Bristol VR	950			

Coaching unit (Pentregethin Road, Ravenhill)

Volvo Expressliner	106							
DAF	189							
Tiger	125	126	707					
Javelin Expressliner	101	102	103	107	108	109	110	111
	112	113	114	115	116	176	177	178
Duple 425	131	132	133	134	135	136	137	139

The latest First Cymru bus livery for non-corporate vehicles is illustrated by Dennis Dart 502, L502HCY, pictured in Kingsway, Swansea. Apart from five buses purchased from Rees & Williams, this batch are the oldest midi buses in the fleet. *John Jones*

Ammanford (Pontardulais Road, Tycroes)

Mercedes-Benz	273	291	292	342	365	378	379	452
	453	454						
Dart	396	397	398	399				
Tiger	156	853	854	855	856			
Leopard	709							

Bridgend (Aneurin Bevan Avenue, Brynmenyn Ind Est)

Mercedes-Benz	306	311	320	385	401	402	403	404
	405	406	407	408	409	410	481	482
	483	484	485					
Dart	509	510	585	586	587	588	589	608
	609	610	617	618	619	620	621	
Lynx	840	841	842					
Tiger	160	180						

The Welsh Bus Handbook

Carmarthen (Dolgwili Road)

Mercedes-Benz	274	310	339	374	375	384	387	388
	390	391	392	393	429	451		
Iveco	201	205	206	212	215	216		
Tiger	140	141	142	143	145	146	147	148
	149	151	152	153	162	166	180	851
Leopard	703	711						

Haverfordwest (Withybush Industrial Estate)

Outstation: Pembroke Dock

Mercedes-Benz	294	297	301	302	326	329	330	331
	335	343	347	348	360	413		

Llanelli (Inkerman Street)

Mercedes-Benz	289	293	296	298	300	304	313	316
	319	323	324	325	332	333	340	341
	344	345	367	368	369	377	394	
Dart	395	501	502	503	504	505	506	549
	561	562	563	564	565	566	567	568
Leopard	710	712						
Tiger	152							

Maesteg (Heol Ty Gwyn Industrial Estate, Tyle Teg)

Mercedes-Benz	334	336	337	338	380	383	431	486
	487	488	489	490				
Volvo	159							
Tiger	165							
Dart	556	557	558	559	601	602	603	604
	615							
Lynx	838	839						

Pontardawe (Tawe Terrace)

Mercedes-Benz	346	349	350	351	352	353	354	355
	356	357	358	359	361	371	372	373
	381	382						
Dart	590	591	592	593	594	595	596	597
	598	599	605	607	631	632	633	634
	635	636	637					
Lance	825	826	827	828				
Bristol VR	978	980	984	990	994			

Port Talbot (Acacia Avenue, Sandfields Estate)

Mercedes-Benz	440	441	442	443	444	445	446	447
	448	449	450					
Dart	611	612	613	615	622	623	624	625
Lance	816	817	818	819	820	821	822	823
	824							
Bristol VR	960	980						

Bristol VRTs and Leyland Olympians largely meet the double-deck requirements of First Cymru. However, the fleet also contains the Metrobuses that were transferred from First Manchester in 1998. Brewers' livery is carried by 922, SND135X in this view taken in Swansea. *John Jones*

Ravenhill (Pentregethin Road)

Outstation: Ludchurch

Iveco	207	208						
Mercedes-Benz	287	290	295	299	305			
	307	309	312	314	315	321	322	370
	418							
Dart	507	508	511	512	513	514	515	516
	517	518	519	520	521	522	523	524
	525	526	527	528	529	530	531	532
	533	534	535	536	537	538	539	540
	541	542	543	544	545	546	547	548
	550	551	552	553	554	555	569	570
	571	572	573	574	575	576	577	578
	579	580	581	582	583	584	626	627
	628	629	630					
Olympian	901	902	903	904	905	906	907	
Metrobus	920	921	922					
Atlantean	956	957	958	963				
Bristol VR	992							

Unallocated

Mercedes-Benz	261	262	270	271	389	308	327	366
	376	419	432	434	435	437		
Iveco	204	209						
Leopard	702							
Toyota	150							
National	797	813						
Heritage	1114							
Bristol VR	946	947	949	976	981	989	995	
Atlantean	951	952	962					

G H A COACHES

EL, G & A Davies, Mill Garage, Bettws Gwerfil Goch, Corwen, Denbighshire LL21 9PU

BTU364S	Bristol VRT/SL3/501	Eastern Coach Works	B43/31F	1978	PMT, 1992
FFR168S	Bristol VRT/SL3/6LXB	Eastern Coach Works	B43/31F	1978	Stagecoach Burnley & Pendle, 1997
FFR172S	Bristol VRT/SL3/6LXB	Eastern Coach Works	B43/31F	1978	Stagecoach Burnley & Pendle, 1997
BWJ68T	Bedford YLQ	Duple Dominant II	C45F	1979	Llew Jones Coaches, Llanrwst, 1991
HBD919T	Bristol VRT/SL3/6LXB	Eastern Coach Works	B43/31F	1979	Stagecoach United Counties, 1998
SGR779V	Bristol VRT/SL3/6LXB	Eastern Coach Works	B43/31F	1979	Northumbria, 1996
SGR792V	Bristol VRT/SL3/6LXB	Eastern Coach Works	B43/31F	1980	Northumbria, 1995
EWE206V	Bristol VRT/SL3/6LXB	Eastern Coach Works	B43/31F	1980	Stagecoach East Midland, 1999
NIL8658	Volvo B58-61	Plaxton Supreme IV	C57F	1980	Redline, Penwortham, 1996
UDM449V	Bristol VRT/SL3/6LXB	Eastern Coach Works	B43/31F	1980	Straffords, Coedpoeth, 1999
APT820W	Bristol VRT/SL3/6LXB	Eastern Coach Works	B42/31F	1980	Northumbria, 1996
DBX548W	Bedford YMQ	Duple Dominant II	C45F	1980	Dyma-Fo, Coaches, 1988
YKS22W	Bedford YLQ	Plaxton Supreme IV Exp	C45F	1980	Munro, Jedburgh, 1991
YMB508W	Bristol VRT/SL3/6LXB	Eastern Coach Works	B43/31F	1981	Straffords, Coedpoeth, 1999
VAH278X	Bristol VRT/SL3/6LXB	Eastern Coach Works	B43/31F	1981	Stagecoach Cambus (Viscount), 2000
VAH279X	Bristol VRT/SL3/6LXB	Eastern Coach Works	B43/31F	1981	Stagecoach Cambus (Viscount), 2000
VAH299X	Bristol VRT/SL3/6LXB	Eastern Coach Works	B43/31F	1981	Stagecoach Cambus (Viscount), 2000
CIB7866	Leyland Tiger TRCTL11/3R	Plaxton Paramount 3500	C49FT	1983	Sargeant's, Kington, 1995
YJI1309	Leyland Tiger TRCTL11/3R	Plaxton Paramount 3500	C49FT	1983	Taylor, Speke, 1999
YLP528	Volvo B10M-61	Van Hool Alizée H	C46FT	1983	Stagecoach Rhondda, 1999
WIB1701	Bedford YNT	Plaxton Paramount 3200	C53F	1983	Luker, Crondall, 1994
552OHU	Leyland Tiger TRCTL11/3R	Plaxton Paramount 3200	C53F	1983	Stagecoach Midland Red, 1999
A132FDC	Leyland National 2 NL116AHLXCT/1R		B49F	1983	Catch-a-Bus, East Boldon, 1998
A279ROW	Leyland Olympian ONLXB/1R	East Lancashire	B46/30F	1984	Village, Bootle, 1998
A15RBL	Volvo B10M-56	Van Hool Alizée L	B51F	1984	Stagecoach Red & White, 1999
MKH87A	Leyland Tiger TRCTL11/3RH	Duple Caribbean	C46FT	1985	SWT (Brewers), 1997
NIL8657	Leyland Royal Tiger RT	Van Hool Alizée	C49FT	1986	Aline, Pelaw, 1996
6689DP	Volvo B10M-61	Irizar Pyrennean	C49FT	1986	Travel Tayside (Greyhound), 1999
D948UDY	Mercedes-Benz L608D	Alexander AM	BC19F	1986	Red & White, 1996
FIL7485	Volvo B10M-61	Van Hool Alizée	C49FT	1987	WGS (Gordons), Rotherham, 1998
E448AFT	Mercedes-Benz 709D	Reeve Burgess Beaver	B20F	1987	Stagecoach Devon, 1998
UBZ3362	Volvo B10M-61	Plaxton Paramount 3200 III	C57F	1987	Blue Iris, Nailsea, 1998
F107NRT	Volvo B10M-61	Plaxton Paramount 3500 III	C49FT	1988	Stagecoach United Counties, 2000
F995DRN	Mercedes-Benz 709D	Reeve Burgess Beaver	BC25F	1988	Stagecoach Burnley & Pendle, 1998
F724FDV	Mercedes-Benz 709D	Reeve Burgess Beaver	B25F	1988	Stagecoach Oxford, 1998
F614XMS	Mercedes-Benz 811D	Alexander AM	B28F	1988	Stagecoach Red & White, 2000
F725USF	Mercedes-Benz 811D	Alexander AM	BC33F	1989	Mainline, 1997
F70LAL	Mercedes-Benz 811D	Alexander AM	BC33F	1989	Mainline, 1997

GHA Coaches' 6689DP ia a Volvo B10M with rare Irizar Purennean coachwork, acquired from Travel Dundee in 1999. It is seen taking part in the afternoon mass exodus from Yale College, Wrexham in September 1999.
John Jones

Two Plaxton MPD buses joined the GHA Coaches fleet in 1999 for use on tendered services. The MPD is a collaboration between Dennis and Plaxton to produce a short version of the Dart. Other bodybuilders have now developed similar bodies including Marshall and Alexander, now a sister company of Dennis within the Mayflower Corporation. V7GHA carries vinyls for *Traxx*, the service network based on Hooton Interchange, and is seen in Mold shortly after entering service. *David Donati*

F725USF	Mercedes-Benz 811D	Alexander AM	BC33F	1989	Mainline, 1997
F70LAL	Mercedes-Benz 811D	Alexander AM	BC33F	1989	Mainline, 1997
G577PRM	Mercedes-Benz 709D	Alexander Sprint	B23F	1990	Stagecoach Ribble, 2000
G183PAO	Mercedes-Benz 709D	Alexander Sprint	B23F	1990	Stagecoach Ribble, 1999
G844UDV	Mercedes-Benz 709D	Carlyle	B29F	1990	Stagecoach Oxford, 1999
H78CFV	Mercedes-Benz 811D	Alexander AM	B31F	1991	Stagecoach Ribble (B&P), 1999
J124AHH	Volvo B10M-60	Plaxton Expressliner	C46FT	1992	Stagecoach Ribble, 1999
K659NGB	Mercedes-Benz 709D	Dormobile Routemaker	B29F	1992	Redline, Penwortham, 1996
N2GHA	Mercedes-Benz 709D	Marshall C19	B27F	1996	
N3GHA	Mercedes-Benz 709D	Marshall C19	B27F	1996	
R5GHA	Mercedes-Benz Vario O814D	Plaxton Beaver 2	BC33F	1998	
S6GHA	Mercedes-Benz Vario O814D	Plaxton Beaver 2	B27F	1998	
V7GHA	Dennis Dart SLF	Plaxton Pointer MPD	N26F	1999	
V8GHA	Dennis Dart SLF	Plaxton Pointer MPD	N26F	1999	

Previous Registrations:

552OHU	A201RHT	NIL8657	C588ORG
6689DP	D491RSU	NIL8658	JJU436V, 999RED, CFR630V
A15RBL	B947ASU	UBZ3362	E328FLD
CIB7866	ANA109Y	WIB1701	VGM244Y, 8466PH, NRV303Y, HSV343, CPE344Y
F995DRN	F95XBV, XFK305	YJI1309	BAJ630Y
HIL7592	E179FFT	HIL7593	E180FFT
FIL7485	D849KVE	YLP528	MSU571Y
MKH87A	B129CTH		

Depots: Mill Garage, Bettws Gwerfil Goch and Gatewen Ind Est, New Broughton, Rhostyllen, Wrexham.
Livery: Grey, red and maroon. Two-tone green (Flintshire Traxx);- V7/8GHA.

G M

R G Millington, Mountain View Garage, Tyfry Road, Cefn Cribwr
Bridgend CF32 0BB

MCO253H	Leyland Atlantean PDR2/1	Park Royal	B49/32D	1970	Light, East Stour, 1989
UKE416H	Leyland Leopard PSU4A/4R	Marshall	B45F	1970	Maidstone & District, 1982
VBA164S	Leyland Atlantean AN68A/1R	Northern Counties	B43/32F	1978	Stagecoach Manchester, 1996
VBA168S	Leyland Atlantean AN68A/1R	Northern Counties	B43/32F	1978	Stagecoach Manchester, 1996
WKE69S	Bedford YMT	Duple Dominant	B61F	1978	Roberts Cs, Maerdy, 1994
AKK174T	Bedford YMT	Duple Dominant	B61F	1978	Roberts Cs, Maerdy, 1994
UHW10T	Leyland Leopard PSU3E/4R	Plaxton Supreme IV	C53F	1978	Blue Iris, Nailsea, 1993
WTG330T	Bristol VRT/SL3/6LXB	Alexander AL	B44/31F	1978	Len Hopkins, Ogmore Vale, 1998
URN153V	Leyland Leopard PSU3E/2R	Duple Dominant	B55F	1979	Green Bus, Great Wyrley, 1997
AUP351W	Leyland Atlantean AN68B/1R	Roe	B43/30F	1980	Go-Ahead (Tynemouth), 1998
AUP371W	Leyland Atlantean AN68B/1R	Roe	B43/30F	1980	Go-Northern, 1999
OIB5880	Volvo B10M-61	Berkhof Esprite 350	C49FT	1983	Brixham Travel, 1993
OIB7915	Volvo B10M-61	Berkhof Esprite 350	C53F	1984	The King's Ferry, 1989
OIB7631	Volvo B10M-61	Berkhof Esprite 340	C53F	1984	The King's Ferry, 1991
MIB284	Volvo B10M-61	Berkhof Esprite 340	C53F	1984	BB, Halesowen, 1999
MIL9466	Iveco Daily 49.10	Robin Hood City Nippy	B25F	1987	Rixon, Porthcawl, 1998

Previous Registrations:

MIB284	B589XNO	OIB7631	A581RVW, 951JNU, A973SKK
MIL9466	D614MKH	OIB7915	A576RVW, 279NDE, A632SKK
OIB5880	ADV147Y, A144JTA, 755HWP, A942RTT		

Livery: Beige and red

GAVENNY BUS

G & K R Lewis, 1 Trinity Terrace, Baker Street, Abergavenny, Monmouthshire, NP7 5BE

D574EWS	Freight Rover Sherpa	Dormobile	B16F	1986	Phil Anslow, Garndiffaith, 1994
D583EWS	Freight Rover Sherpa	Dormobile	B16F	1986	Phil Anslow, Garndiffaith, 1994
D929NDB	Renault-Dodge S56	Northern Counties	B20F	1987	?, 1999
D969PJA	Renault-Dodge S56	Northern Counties	B20F	1987	Bromyard Bus Company, 1999
F463EAX	Freight-Rover Sherpa	Freight-Rover	M8	1989	MoD, 1995
G40HDW	Freight-Rover Sherpa	Carlyle Citybus 2	B20F	1990	Bromyard Bus Company, 1999
J587SOG	Leyland-DAF 200	Leyland-DAF	M8	1992	taxi, Pontypool, 1998

Depot: Horsington's Yard, Lion Street, Abergavenny
Livery: Grey (D929NDB, D969PJA).

GM operate six double-deck buses, the Leyland Atlantean being the dominant type. The latest arrival is Roe-bodied AUP371W which came from Go Northern and is seen returning after its afternoon school run. The body-stying using a 'standard' window bay was much influenced by the former BET companies within NBC, and the PTEs, particularly Manchester who worked closely with Northern Counties. *John Jones*

Gavenny Bus operate local services in Abergavenny, and a service between the Monmouthshire town and Brynmawr, one of the 'Heads of the Valleys' towns. D969PJA is a Dodge S56 bodied by Northern Counties and was originally part of Greater Manchester's Little Gem fleet. *David Donati*

GEORGE EDWARDS & SON

GF & G Edwards, Berwyn, Bwlchgwyn, Wrexham, LL11 5UE

D642DRT	Bedford YNT	Duple Dominant	B63F	1987	Chambers, Bures, 1995
G256EHD	DAF MB230LB615	Van Hool Alizée	C55F	1989	Hanmer, Southsea, 1986
G261EHD	DAF SB2305DHTD585	Plaxton Paramount 3200 III	C57F	1989	
L537EHD	DAF SB3000DKVF601	Van Hool Alizèe HE	C55F	1989	Arriva Bus and Coach, 2000
L407XMR	Dennis Javelin	Plaxton Première 320	C57F	1994	Ellison, Ashton Keynes, 1997
P2WAL	DAF DE02LTSB220	Ikarus CitiBus	B49F	1996	Walls, Sharston, 1998
S403JUA	DAF DE02GSSB220	Optare Delta	B49F	1998	Montague Euro, Northampton, 1999

Livery: Red, maroon and ivory

Walls of Manchester operated several DAF buses on lease from Arriva Bus and Coach. When that operator ceased, this SB220 with Ikarus bodywork moved to George Edwards, retaining its Select index mark P2WAL. It is seen leaving Wrexham bus station for Gwynfryn.
Cliff Beeton

S403JUA is one of the final DAF SB220s to be built by Optare before the old chassis ceased production and a new low-floor SB220 became the standard. Arriva Cymru operated two examples of the model, though these were transferred as part of their rationalisation of types. S403JUA replaced a Duple Dominant-bodied Bedford YMT.
John Jones

GOODSIR

W C Goodsir, 30 Trenwfa Road, Lands End, Holyhead, Anglesey LL65 1LE

NWS288R	Bristol VRT/SL3/6LXB	Eastern Coach Works	B43/28F	1977	Stagecoach C&G (Circle Line), 1999
WBD875S	Bristol VRT/SL3/6LXB	Eastern Coach Works	B43/31F	1977	Stagecoach United Counties, 1996
WDA923T	Leyland Fleetline FE30AGR	MCW	B43/33F	1978	Travel West Midlands, 1997
UEY454T	Leyland National 11351A/2R		B48F	1978	Bajwa, Slough, 1995
JTU597T	Leyland National 10351B/1R		B44F	1979	Jones Llanfaethlu, 1991
SWH376T	Leyland National 10351A/2R		B40D	1979	Hanson, Wordsley, 1998
102UTF	Volvo B10M-61	Jonckheere Jubilee P50	C49FT	1983	Oareís of Holywell, 1994
297EYR	Van Hool T815	Van Hool Alizèe	C53FT	1983	APT, Rayleigh, 1995
GSU368	Volvo B10M-61	Jonckheere Jubilee P90	C51/9FT	1983	Hemisphere, Welwyn Garden, 1997
708EYG	Volvo B10M-53	Plaxton Pimount 4000RS II	C55/9DT	1986	Davies Bros, Pencader, 1998
H466LEY	Mercedes-Benz 709D	Reeve Burgess Beaver	B25F	1991	

Previous Registrations:

102UTF	MRP847Y, NAG455A	UEY454T	YCD85T, BAZ7378
297EYR	TRT182, 827APT, BJS98Y, APT42S, UJN995Y	GSU368	A315XHE
708EYG	D388FBX, 6690DD	SWH376T	AYR347T, JIL8212

Livery: White, black, yellow and orange or white

Goodsir is located in the busy port of Holyhead where it operates several commercial routes. Three Leyland Nationals are included in the fleet the latest arrival being SWH376T, which was new to London Buses and still retains the depot and duty allocation frames. *John Jones*

The Welsh Bus Handbook 71

GLYN WILLIAMS

G J, F J & T G Williams, Risca House, Waunfawr Gardens, Crosskeys, Caerphilly NP1 7BL
Crosskeys Coach Hire Ltd, Pennar Halt Garage, Pentwynmawr,
Pontllanfraith, Caerphilly NP2 2AW

1	RSG821V	Leyland National 2 NL116L11/1R		B52F	1979	Weir, Clydebank, 1995
2	W713DAX	Dennis Dart SLF	Plaxton Pointer MPD	N28F	2000	
3	S787NRV	Dennis Dart SLF	SCC Compass	N44F	1998	
4	P423PBP	Dennis Dart SLF	UVG UrbanStar	N36F	1997	UVG demonstrator, 1997
6	T601DAX	Dennis Dart SLF	Plaxton Pointer MPD	N28F	1999	
7	R409HKG	Dennis Dart SLF	UVG UrbanStar	N43F	1997	
8	T602DAX	Dennis Dart SLF	Plaxton Pointer MPD	N28F	1999	
9	T603DAX	Dennis Dart SLF	Plaxton Pointer MPD	N28F	1999	
10	M1GWT	Mercedes-Benz 811D	Plaxton Beaver	B31F	1995	
11	R410HTG	Dennis Dart SLF	UVG UrbanStar	N44F	1998	
14	R424AOR	Dennis Dart SLF	UVG UrbanStar	N44F	1998	
15	T604DAX	Dennis Dart SLF	Plaxton Pointer MPD	N28F	1999	
17	R407AOR	Dennis Dart SLF	UVG UrbanStar	N42F	1997	
18	HHH371V	Leyland National 2 NL116L11/1R		B52F	1980	Ribble, 1994
19	R421AOR	Dennis Dart SLF	UVG UrbanStar	N44F	1998	
20	MHJ732V	Leyland National 2 NL116L11/1R		B52F	1980	Eastern National, 1994
21	S846SNY	Dennis Dart SLF	UVG UrbanStar	N44F	1998	
22	R408AOR	Dennis Dart SLF	UVG UrbanStar	N44F	1997	
23	MHJ729V	Leyland National 2 NL116L11/1R		B52F	1980	Eastern National, 1995
24	G46TGW	Dennis Dart 8.55SDL3003	Carlyle Dartline	B28F	1990	London United, 2000
25	W714DAX	Dennis Dart SLF	Plaxton Pointer MPD	N28F	2000	
26	M243JHB	Mercedes-Benz 811D	Plaxton Beaver	B31F	1994	
27	M242JHB	Mercedes-Benz 811D	Plaxton Beaver	B31F	1994	
28	M244JHB	Mercedes-Benz 811D	Plaxton Beaver	B31F	1994	
29	LRB200W	Leyland National 2 NL116L11/1R		B52F	1980	Yorkshire Buses, 1994
30	R422AOR	Dennis Dart SLF	UVG UrbanStar	N44F	1998	
31	LRB216W	Leyland National 2 NL116AL11/1R		B52F	1981	Yorkshire Buses, 1994
32	S788NRV	Dennis Dart SLF	SCC Compass	N44F	1998	
33	G514VYE	Dennis Dart 8.55SDL3003	Duple Dartline	B28F	1990	London United, 2000
34	G519VYE	Dennis Dart 8.55SDL3003	Duple Dartline	B28F	1990	London United, 2000
35	G511VYE	Dennis Dart 8.55SDL3003	Duple Dartline	B28F	1990	London United, 2000

Previous Registrations:
M1GWT M528KTG R409HKG R409AOR

Depot: Pennar Halt Garage, Pentwynmawr
Livery: Green and white

Opposite, top: **The Glyn Williams fleet has received many low-floor Dennis Darts. While some have the standard Plaxton body, nine carry UVG UrbanStar bodies and two have Salvador Caetano Coachbuilders' Compass design, following the demise of UVG. Pictured arriving at Newport from Blackwood is 7, R409HKG, one of the UVG products.** *John Jones*
Opposite, bottom: **Four Mini Pointer Darts were placed in service by Glyn Williams in 1999 and, to celebrate 25 years in business, these retain the silver livery in which they arrived. Number 9, T603DAX, is seen climbing up towards Blackwood bus station with the destination blind set for the return journey to Abertillery.** *John Jones*

GWYN WILLIAMS

Gwyn Williams & Sons Ltd, Derlwyn Garage, Lower Tumble, Carmarthenshire SA15 5YT

79	ENY26V	Bedford YMT	Duple Dominant II	C53F	1980	Morris Travel, Pencoed, 1981
95	SJI2154	Leyland Tiger TRCTL11/2R	Plaxton Viewmaster IV Exp	C49F	1982	Vale of Llangollen, 1986
100	5652MT	Leyland Tiger TRCTL11/2R	Plaxton Viewmaster IV Exp	C49F	1982	Vale of Llangollen, 1987
101	E669ECJ	Renault Master T35D	Coachwork Walker	M16	1987	Jenkins, Crickhowell, 1988
105	SJI2155	Leyland Tiger TRCTL11/3R	Duple 320	C53FT	1986	Watson, Annfield Plain, 1989
108	G555HTH	Leyland-DAF 200	Leyland-DAF	M12	1989	
114	G300LEP	Dennis Javelin 12SDA1907	Duple 320	C53F	1990	
117	H930EBX	Renault Trafic	Williams	M12	1990	
121	H20DBW	Dennis Javelin 12SDA1907	Duple 320	C55FT	1991	
122	SJI2156	Renault Master T35D	Cymric	M16	1989	van, 1991
123	SJI2153	Leyland Leopard PSU3B/4R	Plaxton Elite III	C53F	1973	Tenby Bus & Coach, 1991
124	D387SGS	Freight Rover Sherpa	Dormobile	B16F	1987	Smith, Kennford, 1994
125	B634BEP	Mercedes-Benz L207D	Williams	M8L	1985	van, 1994
126	GDZ886	Leyland Tiger TRCTL11/3RZ	Van Hool Alizée	C55F	1985	Merlyns, Skewen, 1994
127	E634YWL	Freight Rover Sherpa	Williams	M8L	1988	van, 1994
129	D958WJH	Freight Rover Sherpa	Dormobile	B8F	1986	Brian Isaac, Morriston, 1994
132	TPL166S	Bedford YMT	Duple Dominant	B53F	1977	Meurig Morgan, Lampeter, 1995
134	VCY401	Dennis Dorchester SDA803	Plaxton Paramount 3200	C53F	1983	Thomas Bros, Llangadog, 1995
136	D458CKV	Freight Rover Sherpa	Rootes	B16F	1986	Midland Red South (G & G), 1995
137	YDR224	DAF MB200DKVL600	Jonckheere Jubilee P50	C50FT	1986	Byronís, Skewen, 1996
138	P10GWS	Renault Master T35D	Cymric	M16	1996	
143	FYJ994V	Bedford YLQ	Duple Dominant II	C45F	1980	Meurig Morgan, Lampeter, 1997
145	BXI637	Leyland Tiger TRCTL11/3R	Plaxton Paramount 3500 III	C49FT	1983	Jones International, Llandeilo, 1997
146	KYV452X	Leyland Titan TNLXB2RR	Leyland	B43/30F	1982	Oxford Cityline, 1997
147	OHV783Y	Leyland Titan TNLXB2RR	Leyland	B43/30F	1983	Oxford Cityline, 1997

Double-deck buses have only recently featured in the Gwyn Williams fleet with three from Oxford Cityline now current. Two are Leyland Titans originally new to London Buses now refurbished and fitted with seat belts. The splendid condition of this fleet is illustrated by 146, KYV452X. *John Jones*

The availability of former Ministry of Defence buses led to the purchase of five by Gwyn Williams during 1998. These Plaxton-bodied Leyland Tigers were placed in service following their conversion from left-hand drive which included repositioning the entrance. The finished product is shown by 150, E601NBX in Kingsway, Swansea. This service now terminates at St Mary's Square. *John Jones*

148	E333NBX	Leyland Tiger TRCTL11/3LZ	Plaxton Derwent 2	BC54F	1987	MoD (87KF41), 1998
149	E591NBX	Leyland Tiger TRCTL11/3LZ	Plaxton Derwent 2	B56F	1987	MoD (87KF36), 1998
150	E601NBX	Leyland Tiger TRCTL11/3LZ	Plaxton Derwent 2	B56F	1987	MoD (64KG05), 1998
151	C007WEP	Leyland Tiger TRCTL11/3LZ	Plaxton Derwent 2	B70F	1987	MoD (87KF30), 1998
152	D409TFT	Mercedes-Benz 709D	Reeve Burgess Beaver	B20F	1986	Stagecoach Devon, 1998
153	S490BBX	LDV Convoy	Van World	M16	1999	
154	KDL121W	Bedford YMT	Plaxton Supreme IV	C53F	1980	Meurig Morgan, Lampeter, 1997
155	HJB462W	Bristol VRT/SL3/6LXB	Eastern Coach Works	B43/31F	1980	Oxford Cityline, 1996
156	E596NBX	Leyland Tiger TRCTL11/3LZ	Plaxton Derwent 2	BC54F	1987	MoD (87KF34), 1998
157	G115PGT	Mercedes-Benz 811D	Alexander Sprint	B30F	1990	Oxford Bus Company, 1999
158	4858DW	Dennis Javelin 12SDA1907	Plaxton Paramount 3200 III	C55F	1988	Lewis, Whitland, 1999
159	GIW2269	Leyland Leopard PSU3C/4R	Duple Dominant	B53F	1976	Lewis, Whitland, 1999

Previous Registrations:

4858DW	E988KJF, 891VDE, E988KJF	SJI2153	NAE887L, 680XAE, JDF149L, 4183MW
5652MT	GCA125X, 467VT, SNT806X	SJI2154	GCA122X, 2378VT, 591DW, LBX948X
BXI637	DVT994Y	SJI2155	D959VTN, GW133, D959VTN
ENY26V	ENY26V, 4858DW	SJI2156	F726UBX
GDZ886	B328AMH	VCY401	A794LCX
GIW2269	MPG153P	YDR224	C422LRP, HBZ4673, C993VDL

Livery: Two-tone blue and red

HAWKES

Hawkes - City Connection

Hawkes Coaches Ltd, The Garage, Bridge Road, Waunarlwydd,
Swansea SA5 4SP

PTD668S	Leyland National 11351A/1R		B49F	1978	Stagecoach East Midland, 1997
FDE362T	Volvo B58-61	Plaxton Supreme IV	C49F	1979	Kim's, Morriston, 1997
OMA503V	Leyland Leopard PSU3E/4R	Duple Dominant II Express	C49F	1979	Pullman, Crofty, 1997
ULS668T	Leyland Fleetline FE30AGR	Eastern Coach Works	B43/31F	1979	Green Lane, Muswell Hill, 1995
EYP30V	Bedford YMT	Plaxton Supreme IV	C53F	1980	Evans, Tregaron, 1995
JNJ365V	Bedford YMT	Duple Dominant II	C53F	1980	Evans, Tregaron, 1995
HJP479V	Volvo B58-61	Duple Dominant II	C53F	1980	Bere Regis & District, 1991
MUE313V	Volvo B58-61	Duple Dominant II	C53F	1980	Bell, New Silksworth, 1992
ETH176V	Volvo B58-61	Duple Dominant II	C53F	1980	Bere Regis & District, 1989
SNS823W	Leyland National 2 NL116L11/1R		B52F	1980	Cooper, Gilesgate Moor, 1999
JSJ426W	Volvo B10M-61	Duple Dominant II	C53F	1981	Smith, Wigan, 1986
TND128X	Volvo B58-61	Duple Dominant IV	C53F	1982	Shearings, 1989
GIL6241	Volvo B10M-61	Duple Dominant IV	C50F	1982	National Travel East, 1987
TJI1698	Volvo B10M-61	Van Hool Alizèe	C52FT	1984	Turner, Bristol, 1994
A616WEP	Mercedes-Benz L608D	Reeve Burgess	C25F	1984	Collins, Roch, 1996
C285EHU	Volvo B10M-61	Duple 340	C57F	1986	Turner, Bristol, 1994
898FCY	Volvo B10M-61	Caetano Algarve	C49FT	1986	Shevill, Carluke, 1994
D204FBK	Leyland Lynx LX112TL11FR1	Leyland Lynx	B51F	1986	Arriva Yorkshire, 1999
D967NCY	Bedford CFL	Steedrive Parflo	M12	1987	Briton Ferry Minibus, 1987
E210HRY	Iveco Daily 49.10	Carlyle Dailybus	B25F	1988	Midland Fox, 1997
E209KCK	Renault-Dodge S46	Northern Counties	B24F	1988	Davies Bros, Pencader, 1999
E940THB	Ford Transit VE6	Ford	M14	1988	Merlynís, Skewen, 1989
E274NVN	Volvo B10M-61	Duple 340	C54F	1988	Walton, Stockton, 2000
GIL6240	Volvo B10M-61	Plaxton Paramount 3500 III	C49FT	1988	Battersby-Silver Grey, Moreibe, 2000
G908UPP	Mercedes-Benz 709D	Reeve Burgess Beaver	B25F	1989	Sovereign, 2000
TAZ9658	Volvo B10M-60	Jonckheere Deauville P599	C51FT	1990	St Brannocks Hotel, Newquay, 1998
723CTH	Volvo B10M-60	Jonckheere Deauville P599	C51FT	1990	St Brannocks Hotel, Newquay, 1998
TAZ9653	Volvo B10M-60	Plaxton Paramount 3500 III	C51FT	1991	Ambassador, Great Yarmouth, 1998

Previous Registrations:

723CTH	G235YVL	GIL6241	OHE272X
898FCY	C644KDS	JNJ365V	DMT904V, 710VCV
C285EHU	C941DHT, 139MDV	JAZ9653	H173EJU, PIJ4317, H149VVG
ETH176V	HJP481V, 898FCY	TAZ9658	G465JNH
FDE362T	EWW234T, 4998LJ	TJI1698	A637EJS, 2080NT, A682VSK
GIL6240	E900UNW, 4148VZ, E138PFV	TND128X	TND128X, GIL6240

Livery: White and blue (coaches); yellow and blue (buses).

The latest arrivals in the Hawkes' fleet are painted in white and blue and retain the City Connection branding. SNS823W is shown in Swansea and is a Leyland National 2 that was new to the Scottish Bus Group subsidiary, Central SMT, in 1980. *John Jones*

During 1999, Hawkes purchased Leyland Lynx D204FBK to displace a Seddon Pennine 7 from service work. Still rather uncommon with independents, the Lynx, here seen in Swansea during the past winter, is the flagship of this fleet's buses. *John Jones*

HENLEY'S

Henley's Bus Services Ltd, Victor Road, Abertillery, Blaenau Gwent NP3 1HU

MFV34T	Leyland Leopard PSU4E/4R	East Lancashire	B47F	1979	Stagecoach Burnley & Pendle, 1996
MFV37T	Leyland Leopard PSU4E/4R	East Lancashire	B47F	1979	Stagecoach Burnley & Pendle, 1996
GTG779W	Leyland Leopard PSU3F/5R	Plaxton Supreme IV Exp	C51F	1980	
PKG702Y	Leyland Tiger TRCTL11/2R	Plaxton Supreme V	C51F	1982	
XIB3942	Setra S215HD	Setra	C48FT	1983	Young, Romsley, 1999
C499FAX	Leyland Tiger TRCTL11/2RZ	Duple Laser 2	C51F	1985	
C810GFM	Ford Transit 150	Economy	M12	1985	Bromyard Bus Co, 1997
JBZ6925	Leyland Tiger TRCTL11/3RZ	Plaxton Paramount 3500 III	C53F	1986	Vale of Llangollen, 1993
D317UTU	Volvo B10M-61	Plaxton Paramount 3500 III	C51F	1987	Vale of Llangollen, 1996
H742TWB	Mercedes-Benz 709D	Reeve Burgess Beaver	BC23F	1991	Nefyn Coaches, 1998
M201RHB	Mercedes-Benz 711D	Alexander Sprint	B29F	1995	
P783BJU	Mercedes-Benz 711D	LCB Eagle	B29F	1998	A-Line, Bedworth, 1999

Previous Registrations:

D317UTU   D288UDM, VLT280, 3810VT, VLT483
JBZ6925   C710LMA, 7052VT, C736NCA, 440VT, C814NCA
XIB3942   4967MW, FLD398Y

Livery: Green white and orange

A sign of reduced passenger numbers is the use of Mercedes-Benz minibuses on services in Abertillery that some years ago were run with full-size buses. P783BJU recently joined a similar vehicle purchased new in 1995. Two Leyland Leopards are still retained. *John Jones*

HOWELLS COACHES

REL & P Howells, Ffos-yr-hebog Farm, Deri, Bargoed, Caerphilly   CF8 8NT

GHV48N	Daimler Fleetline CRL6-30	Park Royal	B45/28D	1975	Diamond-Glantawe, Morriston, 1998
KUC144P	Daimler Fleetline CRL6-30	Park Royal	B45/28D	1975	Diamond-Glantawe, Morriston, 1998
KUC237P	Daimler Fleetline CRL6-30	Park Royal	B45/28D	1975	Diamond-Glantawe, Morriston, 1998
MVK521R	Leyland Atlantean AN68A/2R	Alexander AL	B48/33F	1976	Stagecoach Midland Red, 2000
OJD196R	Leyland Fleetline FE30AGR	MCW	B45/32F	1977	Thamesdown, 1994
OJD234R	Leyland Fleetline FE30AGR	MCW	B45/32F	1977	Thamesdown, 1994
OJD239R	Leyland Fleetline FE30AGR	MCW	B45/32F	1977	Thamesdown, 1994
SCN273S	Leyland Atlantean AN68A/2R	Alexander AL	B49/37F	1980	Stagecoach Midland Red, 2000
TAZ5542	Ford R1114	Plaxton Supreme III	C53F	1978	6060, Merthyr Tydfil, 1997
TAZ5541	Ford R1114	Plaxton Supreme IV	C49F	1979	Hurst & Leek, Goose Green, 1994
ECS875V	Leyland Fleetline FE30AGR	Northern Counties	B44/31F	1979	Stotts, Oldham, 1997
AVK172R	Leyland Atlantean AN68A/2R	Alexander AL	B49/37F	1980	Stagecoach Midland Red, 2000
EJR123W	Leyland Atlantean AN68A/2R	Alexander AL	B49/37F	1980	Stagecoach Midland Red, 2000
TAZ5543	Ford R1114	Plaxton Supreme IV	C53F	1980	E&J Coaches, Batley, 1994
TAZ5539	Ford R1114	Plaxton Supreme IV	C53F	1981	Davis, Church Stretton, 1997
OHV199Y	Ford R1114	Wadham Stringer Vanguard	B32F	1982	Williams, Merthyr Tydfil, 1990
C881KAV	Ford R1115	Plaxton Paramount 3200 II	C53F	1985	Simonds, Botesdale, 1999
C882KAV	Ford R1115	Plaxton Paramount 3200 II	C53F	1985	Simonds, Botesdale, 1999
C926PFL	Ford R1115	Plaxton Paramount 3200 II	C53F	1991	Simonds, Botesdale, 1999
C659HTX	Renault-Dodge S56	Reeve Burgess	B24FL	1986	Gwent CC, 1998
D132WCC	Freight Rover Sherpa	Carlyle	B18F	1987	Owen, Oswestry, 1992
F651SRK	Iveco Daily 40.8	Dormobile	B16FL	1989	London Borough of Merton, 1999
G278MWU	Iveco Daily 49.10	Reeve Burgess Beaver	B23F	1990	Bluebird, Middleton, 1998
G279MWU	Iveco Daily 49.10	Reeve Burgess Beaver	B23F	1990	Bluebird, Middleton, 1998
H835DNE	Iveco Daily 49.10	Pheonix	B23F	1990	Bluebird, Middleton, 1998
H713WGK	Leyland-DAF 400	Dormobile	M15L	1991	LB Lewisham, 1999

Previous Registrations:

SBR87P	JAS521P	TAZ5542	VRY730S, TRX615, BWS263S, FBZ6060
TAZ5539	SRW789W	TAZ5543	JDB952V
TAZ5541	CFX308T		

Livery: various

Howells Coaches' fleet comprises many Ford products. Three late model R1115s with Plaxton Paramount bodywork were acquired from Simonds of Botesdale in 1999. Of these, C882KAV is seen at Pengam cross-roads taking pupils from Lewis Boys School to Cefn Hengoed.
John Jones

IBT - KINGFISHER

Islwyn Borough Transport Ltd, Penmaen Road, Pontllanfraith, Caerphilly   NP12 2DY

01	MAP340W	Leyland Leopard PSU3F/4R	Plaxton Supreme IV Exp	C53F	1980	Cyril Evans, Senghenydd, 1998
02	L4USE	Mercedes-Benz 811D	Dormobile Routemaker	B33F	1993	Patterson, Birmingham, 1995
04	F852LHS	Mercedes-Benz 811D	Alexander Sprint	BC33F	1989	Kelvin Central, 1995
05	H426KPA	Mercedes-Benz 811D	Dormobile Routemaker	B29F	1991	Tillingbourne, Cranleigh, 1999
06	F349TSX	Mercedes-Benz 811D	Alexander Sprint	BC31F	1988	Kelvin Central, 1995
07	H428KPD	Mercedes-Benz 811D	Whittaker Europa	B28F	1991	Tillingbourne, Cranleigh, 1999
08	F94KDS	Mercedes-Benz 811D	Alexander Sprint	BC33F	1989	Kelvin Central, 1995
09	KIB1767	Mercedes-Benz 814D	Reeve Burgess Beaver	C33F	1990	Kelvin Central, 1995
10	N572OUH	Mercedes-Benz 811D	Plaxton Beaver	B29F	1995	
11	N571OUH	Mercedes-Benz 811D	Plaxton Beaver	B29F	1995	
12	N573OUH	Mercedes-Benz 811D	Plaxton Beaver	B29F	1995	
14	H429KPD	Mercedes-Benz 811D	Whittaker Europa	B28F	1991	Tillingbourne, Cranleigh, 1999
20	JSA103V	Leyland Leopard PSU3F/4R	Alexander AT	BC49F	1980	Bluebird Buses, 1999
21	JSA104V	Leyland Leopard PSU3F/4R	Alexander AT	BC49F	1980	Bluebird Buses, 1999
22	GMS305S	Leyland Leopard PSU3E/4R	Alexander AYS	B53F	1978	Bromyard Omnibus Co, 1999
23	YSF83S	Leyland Leopard PSU3E/4R	Alexander AYS	B53F	1977	Highland Country, 1999
27	YDW566T	Leyland Leopard PSU4E/2R	Marshall	B45F	1979	
38	OGE9Y	Leyland Tiger TRBTL11/2R	Duple Dominant	B55F	1983	Rossendale, 1999
39	C195WJT	Leyland Tiger TRBTL11/2R	Duple Dominant	B53F	1985	Tillingbourne, Cranleigh, 1999
40	A774WHB	Leyland Tiger TRBTL11/2RP	Duple Dominant	B55F	1984	Andy James, Tetbury, 1998
41	C41GKG	Leyland Tiger TRBTL11/2RP	East Lancashire	BC47F	1985	
42	C42GKG	Leyland Tiger TRBTL11/2RP	East Lancashire	BC47F	1985	
43	C43GKG	Leyland Tiger TRBTL11/2RP	East Lancashire	BC47F	1985	
44	D44MBO	Leyland Tiger TRBTL11/2RP	East Lancashire	BC47F	1986	
46	D46MBO	Leyland Tiger TRBTL11/2RP	East Lancashire	B47F	1986	
56	IIL7331	DAF MB230 DKVL600	Caetano Algarve	C53FT	1987	Peter Sheffield, Cleethorpes 1988
64	PHB309R	Leyland Leopard PSU3C/2R	Duple Dominant	B53F	1977	Inter Valley Link, 1989
65	PHB310R	Leyland Leopard PSU3C/2R	Duple Dominant	B53F	1977	Inter Valley Link, 1989
70	IIL6443	Bedford YNV Venturer	Caetano Algarve	C53F	1988	Paul Diaper, Newport, 1991
71	SIB7240	Mercedes-Benz 0303/15R	Mercedes-Benz	C49FT	1985	Paul Diaper, Newport, 1991
80	IIL3481	Volvo B10M-61	Jonckheere Jubilee P599	C49FT	1988	Daisy Bus Services, Brigg, 1994
82	LIL3934	Volvo B10M-61	Jonckheere Jubilee P599	C49FT	1988	Victory Tours, Handley, 1995
83	WBC940X	Bedford YNT	Plaxton Supreme V	B53F	1982	Evans, New Tredegar, 1996
84	PIL7240	Volvo B10M-60	Jonckheere Deauville P599	C53FT	1993	APT, Rayleigh, 1996
85	LIL5845	Volvo B10M-61	Van Hool Alizée H	C49FT	1983	Jacobs, Four Oaks, 1996
88	P182NAK	Volvo B10M-62	Plaxton Première 350	C49FT	1997	
89	SIL4467	Mercedes-Benz 609D	North West Coach Sales	BC24F	1989	Skylark, Woodfalls, 1998
90	WJI1726	Kassbohrer Setra S215HD	Setra	C49FT	1983	Geoff Willetts, Pillowell, 1998
91	R979PRD	Volvo B10M-62	Berkhof Axial 50	C51FT	1998	
92	PIL6350	Volvo B10M-60	Jonckheere Deauville P599	C49FT	1992	Thamesdown, 1998
93	RIL1027	MAN 11.190HOCL-R	Caetano Algarve II	C35F	1994	Cyril Evans, Senghenydd, 1999
94	T120JBC	Volvo B10M-62	Jonckheere Mistral 50	C51FT	1999	
95	W868AAY	Volvo B10M-62	Plaxton Excalibur	C49FT	2000	

Previous Registrations:

SIL4467	F46GNS	LIL5845	MSU572Y, CGL905
IIB9140	DDG260T	PIL6350	J533JNH
IIL3481	E33MKV, HS8882, E796NHP	PIL7240	K905RGE, 827APT, K144JVX
IIL6443	E762JAY	RIL1027	L217ETG
IIL7331	D512WNV	SIB7240	C722RJU, DIA4800
KIB1767	H907XGA	WJI1726	CRS327Y, 28JGH, UAB802Y, 890CVJ
LIL3934	E35MVC, HIL8127		

Livery: Blue and white; pink (or silver) and blue (Kingfisher Travel)

Opposite, top: Among recent Mercedes-Benz minibuses in the IBT fleet are three with Plaxton Beaver bodywork, and the only ones bought new. From the trio, 11, N571OUH, is seen passing along Church View in Penmaen in the autumn of 1999. *John Jones*

Opposite, bottom: Following an accident to number 45, only five East Lancashire-bodied Tigers remain. These were joined in 1999 by a similar bus with Duple bodywork, acquired from Tillingbourne. Pictured leaving Blackwood is 39, C195WJT, working the Cardiff-Tredegar service on which Cardiff Bus also operate. *John Jones*

JAMES BROTHERS

Brodyr James

T M G & D E James, Glanyrafon Garage, Llangeitho, Tregaron, Cardiganshire, SY25 6TJ

SFF756T	Bedford YLQ	Plaxton Supreme IV Exp	C45F	1979	D James, Llangeitho, 1980
AUJ746T	Bedford YLQ	Duple Dominant II	C45F	1979	Evans, Tregaron, 1992
WLG999W	Bedford YLQ	Plaxton Supreme IV	C35F	1980	Hanmer, Wrexham. 1983
PNA963W	Bedford YMQ	Duple Dominant II	C45F	1981	Evans, Tregaron, 1992
GVJ522X	Bedford YLQ	Plaxton Supreme IV Exp	C45F	1981	
A44KLF	Mercedes-Benz L307D	Reeve Burgess	M12	1984	M & M, Harrow Weald, 1985
C745TJF	Bedford YNT	Plaxton Paramount 3500 II	C53F	1985	
D372UVL	Leyland Tiger TRCTL11/3R	Duple Caribbean 2	C49FT	1986	Hedon Silverwing, Hull, 1995
E753JAY	Dennis Javelin 11SDA1905	Duple 320	C53F	1988	
E330OMG	Mercedes-Benz 609D	Reeve Burgess Beaver	B20F	1988	Arrow, Bristol, 1993
F426ENB	Mercedes-Benz 609D	Made-to-Measure	C23F	1988	Cunningham, Stanford, 1989
F602HEC	Dennis Javelin 11SDL1906	Duple 320	C53F	1988	Browns, Ambleside, 1994
F407OSR	Dennis Javelin 8.5SDA1926	Plaxton Paramount 3200 III	C35F	1989	Docherty's, Auchterarder, 1999
F790GNA	Leyland Tiger TRCTL11/3ARZ	Duple 320	C53F	1989	Coachstyle, Nettleton, 1999
F21TMP	Mercedes-Benz 709D	Reeve Burgess Beaver	B25F	1989	Jim Stones, Glazebury, 1991
G333LCP	Mercedes-Benz 308D	Mellor	M12	1990	Ferguson, Whitburn, 1999
J291RNE	Mercedes-Benz 609D	Made-to-Measure	B28F	1992	P&O Lloyd, Bagillt, 1999
329UWL	Dennis Javelin 8.5SDA1926	Plaxton Paramount 3200 III	C35F	1992	
K27GVC	Volvo B10M-60	Plaxton Première 350	C49FT	1993	Harry Shaw, Coventry, 1997
164EWN	Toyota Coaster HZB50R	Caetano Optimo III	C21F	1994	
6738UN	Volvo B10M-62	Caetano Algarve II	C49FT	1995	

Previous Registrations:

164EWN	From new	6738UN	From new
329UWL	From new	F407OSR	F407OSR, GSU378

Depots: Glanyrafon Garage, Llangeitho and Heulfryn, Bronant
Livery: Red and white; red, white and gold (most coaches)

JOHN'S TRAVEL

D J Davies, 19 Six Bells Estate, Heolgerrig, Merthyr Tydfil CF48 1TU

RGE900W	Ford R1014	Plaxton Supreme IV	C45F	1980	Frenchay NHS Trust, 1993
D244VNL	Renault-Dodge S56	Alexander AM	BC19F	1987	Red & White, 1994
E267BRG	Renault-Dodge S56	Alexander AM	BC19F	1987	Red & White, 1994
E272BRG	Renault-Dodge S56	Alexander AM	BC19F	1987	Red & White, 1994
E126AAL	Ford Transit VE6	Mellor	B16FL	1988	Nottinghamshire CC, 1996
F107YWO	MCW MetroRider MF150/103	MCW	BC23F	1988	Rhondda, 1996
XJI9612	MCW MetroRider MF158/11	MCW	B31F	1988	HMB Services, Gateshead, 1999
F544JRO	Ford Transit VE6	Ford	M8	1989	private owner, 1992
F338XOV	Ford Transit VE6	Ford	M8	1989	private owner, 1992

Previous registrations

XJI9612	F192YDA

Depot: Winchfawr, Heolgerrig
Livery: Blue and white

Much of James Brothers' work, whether commercial or tendered operations, take the vehicles into Aberystwyth, the largest town in Ceredigion, formerly Cardiganshire. Seen here is 164EWN, a Toyota Coaster with Caetano Optimo bodywork. *John Jones*

John's Travel operate several short commercial routes in Merthyr Tydfil using some Renault-Dodge minibuses and a MCW MetroRider F107YWO. This vehicle was new to InterValleyLink in 1998 and has been joined by a longer example in 1999. *John Jones*

JONES LLANFAETHLU

ORJ Port Handling

O R Jones & Sons Ltd, The Bus & Coach Depot, Llanfaethlu, Anglesey LL65 4NW

WWY905L	Bedford YRT	Plaxton Elite III Express	BC53F	1973	West Yorkshire PTE, 1981
MHL98	Leyland National 1151/2R		B D	1974	R Bullock, Cheadle, 1995
MHL100	Leyland National 1151/2R		B D	1974	Manchester Airport, 1995
PPE658R	Bedford YMT	Duple Dominant II	C53F	1977	Mountford, Harpurhey, 1989
RDC106R	Bristol VRT/SL3/6LXB	Northern Counties	B43/31F	1977	Cleveland Transit, 1990
USE633R	Bedford YMT	Duple Dominant	C49F	1977	Short, Glenrothes, 1990
OBR772R	Bristol VRT/SL3/6LXB	Eastern Coach Works	B43/31F	1979	Northumbria, 1997
APT807R	Bristol VRT/SL3/6LXB	Eastern Coach Works	B43/31F	1980	Northumbria, 1997
APT818W	Bristol VRT/SL3/6LXB	Eastern Coach Works	B43/31F	1980	Northumbria, 1997
A345VEP	DAF MB200DKFL600	Plaxton Paramount 3500	C51FT	1983	McCormick, Airdrie, 1993
A302XWF	Bedford YMP	Plaxton Supreme VI	C35F	1983	South Yorkshire Police, 1997
A8ORJ	Bova FHD12.280	Bova Futura	C53F	1986	South Yorkshire, 1995
C124LHS	Mercedes-Benz L608D	Alexander AM	B20F	1986	PMT, 1998
C353SVV	Scania K92CRB	Jonckheere Citibus	B47D	1986	Dunn-Line, Nottingham, 1998
C934VLB	Scania K112CRS	Plaxton Bustler	BC41D	1986	British Airways, Heathrow, 1997

The largest bus operator based on Anglesey is Jones Llanfaethlu. Many buses run within the ferry terminal at Holyhead while local services are also undertaken. The fleet livery is based on the Welsh colours illustrated here on C124LHS which is seen approaching the Llangefni Post Office terminus on route 52 from Llanrhuddlad. *John Jones*

Another operator to choose a Mercedes-Benz Vario is Jones Llanfaethlu. S91UEY is seen returning towards Holyhead from South Stack, a spectacular nesting site for seabirds. *David Donati*

D166VRP	Mercedes-Benz L608D	Alexander AM	B20F	1986	Crosville Cymru, 1995
D955UDY	Mercedes-Benz L608D	Reeve Burgess	B20F	1986	Crosville Cymru, 1995
E227FLD	Scania N112DRB	Van Hool Alizèe L	BC30D	1987	Capital, West Drayton, 1999
E233FLD	Scania N112DRB	Van Hool Alizèe L	BC30D	1987	Capital, West Drayton, 1999
A0ORJ	Bova FHD12.290	Bova Futura	C53F	1988	Alder Valley, 1992
F947CUA	Freight Rover Sherpa	Carlyle	B18F	1988	Yorkshire Rider, 1993
A7ORJ	Bova FHD12.290	Bova Futura	C49FT	1990	Emblings, Guyhirn, 1996
G134CLF	DAF SB220LC590	Hispano	B45D	1990	Capital, West Drayton, 2000
G194CLF	DAF SB220LC590	Hispano	B45D	1990	Capital, West Drayton, 2000
H964LEY	Mercedes-Benz 709D	Reeve Burgess Beaver	B25F	1990	
H9CCH	Toyota Coaster HBD30R	Caetano Optimo II	C18F	1991	Cross Country Hire, Staplehill, 1994
AEY365	MAN 11.190HOCL-R	Caetano Algarve 2	C35F	1993	Peter Carol, Bristol, 1998
L924SCR	Bova FHD12.340	Bova Futura	C44FT	1994	Flight, Birmingham, 2000
S91UEY	Mercedes-Benz Vario O814D	Plaxton Beaver 2	B31F	1999	

Special Event vehicles:

ECT912	Bedford OB	Duple Vista	C29F	1950	Stevensons, Spath, 1992
XVS913	AEC Regent V 2LD3RA	Park Royal	O40/32F	1959	private owner, 1996
CNP316B	Bedford J2SZ10	Plaxton Consort	C20F	1964	Nippy, Sutton, 1980

Previous Registrations:

A7ORJ	G697VAV	ECT912	From new
A8ORJ	C23EUG, AEY220	L924SCR	L11FTG, L1NER, L11FTG, L1NXF
A9ORJ	E667JNR	XVS913	PFN873, XKO41A
AEY365	L56YJF		

ORJ Port Handling: MHL98, MHL100, C934VLB, C353SVV, E227/233FLD.
Livery: White, red and green; white and blue (B&I Line).

The Welsh Bus Handbook

JONES LOGIN

Jones Motors (Login) Ltd, Login, Whitland, Carmarthenshire, SA34 0UX

UDE351T	Bedford YMT	Plaxton Supreme IV Exp	C53F	1979	Pioneer, Laugharne, 1980
XBX467T	Bedford YMT	Plaxton Supreme IV Exp	C53F	1979	
BDE792V	Bedford YMT	Plaxton Supreme IV	C53F	1980	
GBX484W	Bedford YNT	Duple Dominant IV	C53F	1981	
GDE148X	Volvo B58-56	Plaxton Supreme VI	C53F	1982	Kerricabs, Newport, 1985
YDE679	Volvo B10M-61	Plaxton Paramount 3500	C53F	1984	
963CDE	Volvo B10M-61	Duple 340	C53FT	1987	
526FDE	Volvo B10M-61	Duple 340	C53FT	1988	
LIL9971	Dennis Javelin 12SDA1907	Duple 320	C57F	1988	Shamrock, Pontypridd, 1999
LIL9973	Dennis Javelin 12SDA1907	Duple 320	C57F	1989	Shamrock, Pontypridd, 1999
LIL9974	Dennis Javelin 12SDA1907	Duple 320	C57F	1989	Shamrock, Pontypridd, 1999
521WDE	Dennis Javelin 8.5SDA1915	Plaxton Paramount 3200 III	C31FT	1989	
834TDE	Volvo B10M-60	Plaxton Première 350	C49FT	1992	
K649RDE	Leyland-DAF 400	Crystals	B16F	1992	
K650RDE	Leyland-DAF 400	Crystals	C16F	1992	
L975VDE	Leyland-DAF 400	Autobus Classique	C16F	1994	
M589CDE	LDV 200	LDV	M8	1994	
M459DDE	Dennis Javelin 12SDA2131	Plaxton Première 320	C53F	1995	
M460DDE	Dennis Javelin 12SDA2131	Plaxton Première 320	C53F	1995	
N389KDE	Dennis Javelin 12SDA2155	Plaxton Première 320	C57F	1996	
N390KDE	Dennis Javelin 12SDA2155	Plaxton Première 320	C57F	1996	
P742RDE	Dennis Javelin	Plaxton Première 320	C57F	1996	
R546GDE	Toyota Coaster HZB50R	Caetano Optimo IV	C21F	1997	
R160LDE	Volvo B10M-62	Plaxton Première 350	C49FT	1998	
R161LDE	Volvo B10M-62	Plaxton Première 350	C49FT	1998	
R162LDE	Dennis Javelin	Plaxton Première 320	C53F	1998	
V573DDE	Mercedes-Benz Vario O814	Onyx	C24F	1999	

Previous Registrations:

521WDE	G744YDE	963CDE	D963HDE	LIL9973	F632SAY	
526FDE	E239NDE	GDE148X	NKG98X, 521WDE	LIL9974	F631SAY	
834TDE	J918ODE	LIL9971	E726UHB	YDE679	A475TBX	

Livery: Turquoise, white and blue

D JONES & SON

Bus & Coach Travel

D & G Jones, Clydfan, Hall Street, Rhosllanerchrugog, Wrexham, LL14 2LG

TTA650X	Dennis Lancet SD502	Wadham Stringer Vanguard	B52F	1981	Tillingbourne Valley, 1988
YPD122Y	Leyland Tiger TRCTL11/2R	Duple Dominant IV Express	C53F	1983	Jones, Formby, 1997
E98DMA	Leyland Tiger TRCTL11/3R	Plaxton Derwent	BC52F	1987	MoD(87KF16), 1996
J854PUD	Dennis Dart 9.8SDL3012	Reeve Burgess Pointer	B43F	1992	Tappins, Didcot, 1997
K6BUS	Mercedes-Benz 811D	Dormobile Routemaker	B33F	1992	Acorn, Chester, 1998
K367TJF	Mercedes-Benz 811D	Dormobile Routemaker	B33F	1992	Whitehead, Smithybridge, 1995
V12DJS	Dennis Dart SLF	SCC Compass	N47F	2000	
W	Dennis Dart SLF	SCC Compass	N47F	2000	

Depot: King Street, Acrefair
Livery: Blue and white

Opposite: **Jones Login undertakes several tendered services in the area between Carmarthen and Haverfordwest. R546GDE is seen between Llawhaden and Narberth on a glorious day in 1999. The lower picture shows E98DMA, a Leyland Tiger that D Jones and Son purchased from the MoD and which had been converted from left-hand-drive. The vehicle is seen at Wrexham before it received a revised fleetname.**
John Jones

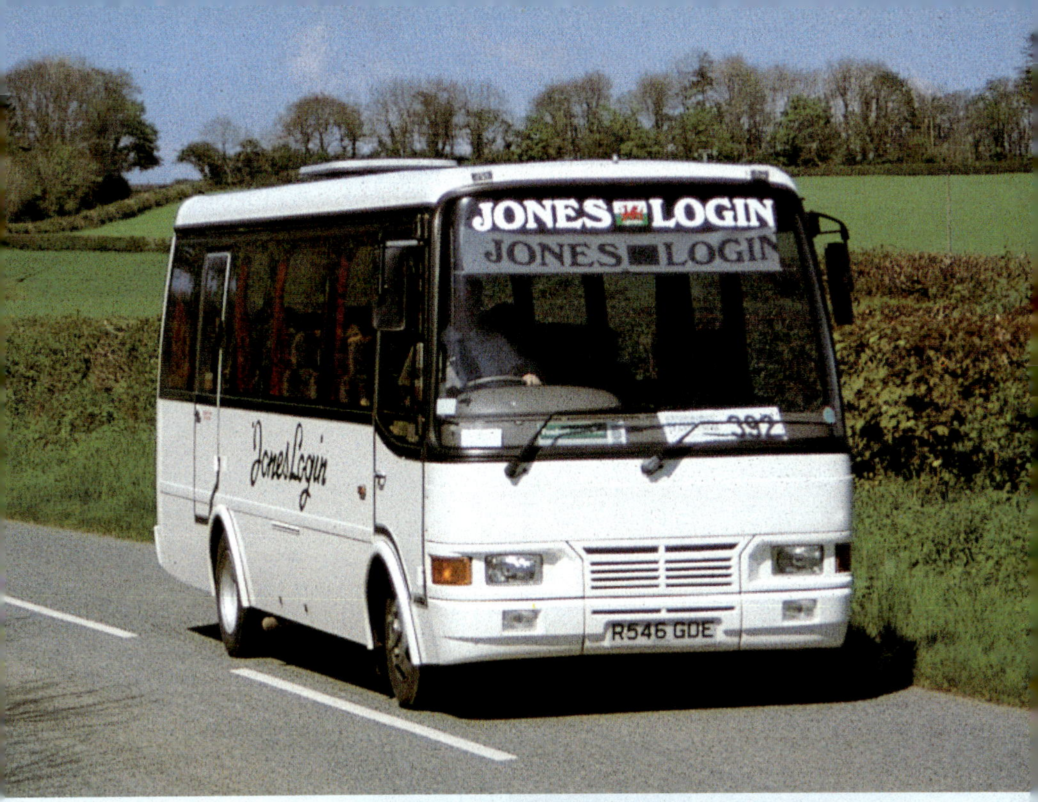
JONES LOGIN
JONES LOGIN
Jones Login
R546 GDE

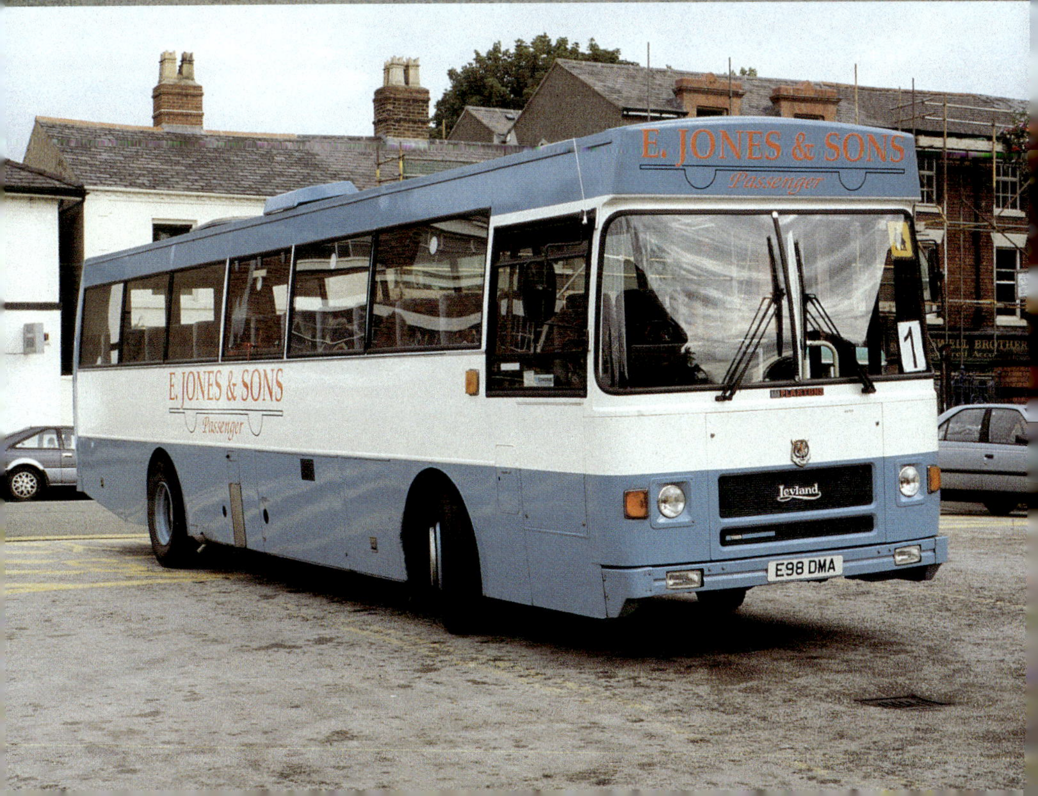
E. JONES & SONS
Passenger
E. JONES & SONS
Passenger
Leyland
E98 DMA
1

E JONES & SONS

Jones of Rhosllanerchrugog

JB & G Jones, Mountain View, Bank Street, Ponciau, Wrexham LL14 1EN

BBM62A	Volvo B58-61	Plaxton Viewmaster IV	C44FT	1980	Sampson, Cheshunt, 1990
C472LKU	Bedford YMT	Duple Dominant	B55F	1986	George Edwards, Bwlchgwyn, 1999
RIW4037	Bedford YNT	Plaxton Paramount 3200 III	C53F	1987	Carter, Litcham, 1999
C7EJS	Volvo B10M-61	Plaxton Paramount 3500 III	C53F	1988	Chase, Chasetown, 1998
L963NWW	Volvo B10M-62	Jonckheere Deauville 45	C50F	1994	Wallace Arnold, 1994
N7EJS	Dennis Dart 9.8SDL30	Plaxton Pointer	B40F	1995	
N937WJL	Mercedes-Benz Vario O814	Autobus Nouvelle 2	C29F	1996	Winrow, Heywood, 1999

Previous Registrations:
BBM62A	KAY10V	RIW4037	E430MSE
C7EJS	E360XSB, PSU906, E360XSB		

Depot: Coppi Industrial Estate, Ponciau
Livery: Blue, white and orange

Other members of the Jones' family trade as E Jones and Sons and operate local services at Wrexham. Orange bands distinguish this fleet from D Jones & Son as shown on N7EJS, a Plaxton-bodied Dennis Dart bought new in 1995. *John Jones*

W E JONES & SON

G E Jones, The Garage, Llanerchymedd, Anglesey LL71 8EB

SEL247H	Leyland Atlantean PDR1A/1	Alexander J	B43/31F	1969	Lancaster, 1989
NSG216M	Bedford YRT	Duple Dominant Express	C53F	1973	Carreglefn Coaches, 1995
SMU919N	Daimler Fleetline CRL6	Park Royal	B44/27D	1974	Woolley, Llanedwen, 1993
ONF25P	Leyland Leopard PSU3C/4R	Plaxton Supreme III Exp	C53F	1976	Hill, Congleton, 1999
SLO514R	Bedford YMT	Duple Dominant	C53F	1977	SilverStar, Caernarfon, 1998
OJV121S	Leyland Fleetline FE30AGR	Roe	B45/29D	1977	East Midland (Grimsby), 1996
SDA778S	Leyland Fleetline FE30AGR	MCW	B43/33F	1978	Express Motors, Bontnewydd, 1996
WKG602	Bedford YMT	Duple Dominant II	C53F	1978	Maye, Astley, 1999
WPJ8S	Bedford YMT	Duple Dominant II	C53F	1978	Browne, Smallfield, 1980
UKH170W	Bedford YMT	Plaxton Bustler	B55F	1981	Williams, Poncian, 2000
A8WEJ	Leyland Royal Tiger B50	Roe Doyen	C44FT	1983	Hart Coaches, Hart, 1994
B218JPH	Mercedes-Benz L608D	Coachcraft	C21F	1984	Evans of Pwllheli, 1991
NIL3279	Volkeswagen LT55	Optare City Pacer	BC25F	1987	Anderson, Ormskirk, 1999

Previous Registrations:

A8WEJ	A213XJR, JCN822, A741DCN	ONF25P	MNU476P, HIL3478
NIL3279	G46RDW	WKG602	XNM822S, XDL696, SCR993S

Depots: Brynteg Farm, Benllech and The Garage, Llanerchymedd
Livery: Red and cream

OJV121S was new to Grimsby-Cleethorpes Transport and purchased by W E Jones & Son from Stagecoach East Midlands who took over that municipality. It is seen at the Brynteg Farm yard on the east coast of Anglesey. *John Jones*

KMP

KMP (Llanberis) Ltd, Y Glyn, Llanberis, Gwynedd, LL55 4EL

HMA564T	Leyland National 10351B/1R		B44F	1978	Jones Llanfaethlu, 1991
JTU596T	Leyland National 10351B/1R		B41F	1979	Midland, 1995
WTH957T	Bristol VRT/SL3/501	Eastern Coach Works	B43/31F	1979	Brewers, 1993
BEP969V	Bristol VRT/SL3/501	Eastern Coach Works	B43/31F	1980	Brewers, 1994
EDT917V	Bristol VRT/SL3/501	Eastern Coach Works	B43/31F	1980	RoadCar, 1995
772URB	Volvo B10M-60	Plaxton Première 350	C49FT	1992	Excelsior, 1996
7CCH	Volvo B10M-62	Plaxton Expressliner	C44FT	1994	Excelsior, Bournemouth, 1999
K7KMP	Volvo B10M-62	Jonckheere Deauville 65	C51FT	1994	Mid Wales, Penrhyncoch, 1997
L77KMP	Volvo B10M-62	Jonckheere Deauville 65	C51FT	1994	
M7KMP	Volvo B10M-62	Jonckheere Deauville 65	C51FT	1994	
M77KMP	Volvo B10M-62	Jonckheere Deauville 65	C51FT	1994	Mid Wales, Penrhyncoch, 1997
M637BEY	Mercedes-Benz 814D	Mellor	B31F	1995	
N776CJC	Mercedes-Benz 814D	Mellor	B31F	1995	
N848FDT	Mercedes-Benz 814D	Mellor	B31F	1996	Mercedes-Benz demo, 1997
6697RU	Volvo B10M-62	Plaxton Première 350	C49FT	1996	Excelsior, 1999
N77KMP	Volvo B10M-62	Plaxton Première 350	C49FT	1996	
N777KMP	Volvo B10M-62	Plaxton Première 350	C49FT	1996	
A7KMP	Volvo B10M-62	Jonckheere Mistral	C49FT	1998	
S377MCC	Dennis Dart SLF	Alexander ALX200	N40F	1998	
T72JCC	Dennis Dart SLF	Plaxton Pointer 2	N40F	1999	
T7KMP	Neoplan N116/2	Neoplan Cityliner	C48FT	1999	

Previous Registrations:

7CCH	M802KJT		K7KMP	M874UEJ
6697RU	N663THO		M77KMP	M875UEJ
772URB	A18XEL, J59NJT			

Livery: Blue and black. Several coaches operate for Eurolines.

Opposite, top: **One of a trio of Mercedes Benz 814s in the KMP fleet converted by Mellor, N776CJC is photographed approaching Llanrug while working this operator's principal service between Llanberis and Caernarfon.** *John Jones*

Opposite, bottom: **KMP still use double-deck Bristols on some journeys from Caernarfon, these providing a spectacular view of the Snowdonia scenery from the upper deck. EDT917V was new to Yorkshire Traction and was pictured at Crawia Bridge.** *John Jones*

KMP's HMA564T is the longest serving vehicle of the current fleet, originally purchased from an operator on Anglesey in 1991. This B-series Leyland National is one of two that originated with Crosville. It is seen leaving Victoria Terrace, Llanberis, the usual terminus for route 88.
John Jones

KEN HOPKINS

Tonna Luxury Coaches Ltd, Tennis View Garage, Heol-y-glo, Tonna, Neath & Port Talbot
SA11 3NJ

125	99KMH	Volvo B10M-61	Plaxton Paramount 3500 III	C53F	1988	
128	CLZ4965	Volvo B10M-61	Duple Dominant IV	C53F	1983	Shearings, 1988
142	XXI7360	Volvo B58-61	Duple Dominant II	C53F	1980	McCulloch, Stoneykirk, 1992
147	IIL6541	Volvo B10M-61	Plaxton Viewmaster IV	C53F	1981	Dereham Coachways, 1993
152	WSU472	Volvo B10M-61	Plaxton Viewmaster IV	C51F	1982	Leisure Travel, Dover, 1994
153	93FYB	DAF MB200DKTL600	Plaxton Viewmaster IV	C53F	1982	Ayres, Dalkeith, 1994
154	WJI8945	DAF MB200DKTL550	Plaxton Supreme IV	C53F	1981	Jones, Birmingham, 1994
155	JIL7652	Volvo B10M-56	Plaxton Supreme VI Exp	C53F	1982	DRM, Bromyard, 1995
157	D338PGO	Mercedes-Benz L307D	Devon Conversions	M12	1987	Oakley Coaches, 1996
158	WYM675	Volvo B10M-61	Plaxton Paramount 3500	C53F	1983	Leon's, Stafford, 1996
159	C818FMC	Mercedes-Benz L608D	Reeve Burgess	C19F	1986	Clews Travel, Wolverhampton, 1997
160	NIL9692	DAF SB2005DHU505	Plaxton Supreme IV	C53F	1982	Haywards, Caversham, 1997
161	BLZ3144	Volvo B58-61	Duple Dominant II	C53F	1982	Haywards, Caversham, 1997
162	PIL2142	Volvo B10M-61	Plaxton Paramount 3500	C51F	1984	Richards Bros, Cardigan, 1996
163	XJI4840	Leyland Tiger TRCTL11/3R	Plaxton Supreme V	C57F	1982	Bysiau, Ffoshelig, 1998
164	JUI4435	Leyland Leopard PSU3F/5R	Plaxton Supreme V	C53F	1982	Parry, Ruyton XI Towns, 1998
165	HUI4958	DAF MB200DKFL600	Plaxton Paramount 3500	C51F	1983	Evans, Tregaron, 1999
166	LIB1181	Leyland Leopard PSU3F/5R	Plaxton Supreme IV Exp	C53F	1981	Jones International, Llandeilo, 1999
167	XBN196	DAF MB200DKFL600	Plaxton Paramount 3500 II	C53F	1985	Parry, Ruyton XI Towns, 1999
168	SIL4275	Leyland Leopard PSU5D/4R	Plaxton Supreme IV	C57F	1980	Bysiau, Ffoshelig, 1999
169	GSC630X	Leyland Atlantean AN68C/1R	Alexander AL	B45/30F	1981	Lothian Buses, 1999
170	GSC645X	Leyland Atlantean AN68C/1R	Alexander AL	B45/30F	1981	Lothian Buses, 2000
171	RIL6494	Leyland Leopard PSU3E/4R	Plaxton Supreme IV Exp	C53F	1980	Jervis, Margam, 2000
172	KUI1350	DAF MB200DKFL600	Plaxton Paramount 3500	C53F	1983	Alpine, Llandudno, 2000
173	GSC649X	Leyland Atlantean AN68C/1R	Alexander AL	B45/30D	1981	Lothian Buses, 2000

Previous Registrations:

93FYB	WUT121X, 791VT
99KMH	E750HJF
BLZ3144	TND136X
CLZ4965	ENF559Y, 561AH
HUI4958	EFK134Y, GDZ760, HCL880Y, GDZ879, HCL880Y
IIL6541	ORR425W
JIL7652	KWP111X, MOI3565, MUY182X
JUI4435	VVT577X
LIB1181	GBO243W
KUI1350	A36EFF
NIL9692	VJT603X
PIL2142	A85GEJ, RBO202, A85GEJ
RIL6494	FSL61W
SIL4275	MRJ268W, WSV550, SVM475W, WJB490, GDE416W
WJI8945	LAK306W
WSU472	YBW472X
WYM675	A111GUE, LOI8643, A120MFA, KMH389
XBN196	C875JCP
XJI4840	VRA3Y, MSU433, ARR956Y
XXI7360	WSW150V

Livery: Blue, grey and red (single-deck); white (double-deck).

The first double-decks for Ken Hopkins are three Leyland Atlanteans recently displaced by Lothian Buses. Used on school duties, two have been converted to single-door layout and GSC645X displays this modification in Tonna.
Byron Gage

LEWIS WHITLAND

F E Lewis, The Garage, King Edward Street, Whitland, Carmarthenshire SA34 0AA

WWP834V	Bedford YMT		Plaxton Supreme IV	C53F	1980	Bysiau Cwm Taf, 1997
OPL77W	Leyland Leopard PSU3F/5R		Plaxton Supreme IV	C53F	1981	Bicknell, Godalming, 1986
RPC59X	Leyland Leopard PSU3F/5R		Plaxton Supreme IV	C53F	1982	Bicknell, Godalming, 1986
SCD693X	Leyland Leopard PSU3F/5R		Plaxton Supreme V	C53F	1982	Bicknell, Godalming, 1989
GSV494	Volvo B10M-61		Plaxton Paramount 3500 III	C53F	1987	Nefyn Coaches, 1998
490ENU	Volvo B10M-61		Duple 320	C57F	1988	Williams, Brecon, 1999
VBX144	Dennis Javelin		Plaxton Paramount 3200 III	C53F	1989	Evans, Tregaron, 1999
L231BUT	Dennis Javelin		Plaxton Paramount 3200 III	C53F	1994	Epsom Coaches, 1999
L234BUT	Dennis Javelin		Plaxton Paramount 3200 III	C53F	1994	Epsom Coaches, 1999
R915GBX	LDV Convoy		Crystals	M16	1998	
W233KDO	Mercedes-Benz Vario O814		Autobus Nouvelle 2	BC31F	2000	

Previous Registrations:

490ENU	E320OPR	GSV494	D106ERU	VBX144	G951WNR

Livery: White, green and gold

Although no further Mercedes-Benz Vario buses are being purchased by the major fleets, the type is still finding buyers in the independent sector. The bus version of the Autobus Nouvelle 2 is displayed in this view of W233KDO which was purchased for the Carmarthenshire tendered route 227 and accordingly displays Bws Caerfyrddin lettering. It is seen in the new bus station at Carmarthen. *Byron Gage*

LEWIS Y LLAN

A H & R M Lewis, Madyn Industrial Estate, Amlwch, Anglesey, LL68 9DL

	MAU615P	Leyland Atlantean AN68/1R	East Lancashire	B47/31D	1975	Lewis, Llanerchymedd, 1999
1	UET680S	Leyland Atlantean AN68A/1R	Alexander AL	B45/29D	1978	Lewis, Llanerchymedd, 1999
	BVJ771V	Ford R1114	Duple Dominant II	C53F	1980	Bennett, Gloucester, 1985
	A482GFF	Leyland Royal Tiger B50	Roe Doyen	C46FT	1983	Gardiner, Holytown, 1993
	UCK177	Volvo B10M-61	Jonckheere Jubilee P50	C51FT	1983	Shaw Hadwin, Silverdale, 1994
	E45RDW	Volkswagen LT55	Optare City Pacer	BC25F	1987	Cambus, 1996
	NIW2232	Volvo B10M-61	Plaxton Paramount 3500 III	C53F	1987	Keir's. Kemnay, 1999
	H272LJC	Mercedes Benz 811D	Optare StarRider	B33F	1990	
	H273LJC	Mercedes Benz 811D	Optare StarRider	B33F	1990	
	S316DLG	Mercedes Benz Vario O814	Plaxton Beaver 2	B31F	1998	

Previous Registrations:

A482GFF   A603KYG, 23PTA, A506RUG, 341TJ   UCK177   A314XHE

Livery: White and blue

The fleet of Lewis-y-Llan includes Optare City Pacer E45RDW which was new to Taff-Ely and passed on to Cambus when only one year old before returning to Wales in 1996. It is seen leaving the terminus outside Kwik Save, on circular route 60 that serves a district west of the town including Carreglefn and Cemmaes. *John Jones*

LLITHFAEN MOTORS

G H Williams, The Garage, Delfryn, Llithfaen, Gwynedd, LL53 6PA

FBX560W	Bedford YMQ	Duple Dominant	B53F	1981	Davies Bros, Pencader, 1988
CEJ939Y	Bedford VAS5	Duple Dominant II	C29F	1983	Nefyn Coaches, 1992
D509MJA	Iveco Daily 49.10	Robin Hood City Nippy	B21F	1987	Nefyn Coaches, 1994

Livery: Red and cream

The villagers of Llithfaen, near the north coast of the Lleyn peninsula can connect to Pwllheli on the south coast by a bus service operated by Llithfaen Motors. Pictured heading for Pwllheli on a market day is FBX560W, a fifty-three seat Bedford YMQ with Duple Dominant bodywork. The vehicle latterly ran with Davies Bros of Pencader. *John Jones*

P & O LLOYD

F, D, GM & R Lloyd, Rhydwen Garage, Bagillt, Flintshire, CH6 6JB

OKW525R	Leyland Fleetline FE30AGR	MCW	B46/31F	1977	Grey Green, Stamford Hill, 1993
TPU73R	Leyland Atlantean AN68A/1R	Eastern Coach Works	B43/31F	1977	Colchester, 1997
OCO120S	Leyland Atlantean AN68A/1R	Roe	B43/30F	1978	London & Country, 1997
WDA969T	Leyland Fleetline FE30AGR	MCW	B43/33F	1978	Phillips, Holywell, 1999
XPG194T	Leyland Atlantean AN68A/1R	Roe	B43/30F	1979	County Bus, 1997
KFM191T	Leyland Fleetline FE30AGR	Northern Counties	B43/29F	1979	Chester, 1993
BCS867T	Leyland Fleetline FE30AGR	Northern Counties	B44/31F	1979	Blue Bus, Derby, 1995
GTO300V	Leyland Fleetline FE30AGR	Northern Counties	B43/30F	1980	Blue Bus, Derby, 1995
WFU468V	Leyland Fleetline FE30AGR	Roe	B45/31F	1980	East Midland (Grimsby), 1996
XFU128V	Leyland Fleetline FE30AGR	Roe	B45/31F	1980	East Midland (Grimsby), 1996
XFU130V	Leyland Fleetline FE30AGR	Roe	B45/31F	1980	South Manchester, Hyde, 1996
KPJ249W	Leyland Atlantean AN68B/1R	Roe	B43/30F	1980	County Bus, 1997
KPJ251W	Leyland Atlantean AN68B/1R	Roe	B43/30F	1980	County Bus, 1997
KPJ280W	Leyland Atlantean AN68B/1R	Roe	B43/30F	1981	Maidstone & District, 1997
PJI7756	Volvo B10M-61	Plaxton Paramount 3200	C50FT	1983	Redline, Penwortham, 1997
A122GSA	Leyland Tiger TRBLXB/2RH	Alexander P	B52F	1984	Stagecoach Bluebird, 2000
A126GSA	Leyland Tiger TRBLXB/2RH	Alexander P	B52F	1984	Stagecoach Bluebird, 2000
MIL7104	Volvo B10M-61	Plaxton Paramount 3500	C51FT	1984	Ross, Grantown on Spey, 1997
PIL4059	Volvo B10M-61	Plaxton Paramount 3200 II	C55F	1985	Plastow, Wheatley, 1997
POI6312	Volvo B10M-61	Plaxton Paramount 3200 II	C53F	1985	Frames Rickards, Brentford, 1992
6709PO	Volvo B10M-61	Plaxton Paramount 3500 III	C53F	1987	Happy Days, Woodseaves, 1997
5373PO	Volvo B10M-61	Plaxton Paramount 3500 III	C51F	1988	Dunn-Line, Nottingham, 1994
5182PO	Volvo B10M-60	Van Hool Alizée	C49FT	1989	Silver Star, Caernarfon, 2000
RIL1067	Optare MetroRider MR03	Optare	B31F	1991	London Central, 1999
RIL1072	Optare MetroRider MR03	Optare	B31F	1991	London Central, 1999

Previous Registrations:

5182PO	G874RNC, JJI4889, G86XRG	PJI7756	LFO900Y, MOI7000, NRV961Y
5373PO	E241BMA, A4BOB, E358ERR	POI2062	GGT334T
6709PO	D883FYL	POI6312	B530BML
IIL8744	JVF818V	RIL1067	H159UUA
MIL7104	B620AMD, YSU990, LBZ4322	RIL1072	H136UUA
PIL4059	B97LUY		

Livery: Cream and red; cream, red and gold (coaches)

The P&O Lloyd fleet contains several double-deck buses for school and contract work, though few venture onto commercial services. Pictured on layover outside the depot is XPG194T, a Roe-bodied Leyland Atlantean purchased by National Bus for London Country work in 1979.
John Jones

LLYNFI COACHES

D H & M Stolzenberg, Birchgrove, Queen Marys Lane, Maesteg, Bridgend, CF34 9SF

	SHP693R	Bedford YMT	Plaxton Supreme III	C53F	1977	Galloway, Mendlesham, 1993	
WTG		Bristol VRT/SL3/6LXB	Alexander AL	B44/31F	1979	Cardiff Bus, 1997-99	
	WTG335T	WTG344T	WTG346T		WTG354T	WTG370T	
	WTG341T	WTG345T	WTG347T		WTG355T	WTG375T	
	F152AWO	MCW MetroRider MF150/119	MCW	B23F	1988	Cardiff Bus, 1997	
	F153AWO	MCW MetroRider MF150/119	MCW	B23F	1988	Cardiff Bus, 1997	
	F154AWO	MCW MetroRider MF150/119	MCW	B23F	1988	Cardiff Bus, 1997	
	F155AWO	MCW MetroRider MF150/119	MCW	B23F	1988	Cardiff Bus, 1997	
	A130SNH	Mercedes-Benz O303	Jonckheere Jubilee P50	C51FT	1990	Williams, Brecon, 1998	
	H366NCY	Ford Transit VE6	Ford	M8	1990	Days Hire, Swansea, 1993	
	H390GAV	Ford Transit VE6	Pearl	M14	1990	Bown Self-drive, Caerphilly, 1992	
	J145UCY	Ford Transit VE6	Ford	M14	1991	Days Hire, Swansea, 1993	
	J149UCY	Ford Transit VE6	Ford	M8	1991	Days Hire, Swansea, 1998	
	N711AHP	Volvo B10M-62	Plaxton Première 350	C53F	1995	Bus Eireann, 1999	
	P96TTX	Toyota Coaster HZB50R	Caetano Optimo III	C21F	1995	Bebb, Llantwit Fardre, 1999	
	P97TTX	Toyota Coaster HZB50R	Caetano Optimo III	C21F	1995	Bebb, Llantwit Fardre, 1999	
	R632VNN	Dennis Javelin GX	Marcopolo Explorer	C53F	1998		
	V979FAV	LDV Convoy	LDV	M16	1999		
	V980FAV	LDV Convoy	LDV	M16	1999		

Previous Registrations:
A130SNH   A130SNH, 5583HA   N711AHP   95D41599

Depot: Heol Ty Gwyn Ind Est, Tyle Teg, Maesteg.
Livery: White and blue.

Bristol VRTs withdrawn recently from Cardiff Bus have migrated to several Welsh operators to meet school tender requirements. Llynfi Coaches currently use ten in an all-white livery. WTG375T is seen at Archbishop McGrath School at Ynysawdre.
John Jones

LONG'S

DG Long & A J Evans, Rheolau Garage, 3 Heol Rheolau, Abercraf, Powys SA9 1TB

OIL4474	Leyland Leopard PSU5/4R	Plaxton Panorama Elite II	C57F	1972	Vale of Llangollen, 1998
OIL4473	Leyland Leopard PSU3B/4R	Plaxton Panorama Elite III	C47F	1974	Vale of Llangollen, 1998
OIL4471	Ford R1114	Plaxton Supreme III	C53F	1975	Joseph Jones & Son, 1990
OIL4472	Bedford YMT	Plaxton Supreme III Exp	B49F	1978	Bromyard Bus Company, 1996
GIL5149	Bristol VRT/SL3/6LXB	Eastern Coach Works	B43/31F	1978	Turner, Bristol, 1998
WTG351T	Bristol VRT/SL3/6LXB	Alexander AL	B44/31F	1978	Cardiff Bus, 1999
WTG367T	Bristol VRT/SL3/6LXB	Alexander AL	B44/31F	1979	Cardiff Bus, 1999
WTG369T	Bristol VRT/SL3/6LXB	Alexander AL	B44/31F	1979	Cardiff Bus, 1999
OIL5276	Ford R1114	Plaxton Supreme IV	C53F	1979	Durbin, Almondsbury, 1992
OIL4470	Leyland Leopard PSU3E/4R	Plaxton Supreme IV	C53F	1979	Joseph Jones & Son, 1990
OIL5274	Leyland Leopard PSU5C/4R	Plaxton Supreme IV	C53F	1980	Eagle Coaches, Bristol, 1994
GIL2339	Bristol VRT/SL3/6LXB	Eastern Coach Works	B43/31F	1980	Turner, Bristol, 1998
CTX384V	Bristol VRT/SL3/6LXB	Alexander AL	B44/31F	1980	Cardiff Bus, 1999
CTX386V	Bristol VRT/SL3/6LXB	Alexander AL	B44/31F	1980	Cardiff Bus, 1999
OIL5271	Ford R1114	Plaxton Supreme IV	C53F	1981	Joseph Jones & Son, 1990
GIL9220	DAF MB200DKTL600	Jonckheere Bermuda	C53F	1982	Eagle, Bristol, 1997
GIL5102	Volvo B10M-61	Plaxton Paramount 3500	C49FT	1983	Sihota, Southall, 1996
GIL6324	Leyland Tiger TRCTL11/3R	Duple Caribbean	C53F	1983	Vale of Llangollen, 1997
GIL7827	Leyland Tiger TRCTL11/3R	Plaxton Paramount 3500	C52F	1983	Venture Travel, Cardiff, 1996
GIL5103	Leyland Tiger TRCTL11/3R	Plaxton Paramount 3500	C53F	1984	Heard, Hartland, 1996
GIL2987	Leyland Tiger TRCTL11/3R	Plaxton Paramount 3500 II	C53F	1985	Vale of Llangollen, 1993

All of Long's coaches and some of the buses have been re-registered with GIL or OIL index marks, though the practice has not spread to the minibuses. GIL4527 is a Leyland Tiger with Van Hool Alizèe bodywork that was new to Shearings. It is seen at Cardiff in February 2000 on an excursion to the France-Wales rugby match.
John Jones

Two Optare MetroRiders joined the fleet of Long's in 1990. Shown here is H170OTG. At the start of 2000 the production of the Metrobus has ceased, giving way to the new Solo. Interestingly, the last Metroriders were supplied to a Welsh operator. *John Jones*

GIL4527	Leyland Tiger TRCTL11/3RZ	Van Hool Alizèe	C53F	1986	Shearings, 1992
GIL4450	Leyland Tiger TRCTL11/3R	Duple Caribbean	C46FT	1986	Vale of Llangollen, 1997
GIL4128	Leyland Tiger TRCTL11/3RZ	Plaxton Paramount 3500 II	C53F	1986	Vale of Llangollen, 1993
D141NON	Freight Rover Sherpa	Carlyle	B18F	1987	Coaches, Bristol, 1994
E348UOH	Freight Rover Sherpa	Carlyle Citybus 2	B21F	1988	D&N Travel, Ystradgynlais, 1995
GIL3217	Volvo B10M-61	Plaxton Paramount 3500 III	C55F	1988	Vale of Llangollen, 1997
GIL7045	Sanos S315	Sanos Charisma	C49FT	1988	Lewis Meridian, Greenwich, 1998
F480SBX	Renault Trafic	Cymric	M10	1988	van, 1992
H168OTG	Optare MetroRider MR01	Optare	B31F	1990	Cardiff Bus, 1999
H170OTG	Optare MetroRider MR01	Optare	B31F	1990	Cardiff Bus, 1999
J986UCY	Ford Transit VE6	Cymric	M14	1991	Days Hire, Swansea, 1994
J189BWJ	Ford Transit VE6	Advanced Vehicle Bodies	M14	1992	Days Hire, Swansea, 1995
K744ECY	Ford Transit VE6	Ford	M7L	1993	Days Hire, Swansea, 1997

Previous Registrations:

Livery: Cream, yellow & maroon

GIL2339	GTX742W
GIL2987	B387DMB, 3810VT, B434FFM
GIL3217	E419CCA, VLT177, 4015VT, E365DMA
GIL4128	C339DND
GIL4450	C137CFB, NAT746A, VLT483, 7052VT
GIL4527	C711LMA, 8177VT, C738NCA, 467VT
GIL5102	RME971Y
GIL5103	A31FVN, GSU347, A695DCN, LXI4455
GIL5149	HPT86N
GIL6324	KGS481Y, ADZ1232, VLT229
GIL7045	F863OVW, IIW372, F78KGO
GIL7827	JNM758Y, 510EKH
GIL9220	WRK4X
OIL4470	YTH930T
OIL4471	KCY187P
OIL4472	ARB528T
OIL4473	YWE506M, 440VT, GAW60M, YSV318, BTU447M, 467VT, GAW122M
OIL4474	MPL11L, 1810VT, RDM356M, 6052VT, EAW611L
OIL5271	PNW329W
OIL5274	BEU809V, 94SHU, BEU809V
OIL5275	ADN51V

The Welsh Bus Handbook

M & H TRAVEL

M Owen, 8 Tre Wen, Denbigh, Denbighshire LL16 3HF

LCC542P	Volvo B58-56	Duple Dominant	C53F	1976	Cerbydau Carreglefn, 1997
KAZ6917	Volvo B58-61	Unicar	C53F	1980	CenturionTravel, Haltwhistle, 1998
FBZ1473	Volvo B10M-61	Duple Goldliner IV	C53F	1982	Safford, Little Gransden, 1993
RJI4378	Volvo B10M-61	Duple Goldliner IV	C50F	1982	Caelloi, Pwllheli, 1992
HIL5659	Volvo B10M-61	Plaxton Paramount 3500 III	C53F	1987	Dodsworth, Boroughbridge, 1996
WAZ4435	Volvo B10M-61	Jonckheere Jubilee	C53F	1987	Go Goodwin, Eccles, 1998
RIL3744	Volvo B10M-60	Plaxton Paramount 3500 III	C44FT	1989	Caelloi, Pwllheli, 1999
SIL1392	Volvo B10M-60	Plaxton Paramount 3500 III	C49FT	1990	Dodsworth, Boroughbridge, 1999
J34UTG	Freight Rover Sherpa (Isuzu)	Carlyle Citybus 2	B20F	1992	Cled Williams, Bargoed, 1996
L65ORB	Mercedes-Benz 711D	Marshall C19	BC29F	1994	Skills, Nottingham, 1997
N118TCN	Iveco TurboDaily 59.12	Mellor	B27F	1996	North Rider, Palmersville, 1997
V107LVH	Optare M850	Optare Solo	B32F	2000	

Previous Registrations:

FBZ1473	FHS744X	RIL3744	F804UDU, KOV2, F317VVC
HIL5659	E563UHS	RJI4378	RSJ812Y
LCC542P	NHP225P, KJC797	SIL1392	G542LWU, 4234NT, G542LWU, USV809
KAZ6917	SFM223V	WAZ4435	D106BNV, WSV553, D877WEY

Depot: Trefnant Garage, Trefnant
Livery: Cream and blue

M&H Travel operate four minibuses alongside their coach fleet. These are used on commercial and tendered routes from a depot at Trefnant near Denbigh. Shown here is N118TCN, a Mellor-bodied Iveco which has recently been joined by a new Optare Solo. *John Jones*

MANSEL DAVID

Movereturn Ltd, 190 Oxford Street, Pontycymmer, Bridgend CF32 8DG

AKK176T	Bedford YMT	Duple Dominant	B51F	1978	Skinner, Saltby, 1998
WTG365T	Bristol VRT/SL3/6LXB	Alexander AL	B44/31F	1978	Cardiff Bus, 1999
WTG374T	Bristol VRT/SL3/6LXB	Alexander AL	B44/31F	1978	Cardiff Bus, 1999
TWS911T	Bristol VRT/SL3/6LXB	Eastern Coach Works	B43/33F	1978	Glenvic, Bristol, 1999
XBO117T	Bristol VRT/SL3/501	Eastern Coach Works	B43/31F	1979	Morris Travel, Pencoed, 1995
APM116T	AEC Reliance 6U2R	Plaxton Supreme IV Exp	C49F	1979	Hague, Sheffield, 1996
WEB409T	AEC Reliance 6U3ZR	Plaxton Supreme IV Exp	C49F	1979	Lincoln, 1991
JBZ6926	AEC Reliance 6U3ZR	Plaxton Supreme IV	C57F	1980	Henleyis, Abertillery, 1995
AVK162V	Leyland Atlantean AN68A/2R	Alexander AL	B49/37F	1980	Stagecoach, 1999
JIL6904	DAF SB2305DHTD585	Plaxton Paramount 3200 III	C53F	1988	Ryan, Bath, 1999

Previous Registrations:

JBZ6926	BBT380V, OAT206V		JIL6904	F281GBW

Livery: Blue and grey

School contracts provide much work for Mansel David who allocate five double-deck buses. Shown here are two variants of Alexander bodywork, Atlantean AVK162V with curved body styling and WTG365T illustrating the peaked front option. *John Jones*

MARTIN

W R & A J Martin & G R Whitcombe (A H Martin & Sons), Cross Ash Garage, Cross Ash, Abergavenny, Monmouthshire NP7 8PL

GRY626N	Bedford YRT	Plaxton Elite III Express	C53F	1975	Leicester, 1984
VEC170R	Bedford YLQ	Plaxton Supreme III	C45F	1977	Nuttall, Modbury, 1997
YDD133S	Bedford YLQ	Plaxton Supreme III	C45F	1978	Aztec, Bristol, 1994
XWS541V	Bedford YLQ	Plaxton Supreme IV Exp	C45F	1979	Sargent, Cardiff, 1990
VBM948W	Bedford YNT	Duple Dominant II	C53F	1980	Palmer, Dunstable, 1987
NWG990X	Bedford YNT	Plaxton Supreme VI	C53F	1982	Angel Motors, Heathrow, 1990
C406WCJ	Bedford CF	Dormobile	M12	1985	Humphreys, Rhayader, 1990
C420WCJ	Bedford CF	Dormobile	M12	1985	
C488JCY	Bedford CF	Dormobile	M12	1986	Briton Ferry Minibus, 1988
D568EWS	Freight Rover Sherpa	Dormobile	B16F	1986	Badgerline, 1989
E762HJF	Bedford YNV	Duple 320	C53FT	1988	Scarlet Coaches, Minehead, 1997
F898LCJ	Freight Rover Sherpa	Freight Rover	M16	1989	
M498DDE	LDV 400	A Line	M16	1994	van, 1997
M536OJH	LDV 400	A Line	M16	1994	van, 1997

Previous Registrations:
YDD133S   YDD133S, PWV693

Depot: Cross Ash Garage, Cross Ash and Station Road, Ross on Wye
Livery: Cream and green

E762HJF, with its Duple 320 body, is one of the last Bedfords built. It is seen near the depot in Cross Ash, a village set in the east Monmouthshire countryside, close to the Herefordshire border. *John Jones*

MERLYN'S

Merlyn's Coaches (Skewen) Ltd, The Lodge, 56 Siding Terrace, Skewen, Neath Port Talbot, SA10 6RD.

ATH352V	Ford R1114	Plaxton Supreme IV	C53F	1979		
WJX478V	Leyland Leopard PSU3E/4R	Plaxton Supreme IV	C53F	1980	Supreme, Hadleigh, 1990	
SFD254W	Leyland Leopard PSU3E/4R	Plaxton Supreme IV	C53F	1980	Supreme, Hadleigh, 1990	
JUH228W	Leyland Leopard PSU4F/2R	Duple Dominant	B47F	1981	Merthyr Tydfil, 1989	
RWN727Y	Leyland Tiger TRCTL11/2R	Plaxton Supreme V	C53F	1983		
IUI2173	Volvo B10M-61	Plaxton Paramount 3500 III	C49FT	1984	Fletcher, Offerton, 1997	
TJI5404	Van Hool T815H	Van Hool Alizée	C49FT	1988		
TJI5405	Volvo B10M-61	Van Hool Alizée	C53F	1988	Time Travel, Thornton Heath, 1995	
F117YVP	MCW MetroRider MF158/16	MCW	B28F	1988	London United, 1997	
F24CWO	Leyland Tiger TRCL10/3ARZM	Plaxton Paramount 3500 III	C53FT	1989	Aintree Coachline, 2000	
J378MBX	Renault Master T35D	Cymric	M14	1991		
J40MCL	Van Hool T815H	Van Hool Acron	C49FT	1992		
K3MCT	Volvo B6	Caetano Algarve II	C35F	1993	MCT, Motherwell, 1998	
T9MCL	Volvo B10M-62	Van Hool Alizée II	C49FT	1999		
T10MCL	Volvo B10M-62	Caetano Enigma	C49FT	1999		

Previous Registrations:

IUI2173	A368YME, 7845UG, A919REO, 792FTA	TJI5404	E291UTH
K3MCT	K698RNR	TJI4505	E315OPR

Livery: White, turquoise, red and yellow

Merlyn's only commercial service links Victoria Gardens in Neath with Birchgrove, a route that requires one vehicle for the hourly service. The normal provider is F117YVP, a MetroRider that was new to London Buses. It was pictured near to its base in Skewen. *John Jones*

MEYERS

M L Meyers, Cilgwyn, Llanpumsaint, Carmarthenshire SA33 6LA

ATH180T	DAF MB200DKL500	Plaxton Supreme IV	C49F	1979	Evans, Tregaron, 1995
B290KPF	Leyland Tiger TRCTL11/3RH	Plaxton Paramount 3200 IIE	C53F	1985	London & Country, 1997
F481WFA	MCW MetroRider MF154/10	MCW	C29F	1989	Dereham Coachways, 1995
H557XNN	Iveco Daily 49.10	Carlyle Dailybus 2	B25F	1990	Pattersons, Birmingham, 1998
L380PAS	Iveco Daily 59.12	Marshall	B25F	1993	Highland Country, 2000

Previous Registrations:
ATH180T   FTW130T, 275NAE   F481WFA   F115UEH, 565LON

Livery: Blue and white; blue and silver

The local index mark allocated to ATH180T disguises that is was new to Harris of Grays who operated some of the first DF MB220s imported into the UK. Showing the Plaxton Supreme IV body styling, it is seen at its home base.
John Jones

Mid Wales Travel acquired this Autobus-bodied Mercedes-Benz 814D at the beginning of 1999, and it is often to be found working local services in Newtown. M568BVL was so employed when seen at the town's small bus station on a very wet Monday morning in April 1999.
John Jones

MID WALES TRAVEL

Mid Wales Travel - Evans

Mid Wales Motorways Ltd, Bwthyn, Penrhyncoch, Aberystwyth,
Cardiganshire SY23 3EH

Reg	Chassis	Body	Type	Year	History
OAO530R	Bedford YMT	Plaxton Supreme III	C53F	1976	King Offa, Westbury, 1996
PUO852S	Bedford YLQ	Duple Dominant II	C45F	1978	Evans, Tregaron, 1999
MAX334X	Leyland Tiger TRCTL11/2R	Plaxton Supreme VI	C53F	1982	Evans, Penrhyncoch, 1991
A114TRP	Leyland Tiger TRCTL11/3RH	Plaxton Paramount 3500 II	C50FT	1983	Stagecoach United Counties, 1999
A702HVT	Leyland Tiger TRCTL11/2R	Duple Dominant	B51F	1984	Arriva Midlands North, 1999
A703HVT	Leyland Tiger TRCTL11/2R	Duple Dominant	B51F	1984	Arriva Midlands North, 1999
A705HVT	Leyland Tiger TRCTL11/2R	Duple Dominant	B51F	1984	Arriva Midlands North, 1999
A706HVT	Leyland Tiger TRCTL11/2R	Duple Dominant	B51F	1984	Arriva Midlands North, 1999
C23MAK	Leyland Tiger TRCLXC/2RH	Duple 340	C49FT	1986	Sunline Tours, Flimwell, 1999
D129VRP	Mercedes-Benz L608D	Dormobile (1990)	B25F	1986	Evans, Tregaron, 2000
D177VRP	Mercedes-Benz L608D	Dormobile (1990)	B25F	1986	Evans, Tregaron, 2000
D140HML	Bedford CF	Dormobile	M8	1986	
E695UNE	Leyland Tiger TRCTL11/3R	Plaxton Paramount 3200 III	C53F	1988	Horseman, Reading, 1999
G464VPG	Mercedes-Benz 709D	Reeve Burgess Beaver	B25F	1988	Eurotravel, Woking, 1995
H179EJU	Leyland Tiger TRCL10/3ARZA	Plaxton Paramount 3500 III	C51FT	1990	Evans, Penrhyncoch, 1991
H942DRJ	Volvo B10M-60	Plaxton Paramount 3500 III	C49FT	1991	Parks of Hamilton, 1996
H943DRJ	Volvo B10M-60	Plaxton Paramount 3500 III	C49FT	1991	Parks of Hamilton, 1996
J447UUK	Ford Transit VE6	Ford	M8	1991	private owner, 1997
M568BVL	Mercedes-Benz 814D	Autobus Nouvelle 2	C25F	1994	Anderson, Bermondsey, 1999
M28TWJ	Leyland-DAF 400	Leyland-DAF	M16	1994	van, 1997

Depots: Brynhyfryd Garage, Penrhyncoch and Pool Road, Newtown, Powys
Livery: White (or cream) and blue

Extensive fleet renewal during 1999 saw the acquisition by Mid Wales Travel of four Leyland Tigers with Dominant bus bodywork from Arriva Midlands North. Now displaying both Evans and Mid Wales names, A703HVT is seen at Newtown bus station. *Roger Pope*

MIDWAY MOTORS

D W & W S Rees, Midway Garage, Crymych, Pembrokeshire, SA41 3QU

PRR449R	Leyland National 11351A/1R		B50F	1976	Trent Buses, 1998
NGL371	Ford R1114	Plaxton Supreme III	C53F	1977	Moss, Sandown, 1991
FFP200V	Ford R1114	Duple Dominant II Express	C53F	1979	Bysiau Ffoshelig, 1994
1885FM	Ford R1114	Duple Dominant IV	C53F	1981	Fraser, Accrington, 1986
JEU803X	Mercedes-Benz L508D	Devon Conversions	BC24F	1981	Gloucestershire CC, 1993
XNK200X	Ford R1014	Plaxton Bustler	B47F	1981	Universitybus, Hatfield, 1993
GIL3276	Volvo B10M-61	Caetano Algarve	C51F	1984	Byron's, Skewen, 1994
MIL6317	Ford R1115	Plaxton Paramount 3500 II	C35F	1985	Norman, Braishfield, 1996
NIL3278	Ford R1115	Plaxton Paramount 3500 II	C35F	1985	Castle Llandovery, 1998
YTH317	Volvo B10M-61	Plaxton Paramount 3500 II	C48FT	1986	Denison, Otley, 1989
E442YAO	Ford Transit VE6	Mellor	M15	1987	Streamline, Bath, 1993
N785ORY	Dennis Javelin 12SDA2134	Caetano Algarve 2	C51FT	1995	Evans, Tregaron, 1998
250DBX	Bova FHD12.290	Bova Futura	C49F	1993	Stratos, Newton, 2000
R721EWV	LDV Convoy	LDV	M16	1997	private owner, 1999

Previous Registrations:

1885FM	JFV295W	MIL6317	C929DYA
250DBX	K123DNT	NIL3278	B997CUS, 973BUS, 627K, 77BUS, B117FCS
GIL3276	B252CUH	NGL371	ODL774R
JEU803X	JEU803X, 250DBX	YTH317	C453CWR

Livery: Blue and silver

NEFYN COACHES

R G Owen, Gerafon, Nefyn, Gwynedd, LL53 6HE

E102DJR	Volvo B9M	Plaxton Paramount 3200 III	C43F	1988	Go-Ahead (OK), 1997
E316ACC	Mercedes Benz 709D	Reeve Burgess Beaver	B25F	1988	
G216EOA	Freight-Rover Sherpa	Carlyle Citybus 2	B20F	1989	Cerbydau Carreglefn, 1999
G60RGG	Volvo B10M-60	Plaxton Paramount 3500 III	C53F	1990	Bakers, Biddulph, 1999
H741TWB	Mercedes-Benz 709D	Reeve Burgess Beaver	C23F	1991	Patterson's, Birmingham, 1995
K805SCC	Leyland-DAF 400	Leyland-DAF	M16	1992	
M829PHN	Volvo B10M-62	Plaxton Première 350	C49FT	1994	Compass Royston, Stockton, 1999
T961ACC	Mercedes-Benz Vario O814	Plaxton Beaver 2	B31F	1999	
T11AGO	Optare M920	Optare Solo	B35F	1999	

Previous Registrations:
E102DJR   E102DJR, 340GUP

Depot: West End Garage, St David's Road, Nefyn
Livery: White (or silver), red, orange and yellow

Opposite, top: **Midway Motors** for many years used buses and coaches based on a variety of Ford chassis. A change came in 1998 when PRR449R, a former Trent Leyland National joined the fleet. It is seen in April 1999 awaiting departure for its home village from Finch's Square in Cardigan. *John Jones*
Opposite, bottom: **Nefyn Coaches** operate several services linking villages on the Lleyn penisula with Pwllheli. Route 8 from Tudweiliog through Nefyn has frequent workings, including tendered operations on Saturday evenings and Sundays. T961ACC, shown here, is a Plaxton-bodied Mercedes-Benz Vario and the first in a new livery using a silver base. It was joined by an Optare Solo later in 1999, the first of the type for an operator based in Wales. *John Jones*

NEWPORT TRANSPORT

Newport Transport Ltd, 160 Corporation Road, Newport   NP19 0WF

1	XFM203		Leyland Tiger TRCL10/3ARZA		Plaxton Paramount 3200 III	C53F	1991		
2	J96NJT		Scania K113CRB		Plaxton Première 350	C49FT	1992		Excelsior, Bournemouth, 1996
3	J97NJT		Scania K113CRB		Plaxton Première 350	C49FT	1992		Smith, High Wycombe, 1997

4-9			Scania N113CRB		Alexander Strider	B48F	1993		
4	K104YTX	6	K106YTX	7	K107YTX	8	K108YTX	9	K109YTX
5	K105YTX								

10-18			Scania L94UB		Wright Axcess Floline	N46F	1998		
10	S110TDW	12	S112TDW	14	S114TDW	16	S116TDW	18	S118TDW
11	S211TDW	13	S113TDW	15	S115TDW	17	S117TDW		

19-26			Scania N112DH		Alexander RH	B47/33F	1984		
19	B219YUH	21	B221YUH	23	B223YUH	25	B225YUH	26	B226YUH
20	B220YUH	22	B222YUH	24	B224YUH				

35-40			Dennis Trident 2		Alexander ALX400	N43/33F	2000		
35	V35HTG	37	V37HTG	38	V38HTG	39	V39HTG	40	V140HTG
36	V36HTG								

41-52			Scania N113DRB		Alexander RH	B47/33F	1988-89		
41	F41YHB	44	F44YHB	47	G47FKG	49	G49FKG	51	G51FKG
42	F42YHB	45	F45YHB	48	G48FKG	50	G50FKG	52	G52FKG
43	F43YHB	46	F46YHB						

53	G53KTX		Optare MetroRider MR09		Optare	B23F	1990		
54	F360URU		MCW MetroRider MF150/108		MCW	B23F	1989		Wilts & Dorset, 2000
55	G55KTX		Optare MetroRider MR09		Optare	B23F	1990		
56	G56KTX		Optare MetroRider MR09		Optare	B23F	1990		
57	G57KTX		Optare MetroRider MR09		Optare	B23F	1990		
58	G58KTX		Optare MetroRider MR09		Optare	B23F	1990		

59-64			Optare MetroRider MR09		Optare	B23F	1991		
59	H59PNY	61	H61PNY	62	H62PNY	63	H63PNY	64	H64PNY
60	H160PNY								

65	M65KTG		Scania N113CRL		Alexander Strider	N48F	1995
66	M166KTG		Scania N113CRL		Alexander Strider	N48F	1995
67	M67KTG		Scania N113CRL		Alexander Strider	N48F	1995

68-73			Scania N113CRB		Alexander Strider	B48F	1994		
68	L68EKG	70	L170EKG	71	L71EKG	72	L172EKG	73	L73EKG
69	L69EKG								

Opposite, top: **January 2000 saw the entry into service of Newport's first low-floor double-deck buses. These are Dennis Tridents, the first for Wales, and are noteworthy in being the first non-Scania full-size buses for almost twenty years, and the first from Dennis since the 1950s. The picture shows the new livery that incorporates a representation of the town's Wave sculpture with the real article behind.** *John Jones*
Opposite, bottom: **Newport uses MetroRiders for its minibus needs. Representing the 1997 intake is 86, R86BDW, seen climbing North Street. The earlier MetroRiders are expected to be replaced during 2000.** *John Jones*

Route 30 from Cardiff to Newport is a jointly operated service. Newport 17, S117TDW, is seen between Tredegar Park and Castleton. The purchase of this batch of Scania L94s with Wright Axcess Floline bodywork introduced a darker shade of green to the larger buses. *John Jones*

74-83		Scania N113CRL		Alexander Strider		N48F	1995-97		
74	M74KTG	76	M76KTG	78	N78PDW	80	N180PDW	82	N82PDW
75	M75KTG	77	P177VDW	79	N79PDW	81	N81PDW	83	N83PDW
86	R86BDW		Optare MetroRider MR31	Optare		B25F	1997		
87	R87BDW		Optare MetroRider MR31	Optare		B25F	1997		
88	R188BDW		Optare MetroRider MR31	Optare		B25F	1997		
89	R89BDW		Optare MetroRider MR31	Optare		B25F	1997		
90-94		Scania N113CRL		Alexander Strider		N48F	1997		
90	P190VDW	91	P91VDW	92	P92VDW	93	P93VDW	94	P94VDW

Special event vehicles:

102	YDW752K	Metro-Scania BR111MH	MCW	B40D	1972	
178	PDW484	Leyland Titan PD2/40	Longwell Green	B30/28R	1958	

Ancilliary vehicles:

117	RUH17Y	Scania BR112DH	Wadham Stringer Vanguard TV		1983	
174	XGM450L	Leyland Leopard PSU3/3R	Alexander Y	TV	1972	Morris Travel. Pencoed, 1991

Stored vehicles with duplicate numbers:

11	RUH11Y	Scania BR112DH	Wadham Stringer Vanguard B42F	1983
13	RUH13Y	Scania BR112DH	Wadham Stringer Vanguard B42F	1983

Previous Registrations:

J96NJT	A15XEL	XFM203	J905UBO
J97NJT	A16XEL		

Livery: Green and cream: **On order:** 5 low floor Dennis Dart for May/June 2000

OARE'S OF HOLYWELL

G A Oare, Ty Draw, Brynford, Holywell, Flintshire CH8 8LP

TXI8754	Volvo B58-56	Plaxton Panorama Elite III	C53F	1973	Pat's, New Broughton, 1999
JYG432V	Bristol VRT/SL3/6LXB	Eastern Coach Works	B43/31F	1979	Devaway, Bretton, 1999
SIB4631	Volvo B58-56	Duple Dominant II Express	C53F	1980	Patis, New Broughton, 1998
FIL3825	DAF SBR2300DHS553	Jonckheere Jubilee P99	C55/13CT	1982	Crescent, North Walsham, 1992
TIB4921	DAF MB200DKTL600	Plaxton Paramount 3500	C53F	1983	Lavender, Shirley, 1995
HUI4199	Van Hool T815	Van Hool Alizée	C53FT	1984	Arvonia, Llanrug, 1995
HIL7642	Volvo B10M-61	Duple 340	C49FT	1987	Ross, Featherstone, 1998
HIL5698	Volvo B10M-61	Van Hool Alizée	C49FT	1987	Dereham Coachways, 1998
F345ONO	Ford Transit VE6	Dormobile	B20F	1988	Sel's, Llanrwst, 1991
G439GJC	Volvo B10M-60	Plaxton Expressliner	C46FT	1990	Benson, Greasby, 1999
H127YGG	Ford Transit VE6	Made-to-Measure	BC20F	1990	Out & About, Trefnant, 1999
H175ANE	Ford Transit VE6	Ford	M14	1990	Flanagan, Grappenhall, 1999
M762JCU	Ford Transit VE6	Oare	M14	1995	van, 1999
N919ETU	Ford Transit VE6	Ford	M14	1995	Hanmer, Southsea, 1998
R10ARE	Mercedes-Benz Vario O814D	Plaxton Beaver 2	BC30F	1998	

Previous Registrations:

FIL3825	DLX46Y, 103UTW	SIB4631	XRN28V
HIL5698	D638MSJ	TIB4921	EFK135Y, MIB516, FFA545Y
HIL7642	D530YCK	TXI8754	LVD814L
HUI4199	A947GPM, 367ARV		

Livery: White, red and silver, or white. A number of minibuses are operated as non-PCVs in addition to the fleet above.

The latest arrival for tendered services at Oare's of Holywell is R10ARE (R1 OARE), a Mercedes-Benz Vario with Beaver 2 bodywork. It is seen in Holywell on a local service, though it is also used on longer routes to Mold and Denbigh. *John Jones*

OWENS MOTORS

Owen's Motors Ltd, Temeside House, Station Road, Knighton, Powys, LD7 1DT

MSF679T	Bedford YLQ	Plaxton Supreme IV	C45F	1979	Smith's, High Wycombe, 1990
CRL918R	Bedford YMT	Plaxton Supreme IV Exp	C53F	1979	Norris, Hawkhurst, 1997
TUA161W	Bedford YMT	Plaxton Supreme IV	C53F	1981	Bakers, Weston-super-Mare, 1999
NJI5235	Bedford YNT(Cummins)	Plaxton Supreme VI Exp	C49F	1982	Teme Valley, Leintwardine, 1997
PJI6076	Bedford YNT	Plaxton Supreme V Exp	C53F	1982	Searle, Seaton, 1997
SIL2243	Bedford YMP	Plaxton Paramount 3200	C35F	1983	Evans, Tregaron, 2000
572RKJ	Bedford YNV Venturer	Plaxton Paramount 3200 III	C53F	1987	Newbury, Ledbury, 2000
E712UHB	Bedford YNV Venturer	Duple 320	C57F	1988	Waddon, Bedwas, 1993
LAZ3830	Hestair Duple SDA1512	Duple 425	C55F	1990	Bywater, Rochdale, 1995
RJI2713	Setra S215HD	Setra	C49FT	1990	The King's Ferry, 1997
L220JAW	Ford Transit VE6	Ford	M8	1994	private owner, 1997
N716SOP	LDV 400	ALine	M16	1996	van, 1997
T931KNW	LDV Convoy	LDV	M16	1999	private owner, 2000

Previous Registrations:

572RKJ	E830EUT		PJI6076	SNU689X
LAZ3830	G137TNU		RJI2713	G506YFE
NJI5235	PNT849X, GBB254, MAB117X, XKH455, MUY121X		SIL2243	RYL181Y, HSV389, WWE332Y

Livery: Blue and grey

Owens Motors' depot is situated just on the Shropshire side of the border on the outskirts of Knighton in Powys. Seen on a market day service to Newtown is MSF679T, a Bedford 10-metre YLQ with Plaxton Supreme bodywork that was fitted with 'grant' doors. *David Donati*

PENCOED TRAVEL

Morris Travel Ltd, Wellhouse Garage, Penprysg Road, Pencoed, Bridgend CF35 6LT

SRJ751R	Leyland Atlantean AN68A/1R	Northern Counties	B43/32F	1977	Maidstone & District, 1997
UDT183S	Leyland Atlantean AN68A/2R	East Lancashire	B45/31D	1978	Armchair, Brentford, 1997
EPH215V	Leyland Atlantean AN68A/1R	Roe	B43/30F	1979	Kentish Bus, 1997
BUH238V	Bristol VRT/SL3/501	Eastern Coach Works	B43/31F	1980	Rhondda, 1992
FWA499V	Leyland Leopard PSU3E/4R	Duple Dominant II Express	C53F	1980	Happy Days, Woodseaves, 1998
PSN916Y	Leyland Tiger TRCTL11/3R	Duple Goldliner III	C46FT	1982	Strathtay Scottish, 1991
TXI2425	DAF MB200DKFL600	Jonckheere Jubilee P50	C51FT	1983	Pan Atlas, Acton, 1989
HIL7540	DAF MB230DKFL615	Duple 340	C55F	1987	
GIL8494	DAF SB2305DHS585	Van Hool Alizée	C51FT	1988	Hardings, Redditch, 1999
LIL7332	DAF SB2305DHS585	Jonckheere Deauville P599	C49FT	1988	Gray Line, Bicester, 1996
HIL7542	Dennis Javelin GX	Berkhof Excellence 1000L	C51FT	1995	The Londoners, 2000

Previous Registrations:

GIL8494	E447LNP, DSK593, E681MWP	PSN916Y	SSJ135Y, WLT943
HIL7540	D27MTG	TXI2425	NNV610Y
HIL7542	M784SRX	UDT183S	UDT183S, OIL8494
LIL7332	E670WKW, SPV860, E750DJO		

Livery: White, blue and yellow

While confined to school tendered routes, SRJ751R is seen in Penllwyngwent in the Ogmore Valley. The coach fleet now comprises mostly DAF products. John Jones

The Welsh Bus Handbook

PHIL ANSLOW TRAVEL

P Anslow/S J Anslow/Gwent Omnibus Co Ltd, 10 Pontnewynydd Ind Est, Pontnewynydd,
Pontypool, Torfaen   NP4 6YW

PIL2859	Leyland Leopard PSU3E/4R	Duple Dominant	B49F	1980	Blue Bus, Horwich, 1996
PIL2861	Leyland National 2 NL116L11/1R		B52F	1980	Glyn Williams, Crosskeys, 1998
PIL2862	Leyland National 2 NL116L11/1R		B49F	1980	Glyn Williams, Crosskeys, 1998
NIL8647	Leyland National 2 NL116L11/1R		BC48F	1980	Arriva Cymru, 1999
NIL8656	Leyland National 2 NL116L11/1R		B49F	1980	Arriva Cymru, 1999
FIL8275	Leyland National 2 NL116L11/1R		B49F	1980	Glyn Williams, Crosskeys, 1998
VBG91V	Leyland National 2 NL116L11/1R		B49F	1980	Arriva Cymru, 1999
NIL8646	Leyland Leopard PSU4F/2R	Duple Dominant	B45F	1981	Porthcawl Omnibus Co, 1996
PSO178W	Leyland Tiger TRCTL11/3R	Duple Goldliner	C46F	1981	Western Buses, 1997
NIL8645	Leyland Leopard PSU3G/2R	Duple Dominant	BC49F	1982	Blue Bus, Horwich, 1996
XUA76X	Leyland National 2 NL116L11/1R		B49F	1982	Arriva Cymru, 1999
EWT207Y	Leyland National 2 NL116L11/1R		B49F	1982	Arriva Cymru, 1999
EWT209Y	Leyland National 2 NL116L11/1R		B49F	1983	Arriva Cymru, 1999
EWX215Y	Leyland National 2 NL116L11/1R		B49F	1983	Arriva Cymru, 1999
TJI4123	Leyland Tiger TRCTL11/2R	Duple Dominant	B55F	1984	Bennett, Gloucester, 1998
NIL8655	Leyland Tiger TRCTL11/3RH	Duple 340	C49F	1986	Arriva Cymru, 1999
NIL8653	Mercedes-Benz 811D	Optare StarRider	B31F	1988	London Central, 1998
NIL8654	Mercedes-Benz 811D	Optare StarRider	B31F	1989	London Central, 1998
LIL9975	Leyland Tiger TRCL10/3ARZM	Plaxton Paramount 3500 III	C49FT	1989	Shamrock, Pontypridd, 1999
TJI4124	Leyland Tiger TRCL10/3ARZ	Plaxton Paramount 3200 III	C53F	1989	Jay, Greengairs, 1999
PIL2841	Leyland Tiger TRCTL11/3ARZ	Duple 320	C53F	1989	Parks of Hamilton, 1994
NIL8649	Volvo B10M-60	Plaxton Excalibur	C49FT	1992	Excelsior, Bournemouth, 1997
J114NJT	Volvo B10M-60	Plaxton Première 320	C49FT	1992	Excelsior, Bournemouth, 1997
J115NJT	Volvo B10M-60	Plaxton Première 320	C49FT	1992	Excelsior, Bournemouth, 1997
K336RCN	Iveco TurboDaily 59.12	Dormobile Routemaker	B27F	1992	Stagecoach Busways, 1997
K337RCN	Iveco TurboDaily 59.12	Dormobile Routemaker	B27F	1992	Stagecoach Busways, 1997
K197XEL	Volvo B10M-62	Plaxton Première 350	C49FT	1993	Excelsior, Bournemouth, 1997
K61BAX	Volvo B10M-60	Jonckheere Deauville	C53F	1993	Ralphs, Langley, 1997

Fourteen Mercedes-Benz Vario minibuses are operated by Phil Anslow Travel. Pictured here is T38PTG, an example with Plaxton Beaver 2 bodywork.
John Jones

K205OHS K206OHS		Mercedes-Benz 709D K97RGA	Dormobile Routemaker L914UGA	B29F	1993 L927UGA	 L928UGA
L51CNY	Volvo B10M-60	Plaxton Première 350	C53F	1993	Westbus, Hounslow, 1996
M134SKY	Volvo B10M-62	Van Hool Alizée HE	C51F	1995	Skyeways, Kyle, 1998
M135SKY	Volvo B10M-62	Van Hool Alizée HE	C51F	1995	Skyeways, Kyle, 1998
M91JHB	Mercedes-Benz 709D	WS Wessex II	B29F	1995	
M92JHB	Mercedes-Benz 709D	WS Wessex II	B29F	1995	
M93JHB	Mercedes-Benz 811D	WS Wessex II	B33F	1995	
	Iveco TurboDaily 59.12	UVG Citi Star	BC29F*	1996-97	*R617 is B29F
N419UWN	P969UKG	P970UKG		P971UKG	R617BWO
R624CTX	Mercedes-Benz Vario O814	UVG Citi Star	B29F	1997	
	Mercedes-Benz Vario O814	Plaxton Beaver 2	B31F	1999	
T56JKG	T38PTG	T584SKG		T587SKG	T589SKG
T57JKG	T582SKG	T585SKG		T588SKG	T590SKG
T58JKG	T583SKG	T586SKG			

Previous Registrations:

FIL8275	EON827V
J114NJT	A10XEL, J114NJT, NIL8655
J115NJT	A11XEL, J115NJT, NIL8647
K61BAX	K61BAX, TJI4124
K197XEL	K105VJT, A8XCL, K197XEL, NIL8656
K889BRW	K889BRW, PIL2863
L51CNY	L51CNY, NIL8653
L53CNY	L53CNY, NIL8654
LIL9975	F593BTG
NIL8645	OWO234Y
NIL8646	JHU230W
NIL8647	CCY820V
NIL8649	A9XEL, J405NJT
NIL8653	F923YWY
NIL8654	F163FWY
NIL8655	C63JTU
NIL8656	SNS824W
PIL2841	G797RNC, NIL8651, G797RNC
PIL2859	VUP514V
PIL2861	NAT201V
PIL2862	RSG818V
PSO178W	BSG547W, WLT741, WGB176W, CSU921, PSO178W, IIB9140
TJI4123	B472ENT
TJI4124	F779GNA, 8733CD, F806PSN

Livery: Green, yellow, and white (buses); white, red and blue (coaches).

The Phil Anslow Travel fleet includes several buses dedicated to school duties. Recent arrivals for this purpose include Leyland National 2s. Pictured on such duties is TJI4123, a Leyland Tiger with Duple Dominant bodywork. *John Jones*

PHILLIPS

H O, J & A S Phillips, St John's House, Brynford Road,
Holywell, Flintshire CH8 7RP

	WDA926T	Leyland Fleetline FE30AGR	MCW	B43/33F	1978	Travel West Midlands, 1997
	PRN117T	Bedford YMT	Duple Dominant II	C53F	1979	T Williams & Sons, Ponciau, 1995
9	OLG601V	Bedford YMT	Plaxton Supreme IV Exp	C53F	1979	
8	EWX213Y	Leyland National 2 NL116HLXB/1R		B49F	1983	Arriva Cymru, 1999
16	PAZ4945	Leyland Royal Tiger B50	Plaxton Paramount 3500	C49FT	1984	Eastham Garage, 1999
	B679EWE	Bedford YNT	Duple Laser 2	C53F	1985	Whitehead, Conisbrough, 1995
12	C830XCJ	Bedford YNT	Duple Laser 2	C53F	1986	
	G729WJU	Iveco Daily 40.10	Carlyle DailyBus 2	B25F	1989	Horrocks, Brockton, 1999
15	T91JBA	Mercedes-Benz Vario O814	Plaxton Beaver 2	B31F	1999	

Previous Registrations:
PAZ4945   A326XHE, MKA980

Depots: Greenfield, Holywell
Livery: Red and cream

As with some other operators in Flintshire, the Phillips fleet received a new Mercedes-Benz Vario for tendered services during 1999. This displaced an older minibus and is generally to be found working the Holywell to Mold service. T91JBA is seen at Holywell bus terminus in September 1999. *John Jones*

PIED BULL COACHES

R Williams, 53 Woodlands Close, Mold, Flintshire CH7 1UU

CUN669L	Ford R192	Duple Dominant	C45F	1973	Wright, Pen-y-Cae, 1977
HIL9374	Leyland Tiger TRCTL11/3R	Plaxton Supreme V Exp	C53F	1982	Allmey, Eastcote, 1996
AEF868A	Leyland Tiger TRCTL11/2R	Plaxton Supreme VIExp	C53F	1982	Acorn, Sealand, 1997
LIJ6832	Ford R1115	Plaxton Paramount 3200	C49F	1983	Roger Hill, Congleton, 1988
C284AOR	Iveco-Fiat 79.14	Robin Hood	C28FL	1985	Mawbey, Ombersley, 1993
C315DVU	Ford Transit 160	Deansgate	M12	1986	
G278HDW	Freight Rover Sherpa	Carlyle Citybus 2	B20F	1990	Executive Travel, Fenton, 1993

Previous Registrations:

AEF868A	SND353X	LIJ6832	BLJ711Y
HIL9374	VAV254X		

Depot: Gas Lane, Mold
Livery: Blue and white(or grey)

The large 'Bustler' fleet of minibuses acquired by National Welsh is now spread far and wide. One to have joined the Pied Bull Coaches fleet is G278HDW which is seen at work in Ruthin. *John Jones*

PORTHCAWL OMNIBUS Co

The Porthcawl Omnibus Co Ltd, Old Station Lane, Porthcawl,
Bridgend   CF36 5TL
J Williams, The Little Grange, 176 New Road, Porthcawl, Bridgend CF36 5BH

WDA913T	Leyland Fleetline FE30AGR	MCW	B43/33F	1978	Travel West Midlands, 1997
WDA977T	Leyland Fleetline FE30AGR	MCW	B43/33F	1978	Travel West Midlands, 1997
XTE229V	Leyland Fleetline FE33ALR	Northern Counties	B49/31D	1979	Arriva The Shires (S), 1999
AAL423A	Leyland Leopard PSU5D/4R	Plaxton P3200 III (1987)	C53F	1980	Birmingham Coach Co, 1992
KBC1V	Volvo B58-61	Plaxton Supreme IV	C57F	1980	Wiffen, Roehampton, 1998
LNV795	Volvo B58-61	Jonckheere Bermuda	C51F	1980	Baker, Weston-s-Mare, 1989
LWG533W	Leyland Leopard PSU3E/4R	Plaxton Supreme IV	C49F	1981	Reedis Travel, Kinsley, 1992
LWN790X	Bedford YNT	Duple Dominant IV	C53F	1982	Rees & Williams, 1986
VKN835X	Leyland Leopard PSU3F/4R	Willowbrook 003	C47F	1982	Maidstone & District, 1994
VKN837X	Leyland Leopard PSU3F/4R	Willowbrook 003	C47F	1982	Maidstone & District, 1994
RIL3747	Volvo B10M-61	Plaxton Paramount 3500 III	C49FT	1987	Atkinson, Ingleby Arncliffe, 1995
JIL2284	Volvo B10M-61	Plaxton Paramount 3200 III	C57F	1988	Grahamis, Talke, 1998

Previous Registrations:

AAL423A	BUH223V	LNV795	GPA628V
JIL2284	E881RGL	RIL3747	D820SGB

Livery: Maroon and beige or maroon and white

Shown at the entrance to Porthcawl Omnibus' depot is Volvo B58 KBC1V which was new to Leicester City Transport in 1980. The bodywork is Plaxton Supreme IV, a type regularly found on school duties. *John Jones*

PULLMAN COACHES

Pullman Coaches Ltd; CW Lewis & HS Rees, 41 Penclawdd Industrial Estate, Crofty, Swansea SA4 3RS

Reg	Chassis	Body	Type	Year	Notes
F854YJX	DAF SB2305DHTD585	Duple 340	C57F	1989	Arvonia, Llanrug, 1997
F924YWY	Mercedes-Benz 811D	Optare StarRider	B26F	1988	London Central, 1998
G121KUB	Mercedes-Benz 811D	Optare StarRider	B26F	1989	London Northern, 1998
TJI4700	DAF MB230LB615	Van Hool Alizée H	C51FT	1990	Freestone Cs, Beetley, 1995
J47UFL	DAF SB3000DKV601	Van Hool Alizée HE	C53F	1992	Wootton, Northampton, 1999
J781KHD	DAF MB230LB615	Van Hool Alizée HE	C51FT	1992	Berkeley, Hemel Hempstead, 2000
J782KHD	DAF MB230LB615	Van Hool Alizée HE	C51FT	1992	Oates, Lelant, 2000
J792KHD	DAF SB3000DKV601	Van Hool Alizée HE	C51FT	1992	Cosgroves, Preston, 2000
M884WAK	Volvo B10M-62	Plaxton Première 350	C49FT	1995	Logan, Dunloy, 1997
N2PCL	Dennis Javelin 12SDA2159	Plaxton Première 350	C51FT	1995	
N753VCY	DAF MB230LT615	Van Hool Alizée HE	C49FT	1996	
N990FWT	Mercedes-Benz Vario O814	Autobus Nouvelle 2	C29F	1996	
P690CWN	LDV Convoy	LDV	M16	1997	
P5PCL	Volvo B10M-62	Plaxton Première 350	C49FT	1997	
P731FCY	DAF DE33WSSB3000	Plaxton Première 350	C53F	1997	
R997FNW	DAF DE33WSSB300	Van Hool Alizée HE	C51FT	1998	
R3PCL	Dennis Javelin	Berkhof Axial 50	C51FT	1998	
S6PCL	Dennis Javelin	Neoplan Transliner	C49FT	1999	
S794JTH	DAF DE33WSSB300	Van Hool Alizée HE	C49FT	1999	
T606SBX	Renault Espace	Cymric	M7	1999	
T4PCL	MAN 11.220 HOCL-R	Caetano Enigma	C35F	1999	
V7PCL	DAF DE33WSSB3000	Plaxton Première 320	C55F	1999	
V670LWT	Mercedes-Benz Vario O814	Alexander ALX100	B27F	1999	
V703LWT	Dennis Dart SLF	Alexander ALX200	N31F	2000	
V705LWT	DAF DE33WSSB3000	Van Hool Alizée HE	C51FT	2000	
V8PCL	Volvo B10M-62	Plaxton Excalibur	C53FT	2000	
V9PCL	Volvo B10M-62	Plaxton Excalibur	C53FT	2000	

Previous Registrations:
TJI4700   G970KJX

Livery: Cream/white, red and fawn

The first low floor bus for Pullman Coaches entered service in the Spring of 2000. V703LWT is seen in Swansea.
John Jones

RICHARDS BROS

CH, WJM, R & DN Richards, Moylgrove Garage, Pentood Ind Est, Cardigan, SA43 3AD.

Reg	Chassis	Body	Code	Year	Notes
JKO63N	Bedford YRT	Duple Dominant	B53F	1975	Maidstone, 1981
JKO64N	Bedford YRT	Duple Dominant	B53F	1975	Maidstone, 1981
HPB674N	Bedford YRQ	Duple Dominant	B47F	1975	Marchwood, Haverfordwest, 1981
TPX332P	Bedford YRQ	Duple Dominant	BC45F	1975	Marchwood, Haverfordwest, 1981
NKE306P	Bedford YRT	Duple Dominant	B53F	1976	Maidstone, 1982
LVS433P	Bedford YLQ	Plaxton Supreme III	C41F	1976	Stanley, Hersham, 1985
LDE547P	Bedford YLQ	Duple Dominant	B47F	1976	
VUP745R	Bedford YLQ	Duple Dominant	B47F	1977	Wilson, Middlesbrough, 1988
YDE350	Bedford YMT	Willowbrook Warrior (1988)	B51F	1977	Safeway, Dagenham, 1988
OBX345R	Bedford YLQ	Duple Dominant I	C45F	1977	
OBX346R	Bedford YLQ	Duple Dominant I	C45F	1977	
RGS99R	Bedford YLQ	Plaxton Supreme III	C41F	1977	Stanley, Hersham, 1985
BBR738S	Bedford YMT	Duple Dominant	B53F	1977	Barwick, Barlow, 1990
DTT496T	Bedford YMT	Duple Dominant	B53F	1979	Berkeley, Paulton, 1992
FFW508T	Bedford YMT	Duple Dominant	B55F	1979	Evans, Tregaron, 1994
GPA625V	Bedford YLQ	Plaxton Supreme IV	C45F	1980	TM Daniel, Cardigan, 1997
HVC9V	Bedford YMT	Plaxton Supreme IV	C53F	1979	Gastonia, Cranleigh, 1984
ADE612V	Bedford YMT	Plaxton Supreme IV Exp	C53F	1979	
BBX190V	Bedford YMT	Plaxton Supreme IV Exp	C53F	1980	
JTM114V	Bedford YMT	Duple Dominant	B55F	1980	Stanley, Hersham, 1985
LVO801W	Bedford YLQ	Duple Dominant II	C45F	1980	Evans, Dinas Mawddwy, 1994
MCH352W	Bedford YMT	Duple Dominant	B53F	1981	National Plant & Transport, 1991
HBX971X	Bedford YNT	Plaxton Supreme IV Exp	C53F	1981	TM Daniel, Cardigan, 1997
RVO839X	Bedford YMT	Duple Dominant	B53F	1981	National Plant & Transport, 1991
XNN890Y	Bedford YMT	Duple Dominant	B53F	1983	National Plant & Transport, 1991
NDE481Y	Bedford CF	Dormobile	M12	1983	
RBO350	Volvo B10M-61	Plaxton Paramount 3500	C49FT	1983	
D44AVJ	Bedford CF	Dormobile	M12	1986	
D983OEJ	DAF SB2300DHS585	Duple 340	C53FT	1986	
RBO202	DAF SB2300DHS585	Duple 340	C53FT	1986	
RBO284	DAF SB2300DHS585	Duple 340	C53FT	1986	
E36RBO	Renault-Dodge S56	Reeve Burgess Beaver	B25F	1987	Newport, 1991
E788MDE	Volvo B10M-61	Plaxton Paramount 3500 III	C49FT	1988	
E238MBX	Mercedes-Benz 609D	Reeve Burgess Beaver	B20F	1988	Ffoshelig, Newchurch, 1996
F876RDE	Mercedes-Benz 609D	Reeve Burgess Beaver	C19F	1988	
F482WFX	Mercedes-Benz 811D	Reeve Burgess Beaver	BC29F	1989	Elcock Reisen, Telford, 1997
F566ABV	Freight Rover Sherpa	Elme Orion	B21F	1989	Bellview Cs, Paisley, 1993
F133UDE	DAF MB230LT615	Plaxton Paramount 3500 III	C51FT	1989	
F136LJO	DAF SB3000DKV601	Plaxton Paramount 3500 III	C53F	1989	Cityline, Oxford, 1998
F137LJO	DAF SB3000DKV601	Plaxton Paramount 3500 III	C53F	1989	Cityline, Oxford, 1998
F138LJO	DAF SB3000DKV601	Plaxton Paramount 3500 III	C53F	1989	Cityline, Oxford, 1998
F334FWW	DAF SB220LC550	Optare Delta	BC48F	1989	BAA, Gatwick, 1994
G837LWR	DAF SB220LC550	Optare Delta	B49F	1990	Optare demonstrator, 1992
G978KJX	DAF SB3000DKV601	Van Hool Alizée	C53F	1990	Smith, Alcester, 1992
G112PGT	Mercedes-Benz 811D	Alexander AM	B26F	1990	Cityline, Oxford, 2000
G119PGT	Mercedes-Benz 811D	Alexander AM	B26F	1990	Cityline, Oxford, 1999
H704FDE	DAF SB220LC550	Optare Delta	B49F	1990	
H332FEJ	Volkswagen Microbus 252	Devon Conversions	M9	1990	
7289DD	Volvo B10M-60	Van Hool Alizée	C49FT	1990	Davies Bros, Pencader, 1999
H931DRJ	Volvo B10M-60	Plaxton Paramount 3200 III	C53F	1991	Capital, West Drayton, 1997
H158HDE	Dennis Dart 9.8SDL3004	Carlyle Dartline	B35F	1991	
J64PDE	Volvo B10M-60	Jonckheere Deauville P599	C51FT	1992	
K530RJX	DAF SB3000DKVF601	Van Hool Alizée	C51FT	1993	C&H Coaches, Fleetwood, 1994
L485XDE	Dennis Dart 9.8SDL3035	Plaxton Pointer	B40F	1994	

Opposite, top: **Plaxton Beaver-bodied Vario S775BLG of Richards Bros was new to the fleet in 1998. It is seen in Cardigan after completing a run from Tresaith and Aberporth.** *John Jones*

Opposite, bottom: **Richards Bros acquired two Northern Counties-bodied DAF SB220 buses that had previously worked at Leeds-Bradford Airport. The combination of Palatine body and DAF was only supplied for this order, the body mostly appearing on midi chassis such as the Dart and B6.** *John Jones*

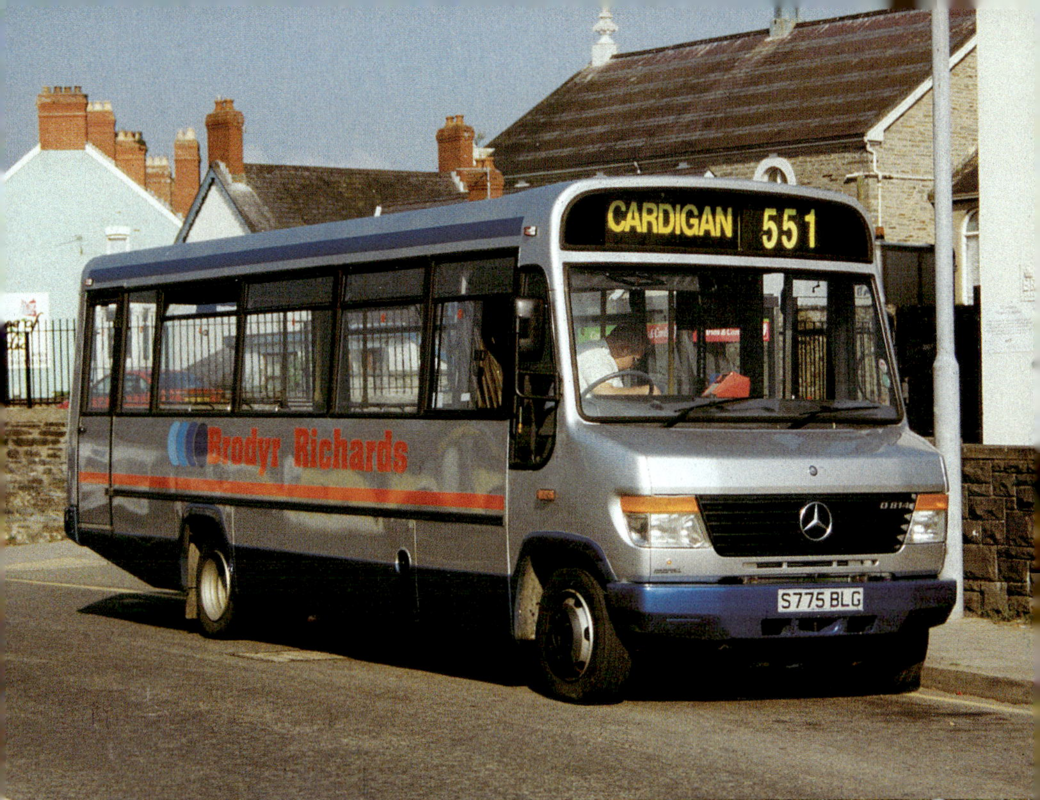
CARDIGAN 551
Brodyr Richards
S775 BLG

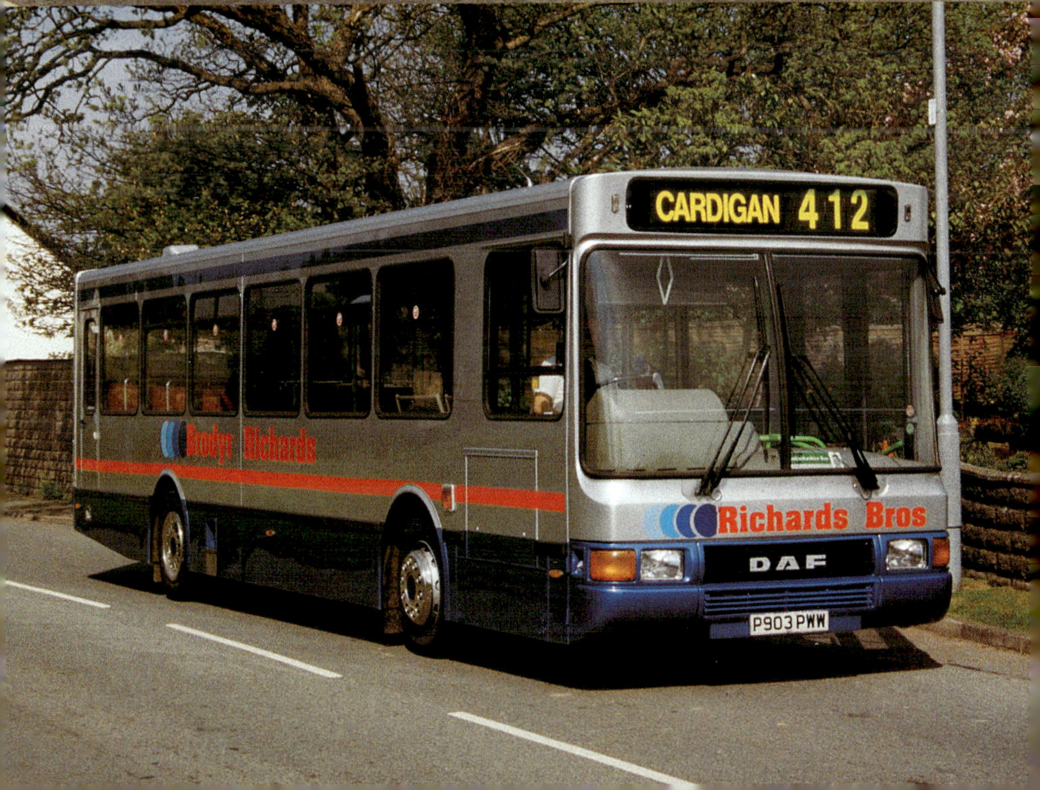
CARDIGAN 412
Brodyr Richards
Richards Bros
DAF
P903 PWW

In April 1999, Richard Bros were using G119PGT, an Alexander-bodied Mercedes-Benz 811 on a local service in Cardigan. It is seen crossing the narrow bridge over the river Teifi now relieved by a by-pass around the town that crosses some 500 metres upstream.
John Jones

M197CDE	MAN 11.190	Optare Vecta	B40F	1994	
M591CDE	LDV 400	LDV	M16	1995	
M680DDE	Mercedes-Benz 811D	Marshall C16	B31F	1995	
M740DDE	Dennis Dart 9.8SDL3040	Plaxton Pointer	B40F	1995	
M798DDE	DAF SB3000WS601	Van Hool Alizèe	C51FT	1995	
P260SDE	Dennis Dart	Marshall C37	B40F	1996	
P97SDE	LDV Convoy	LDV	M16	1996	
P901PWW	DAF SB220LT550	Northern Counties	B49F	1996	Leeds-Bradford Airport, 1998
P902PWW	DAF SB220LT550	Northern Counties	B49F	1996	Leeds-Bradford Airport, 1998
N960LDE	DAF DE33WSSB3000	Ikarus Blue Danube 350	C55F	1996	
P916DEJ	DAF DE33WSSB3000	Van Hool Alizèe II	C51FT	1997	
S775BLG	Mercedes-Benz Vario O814	Plaxton Beaver 2	B27F	1998	
T941RDE	Mercedes-Benz Sprinter 614D	Autobus Classique	C24F	1999	
T510RDE	DAF DE33WSSB3000	Van Hool Alizèe II	C49FT	1999	
W439NDE	DAF DE33WSSB3000	Van Hool Alizèe II	C51FT	2000	
W-----DE	DAF DE33WSSB3000	Van Hool Alizèe II	C51FT	2000	

Previous Registrations:

7289DD	H595EBX	RBO350	NDE760Y
RBO202	D982OEJ	YDE350	TMJ952R
RBO284	C785CDE		

Depots: Moylgrove Garage, Pentood Ind Est, Cardigan and Cardigan Road, Newport
Livery: Silver, red and blue (buses); white, red and silver (coaches)

SHAMROCK Group

RH &DT Edwards Ltd (Venture Travel - Eros Travel)
A Jones (Shamrock - Thomas of Barry)
34 Taff Street, Pontypridd, Rhondda Cynon Taff, CF37 3JP

WTG331T	Bristol VRT/SL3/6LXB	Alexander AL	B44/31F	1979	Venture Travel, Cardiff, 2000
CJH125V	Bristol VRT/SL3/6LXB	Eastern Coach Works	BC41/25F	1980	Coobes, Weston-super-Mare, 1997
GWE617V	Leyland National 2 NL116L11/1R		B49F	1980	Stagecoach East Midlands, 1999
GWE618V	Leyland National 2 NL116L11/1R		B49F	1980	Stagecoach East Midlands, 1999
ALZ7317	Bristol VRT/SL3/6LXB	Eastern Coach Works	B43/31F	1981	Happy Als, Birkenhead, 1998
MIL6782	Leyland Tiger TRCTL11/2R	Plaxton Viewmaster IV Exp	C53F	1981	Venture Travel, Cardiff, 2000
MIL6897	Leyland Tiger TRCTL11/2R	Plaxton Supreme VI Exp	C53F	1982	Venture Travel, Cardiff, 2000
OHV687Y	Leyland Titan TNLXB2RR	Leyland	B44/24D	1983	London Central, 2000
OHV693Y	Leyland Titan TNLXB2RR	Leyland	B44/24D	1983	London Central, 2000
OHV764Y	Leyland Titan TNLXB2RR	Leyland	B44/24D	1983	London Central, 2000
OHV775Y	Leyland Titan TNLXB2RR	Leyland	B44/24D	1983	London Central, 2000
A901SYE	Leyland Titan TNLXB2RR	Leyland	B44/26D	1983	London Central, 2000
A930SYE	Leyland Titan TNLXB2RR	Leyland	B44/26D	1904	London Central, 2000
A973SYE	Leyland Titan TNLXB2RR	Leyland	B44/26D	1984	London Central, 2000
C331MLG	Mercedes-Benz L608D	LCB Eagle (1997)	B20F	1986	
C327UFP	Mercedes-Benz L608D	LCB Eagle (1997)	B20F	1986	
D985ARE	Mercedes-Benz L608D	LCB Eagle (1997)	B20F	1986	
E807FRY	Mercedes-Benz 709D	Reeve Burgess Beaver	B25F	1988	Reeve Burgess demonstrator
LIL9972	Dennis Javelin 12SDA1907	Duple 320	C55F	1988	
F918YWY	Mercedes-Benz 811D	Optare StarRider	B26F	1988	Swiftlink, Harry Stoke, 1998
F671DBO	Mercedes-Benz 811D	Reeve Burgess Beaver	B33F	1989	
G97KUB	Mercedes-Benz 811D	Optare StarRider	B26F	1989	Swiftlink, Harry Stoke, 1998
G102KUB	Mercedes-Benz 811D	Optare StarRider	B26F	1989	Swiftlink, Harry Stoke, 1998
G847VAY	Dennis Javelin 11SDL1909	Duple 300	B55F	1989	
G584RNC	Peugeot-Talbot Express	Made-to-Measure	M14	1989	Venture Travel, Cardiff, 2000

January 2000 saw the arrival of a pair of Optare Solo buses that had latterly performed the role of demonstrators for Optare. V236LWU is seen at Pontypridd while heading for Ynysybwl on a route that some years ago was operated jointly by Pontypridd UDC, Red & White and Rhondda Transport. *John Jones*

Reg	Chassis	Body	Layout	Year	Notes
H368NDW	Dennis Javelin 12SDA1919	Duple 320	C57F	1990	
H787NUH	Mercedes-Benz 811D	Reeve Burgess Beaver	B33F	1990	
H788NUH	Mercedes-Benz 811D	Reeve Burgess Beaver	B33F	1990	
H492OHB	Mercedes-Benz 811D	Reeve Burgess Beaver	B31F	1990	
H493OHB	Mercedes-Benz 811D	Reeve Burgess Beaver	B33F	1990	
H494OHB	Mercedes-Benz 811D	Reeve Burgess Beaver	B33F	1990	
H687UHH	Mercedes-Benz 709D	Made-to-Measure	B28F	1991	
H688UHH	Mercedes-Benz 709D	Made-to-Measure	B28F	1991	
H689UHH	Mercedes-Benz 709D	Made-to-Measure	B28F	1991	
K928AEP	Mercedes-Benz 811D	Dormobile Routemaker	BC33F	1992	
K929AEP	Mercedes-Benz 811D	Dormobile Routemaker	BC33F	1992	
K365TJF	Mercedes-Benz 811D	Dormobile Routemaker	BC33F	1992	
K366TJF	Mercedes-Benz 811D	Dormobile Routemaker	BC33F	1992	
K586MHY	Mercedes-Benz 709D	Dormobile Routemaker	B27F	1993	
K588MHY	Mercedes-Benz 709D	Dormobile Routemaker	B27F	1993	
K589TRY	Mercedes-Benz 814D	Dormobile Routemaker	BC33F	1993	
K590TRY	Mercedes-Benz 814D	Dormobile Routemaker	BC33F	1993	
K451VAY	Bluebird Q Bus	Bluebird	BC31F	1992	Bluebird demonstrator, 1993
L466XNR	Mercedes-Benz 811D	Dormobile Routemaker	B33F	1993	
L467XNR	Mercedes-Benz 811D	Dormobile Routemaker	B33F	1993	
L536XNR	Mercedes-Benz 811D	Dormobile Routemaker	B33F	1993	
L552XNR	Mercedes-Benz 811D	Dormobile Routemaker	B33F	1993	
L553XNR	Mercedes-Benz 811D	Dormobile Routemaker	B33F	1993	
L361ANR	Mercedes-Benz 811D	Dormobile Routemaker	B33F	1993	
L362ANR	Mercedes-Benz 811D	Dormobile Routemaker	B33F	1993	
L370XBX	Leyland Tiger TRCTL11/3L	Marshall Campaigner	B54F	1993	Davies Bros, Pencader, 1999
L38DBC	Dennis Javelin 12SDA2136	Caetano Algarve II	C55F	1994	
L957JGS	Iveco TurboCity 480.10.21	WS Vanguard II	B47F	1994	
L775GNM	Iveco TurboCity 480.10.21	WS Vanguard II	B47F	1994	
M851JHB	Dennis Dart 9.8SDL3040	Plaxton Pointer	B40F	1994	
M852JHB	Dennis Dart 9.8SDL3040	Plaxton Pointer	B40F	1994	
M737JKG	Dennis Dart 9.8SDL3040	Plaxton Pointer	B40F	1994	
M738JKG	Dennis Dart 9.8SDL3040	Plaxton Pointer	B40F	1994	
M425JNY	Dennis Dart 9.8SDL3040	Plaxton Pointer	B40F	1994	
M426JNY	Dennis Dart 9.8SDL3040	Plaxton Pointer	B40F	1994	
M710HBC	Dennis Javelin 12SDA2131	Plaxton Première 320	C53F	1995	
M711HBC	Dennis Javelin 12SDA2131	Plaxton Première 320	C53F	1995	
M982KKG	Dennis Dart 9.8SDL3054	Northern Counties Paladin	B40F	1995	
M983KKG	Dennis Dart 9.8SDL3054	Northern Counties Paladin	B40F	1995	
M984KKG	Dennis Dart 9.8SDL3054	Northern Counties Paladin	B40F	1995	
M985KKG	Dennis Dart 9.8SDL3054	Northern Counties Paladin	B40F	1995	
M986KKG	Dennis Dart 9.8SDL3054	Northern Counties Paladin	B40F	1995	
M987KKG	Dennis Dart 9.8SDL3054	Northern Counties Paladin	B40F	1995	
M252KNR	Morcodoc Bonz 700D	Alexander Sprint	B29F	1995	
M31KUT	Bluebird Q Bus	Bluebird	BC47F	1995	
N755NAY	Dennis Javelin 12SDA2136	Marcopolo Explorer	C53F	1995	
N461OTX	Dennis Dart 9.8SDL3054	Marshall C37	B40F	1995	
N462OTX	Dennis Dart 9.8SDL3054	Marshall C37	B40F	1995	
N463OTX	Dennis Dart 9.8SDL3054	Marshall C37	B40F	1995	
N511PNY	Dennis Dart 9.8SDL3054	Marshall C37	B40F	1996	
N512PNY	Dennis Dart 9.8SDL3054	Marshall C37	B40F	1996	
N513PNY	Dennis Dart 9.8SDL3054	Marshall C37	B40F	1996	
N143XEG	Dennis Dart 9.8SDL3054	Marshall C37	B40F	1996	
N144XEG	Dennis Dart 9.8SDL3054	Marshall C37	B40F	1996	
N145XEG	Dennis Dart 9.8SDL3054	Marshall C37	B40F	1996	
N121YLS	Bova Futura FHD12.340	Bova	C53FT	1996	Silver Choice, East Kilbride, 1997
N122YLS	Bova Futura FHD12.340	Bova	C53FT	1996	Silver Choice, East Kilbride, 1997
N74WSB	Bova Futura FHD12.340	Bova	C53FT	1996	Silver Choice, East Kilbride, 1997
N289DWY	Optare MetroRider MR17	Optare	B29F	1996	Black Prince, Morley, 1999
N854PDW	Mercedes-Benz 711D	LCB Eagle 29	B29F	1996	
N855PDW	Mercedes-Benz 711D	LCB Eagle 29	B29F	1996	
N856PDW	Mercedes-Benz 711D	LCB Eagle 29	B29F	1996	
N857PDW	Mercedes-Benz 711D	LCB Eagle 29	B29F	1996	
P742UWW	Mercedes-Benz 711D	Crest	BC25F	1996	

Opposite, top: **A pair of Dennis Lances with the first styling of Northern Counties Paladin bodywork joined the Shamrock fleet in 1996. While one is painted in Thomas' livery P224WBV is in Shamrock colours. It is seen on the Llantrisant road at Capel Llanilltern while operating the Cardiff to Pencoed service.** *John Jones*
Opposite, bottom: **The first low-floor Dennis Darts for Shamrock were a batch of six with UVG bodywork that entered service in 1997. From that delivery, R708TRV is seen turning into Pontypridd bus station.** *John Jones*

Reg	Chassis	Body	Type	Year	Notes
P98VGD	Volvo B10M-62	Jonckheere Mistral 50	C51FT	1996	Silver Choice, East Kilbride, 1997
P176ANR	MAN 11.190 HOCL-R	Caetano Algarve 2	C35F	1996	
P177ANR	Dennis Javelin 12SDA2136	Caetano Algarve 2	C53F	1996	
P224WBV	Dennis Lance 11SDA3113	Northern Counties Paladin	B49F	1996	
P225WBV	Dennis Lance 11SDA3113	Northern Counties Paladin	B49F	1996	
P122DMS	Dennis Dart	Alexander Dash	B40F	1996	
P575GCF	Dennis Javelin	Berkhof Excellence 1000L	C57F	1997	Q Drive, Battersea, 1998
P576GCF	Dennis Javelin	Berkhof Excellence 1000L	C56F	1997	Q Drive, Battersea, 1998
P895FMO	Dennis Javelin	Berkhof Axial 50	C53F	1997	Q Drive, Battersea, 1998
P896FMO	Dennis Javelin	Berkhof Axial 50	C53F	1997	Q Drive, Battersea, 1998
P897FMO	Dennis Javelin	Berkhof Axial 50	C53F	1997	Q Drive, Battersea, 1998
P898FMO	Dennis Javelin	Berkhof Axial 50	C53F	1997	Q Drive, Battersea, 1998
P633KTF	Volvo B10M-62	Berkhof Axial 50	C49FT	1997	Q Drive, Battersea, 1998
P634KTF	Volvo B10M-62	Berkhof Axial 50	C49FT	1997	Q Drive, Battersea, 1998
R703TRV	Dennis Dart SLF	UVG UrbanStar	N44F	1997	
R704TRV	Dennis Dart SLF	UVG UrbanStar	N44F	1997	
R705TRV	Dennis Dart SLF	UVG UrbanStar	N44F	1997	
R706TRV	Dennis Dart SLF	UVG UrbanStar	N44F	1997	
R707TRV	Dennis Dart SLF	UVG UrbanStar	N44F	1997	
R708TRV	Dennis Dart SLF	UVG UrbanStar	N44F	1997	
R916ULA	Volvo B10M-62	Berkhof Axial 50	C49FT	1998	Q Drive, Battersea, 1998
R921ULA	Volvo B10M-62	Berkhof Axial 50	C49FT	1998	Q Drive, Battersea, 1998
R180EOT	Mercedes-Benz Vario O814	Robin Hood 2000	BC25F	1998	
R183EOT	Mercedes-Benz Vario O814	Robin Hood 2000	BC25F	1998	
R184EOT	Mercedes-Benz Vario O814	Robin Hood 2000	BC25F	1998	
R631EYS	Mercedes-Benz Vario O814	Plaxton Beaver 2	BC---F	1998	
R713TRV	Dennis Javelin	UVG S320	C57F	1998	
R720TRV	Dennis Javelin	UVG S320	C57F	1998	
R749XPO	Dennis Javelin	UVG S320	BC69F	1998	
R751XPO	Dennis Dart SLF	UVG UrbanStar	N44F	1998	
R752XPO	Dennis Dart SLF	UVG UrbanStar	N44F	1998	
R190TKU	Dennis Dart SLF	Plaxton Pointer 2	N39F	1998	Bluebird, Middleton,1998
S58BTX	Dennis Dart SLF	Marshall Capital	N43F	1999	
S895SNY	Mercedes-Benz Vario O814	Plaxton Beaver 2	B33F	1998	
S896SNY	Mercedes-Benz Vario O814	Plaxton Beaver 2	B33F	1998	
T943BWO	Mercedes-Benz Vario O814	Plaxton Beaver 2	B27F	1999	
T944BWO	Mercedes-Benz Vario O814	Plaxton Beaver 2	B27F	1999	
T491SKG	Mercedes-Benz Vario O814	Plaxton Beaver 2	B27F	1999	
T492SKG	Mercedes-Benz Vario O814	Plaxton Beaver 2	B27F	1999	
T493SKG	Mercedes-Benz Vario O814	Plaxton Beaver 2	B27F	1999	
T158PNY	Mercedes-Benz Vario O814	Plaxton Beaver 2	B27F	1999	
T159PNY	Mercedes-Benz Vario O814	Plaxton Beaver 2	B27F	1999	
T160PNY	Mercedes-Benz Vario O814	Plaxton Beaver 2	B27F	1999	
T161PNY	Mercedes-Benz Vario O814	Plaxton Beaver 2	B27F	1999	
T162PNY	Mercedes-Benz Vario O814	Plaxton Beaver 2	B27F	1999	
T163PNY	Mercedes-Benz Vario O814	Plaxton Beaver 2	B27F	1999	

Although a number of Shamrock's Dormobile Routemaster-bodied Mercedes-Benz 811Ds have been withdrawn, others have been repainted in the latest version of fleet livery as applied to the majority of Mercedes-Benz varios received in 1999. A freshly painted L362ANR is seen in March 2000 arriving at Caerphilly from Pontypridd.
John Jones

T164PNY	Mercedes-Benz Vario O814	Plaxton Beaver 2	B27F	1999	
T303PNY	Mercedes-Benz Vario O814	Plaxton Beaver 2	B27F	1999	
T304PNY	Mercedes-Benz Vario O814	Plaxton Beaver 2	B27F	1999	
T305PNY	Mercedes-Benz Vario O814	Plaxton Beaver 2	B27F	1999	
V629KWR	Mercedes-Benz Sprint 412D	Olympus	BC16F	1999	
V116LVH	Optare MetroRider MR17	Optare	B31F	1999	
V117LVH	Optare MetroRider MR17	Optare	B31F	1999	
V304EAK	Scania N113DRB	East Lancashire Cityzen	B47/31F	1999	
V305EAK	Scania L94IB	Irizar InterCentury 12.32	C55F	1999	
V307EAK	Scania N113DRB	East Lancashire Cityzen	B47/31F	1999	
V309EAK	Scania N113DRB	East Lancashire Cityzen	B47/31F	1999	
V235LWU	Optare M850	Optare Solo	B30F	1999	Optare demonstrator, 2000
V236LWU	Optare M850	Optare Solo	B30F	1999	Optare demonstrator, 2000
W391WPX	Dennis Dart SLF	SCC Compass	N44F	2000	
W392WPX	Dennis Dart SLF	SCC Compass	N44F	2000	
W393WPX	Dennis Dart SLF	SCC Compass	N38F	2000	
W394WPX	Dennis Dart SLF	SCC Compass	N38F	2000	
W395WPX	Dennis Dart SLF	SCC Compass	N38F	2000	
W396WPX	Dennis Dart SLF	SCC Compass	N38F	2000	
W397WPX	Dennis Dart SLF	SCC Compass	N38F	2000	
W875UWO	Mercedes-Benz Vario O814	Plaxton Cheetah	C29F	2000	
W301MKY	Scania N113DRB	East Lancashire Cityzen	B47/31F	2000	
W302MKY	Scania N113DRB	East Lancashire Cityzen	B47/31F	2000	
W303MKY	Scania N113DRB	East Lancashire Cityzen	B47/31F	2000	
W671DDN	Optare MetroRider MR17	Optare	B31F	2000	
W672DDN	Optare MetroRider MR17	Optare	B31F	2000	
W673DDN	Optare MetroRider MR17	Optare	B31F	2000	
W674DDN	Optare MetroRider MR17	Optare	B31F	2000	
W675DDN	Optare MetroRider MR17	Optare	B31F	2000	

Previous Registrations:

LIL9972	F106AKG		MIL6782	VOY180X
L370XBX	20KB79	MIL6897	NDW141X	

Depots: Pontcynon Ind Est, Abercynon; Cardiff Road, Cadoxton, Barry and Stephenson Road Ind Est, Newport
Livery: White, yellow and green; cream and red (Thomas of Barry).

Double-deck buses have been used by Shamrock only for contracts until three new Scania N113s arrived in 1999. These are likely to be the last non low-floor double-decks built in the UK and can be seen on commercial services in the Pontypridd area between contracts and on Saturdays. Seen working the cross-town service shortly after delivery is V307EAK.
John Jones

SHUTTLE

Harris Coaches - Shuttle

Harris Coaches (Pengam) Ltd, Bryn-Gwyn, Fleur-de-Lys, Blackwood, Caerphilly NP2 1RZ

YYE273T	Leyland National 10351A/2R		B38F	1978	London Buses, 1990
CKC928X	Leyland National 2 NL116AL11/1R		B52F	1982	Arriva Cymru, 1998
EWM630Y	Leyland National 2 NL116AL11/1R		B52F	1983	Arriva Cymru, 1998
2039NU	DAF MB200DKFL600	Caetano Algarve	C52FT	1984	
F982EDS	Mercedes-Benz 609D	North West Coach Sales	C24F	1988	Clydeside 2000, 1993
F130YVP	MCW MetroRider MF158/16	MCW	B28F	1988	Stagecoach East London, 1996
F131YVP	MCW MetroRider MF158/16	MCW	B28F	1988	Stagecoach East London, 1996
F951BMS	Mercedes-Benz 811D	Alexander AM	B26F	1989	First Centrewest, 1998
F757GUS	Mercedes-Benz 609D	Scott	C24F	1989	Clydeside 2000, 1993
F68LNR	Mercedes-Benz 709D	Robin Hood	B29F	1989	Filer, Ilfracombe, 1999
F921MTM	Mercedes-Benz 709D	Robin Hood	B29F	1989	North Mymms, 1991
F322EJO	Mercedes-Benz 709D	Reeve Burgess Beaver	BC25F	1988	Tim's Travel, Sheerness, 2000
F150TRY	DAF SB2305DHS585	Caetano Algarve	C53FT	1989	James Brothers, Llangeitho, 1995
F427RRY	DAF SB2300DHS585	Caetano Algarve H-SDH	C53F	1989	Clarke, Burbage, 1996
G99PCK	Mercedes-Benz 709D	Reeve Burgess Beaver	B25F	1990	Stagecoach Burnley & Pendle, 1998
H754DTM	Mercedes-Benz 811D	Reeve Burgess Beaver	B33F	1990	Ashford Luxury Travel, 1999
2375RU	DAF SB2305DHS585	Caetano Algarve	C53FT	1990	
M777GSM	Dennis Javelin 12SDA2131	Berkhof Excellence 1000LD	C53F	1995	Mayne's, Buckie, 1998
P220OLC	Mercedes-Benz Vario 0814D	Autobus Nouvelle 2	C29F	1997	
P502HEG	Marshall Midi	Marshall MM	B26F	1996	First CentreWest, 2000
P503HEG	Marshall Midi	Marshall MM	B26F	1996	First CentreWest, 2000
P504HEG	Marshall Midi	Marshall MM	B26F	1996	First CentreWest, 2000
P505HEG	Marshall Midi	Marshall MM	B26F	1996	First CentreWest, 2000
R294RJM	Volvo B10M-62	Berkhof Axial 50	C51FT	1998	

Previous Registrations:

2375NU	G168XJF	2039NU	From new	F150TRY	F425RRY, 6738UN

Livery: Cream, maroon and red

While the larger buses are confined to contract work, service work is undertaken by minibuses. Shown here is MetroRider E128KYW which was new to Rhondda Buses and was pictured when working to Bargoed shortly before it was replaced by Marshall Midi buses from London. *John Jones*

128

SILCOX

Silcox Motor Coach Company Ltd, Waterloo Garage, Pembroke Dock, Pembrokeshire SA72 4RR

1	M361CDE	Mercedes-Benz 709D	WS Wessex II	B27F	1994	
2	H227GDE	Mercedes-Benz 811D	Dormobile Routemaker	B33F	1991	
3	H743EDE	Mercedes-Benz 709D	Dormobile Routemaker	B29F	1990	
4	H754EDE	Mercedes-Benz 709D	Dormobile Routemaker	B29F	1990	
5	J387ODE	Mercedes-Benz 811D	Crystals	B31F	1992	
6	H736EDE	Mercedes-Benz 709D	Dormobile Routemaker	B29F	1990	
7	M674CDE	Mercedes-Benz 709D	Mellor	B27F	1994	
8	M368CDE	Mercedes-Benz 709D	Mellor	B27F	1994	
9	K651TDE	Mercedes-Benz 811D	Crystals	B33F	1992	
10	D603MKH	Iveco Daily 49.10	Robin Hood Dailybus	B25F	1987	Rixon, Porthcawl, 1999
12	H681YGO	Optare MetroRider MR03	Optare	B26F	1991	Epsom Buses, 1999
14	H689YGO	Optare MetroRider MR03	Optare	B26F	1991	Epsom Buses, 1999
16	M16SMC	Dennis Dart 9SDL3053	Marshall C36	BC31F	1994	
17	M17SMC	Dennis Dart 9SDL3053	Marshall C36	BC31F	1994	
18	M18SMC	Dennis Dart 9SDL3053	Marshall C36	BC31F	1994	
54	VAW527	Leyland Leopard PSU3D/4R	Willowbrook Crusader (1989)	C51F	1977	Perry, Bromyard, 1989
59	PVO624	Leyland Leopard PSU3C/4R	Plaxton Supreme III	C53F	1976	Stephenson, Rochford, 1992
66	9195PU	Leyland Leopard PSU3E/4R	Duple Dominant	C57F	1978	Lattimore, Markyate, 1992
102	A2WLS	Duple 425 SDA1512	Duple 425	C57F	1988	
104	A4WLS	Volvo B10M-60	Van Hool Alizèe	C49FT	1989	Gain Travel, Wibsey, 1994
106	A6WLS	Volvo B10M-60	Caetano Algarve	C53F	1989	Daisy, Broughton, 1996
111	A11WLS	DAF SB2300DHS585	Plaxton Paramount 3200 II	C55F	1986	
131	KSU409	Leyland Leopard PSU3E/4R	Plaxton Supreme III	C53F	1978	Hants & Dorset, 1983
132	817FKH	Leyland Leopard PSU3E/4R	Plaxton Supreme III	C53F	1978	South Wales, 1987
143	NDE86R	Leyland Leopard PSU3C/4R	Duple Dominant	B65F	1977	
149	WBX871T	Leyland Leopard PSU3E/4R	Duple Dominant II Express	C53F	1979	
150	804SHW	Leyland Leopard PSU5C/4R	Duple Dominant II	C57F	1979	
151	BBX915V	Leyland Leopard PSU3E/4R	Duple Dominant II Express	C53F	1980	
152	BDE140V	Leyland Leopard PSU3E/4R	Duple Dominant	B63F	1980	
153	BDE143V	Leyland Leopard PSU3E/4R	Duple Dominant II Express	C53F	1980	
179	P779WDE	Dennis Javelin	Caetano Algarve 2	C49FT	1997	
180	P780WDE	Dennis Javelin	UVG S320	C53F	1997	
181	H530HDE	Volvo D10M 62	Caetano Algarve 2	C49FT	1998	
182	R531HDE	Dennis Javelin	Marcopolo Explorer 2	C53F	1998	

VAW527 is a Leyland Leopard PSU3 which was rebodied in 1989 with Willowbrook Crusader-style coachwork type and now used by Silcox where it carries fleet number 54.
John Jones

Three Marshall-bodied Dennis Darts were new to Silcox in 1994 and are often found on the Carmarthen to Tenby route. M16SMC is seen on Blue Street in Carmarthen bound for the south Pembrokeshire resort.
John Jones

183	R532HDE	Dennis Javelin	Plaxton Première 320	C53F	1998	
184	S224BDE	Dennis Javelin	Marcopolo Explorer 2	C53F	1998	
185	T141RDE	Dennis Javelin	Caetano Enigma	C53FT	1999	
186	T142RDE	Dennis Javelin	SCC Cutlass	C53F	1999	
187	T143RDE	MAN 18.310 HOCL-R	Marcopolo Continental 340	C49FT	1999	
188	W108NDE	Dennis Javelin	Berkhof Axial 50	C51FT	2000	
189	W109NDE	Dennis Javelin	Marcopolo Continental 340	C53F	2000	
190	K780UDE	Dennis Javelin	Wadham Stringer Vanguard	BC53F	1992	MoD, 1999
191	K726DWN	Dennis Javelin	Wadham Stringer Vanguard	BC53F	1992	MoD, 1999
192	N356MDE	Dennis Javelin	UVG Vanguard III	C55F	1996	MoD, 1999
200	E98LLP	Leyland Tiger TRCTL11/3LZ	Plaxton Derwent II	B54F	1987	MoD (87KF43), 1997
201	E628WWD	Leyland Tiger TRCTL11/3LZ	Plaxton Derwent II	B54F	1987	MoD (87KF28), 1997
202	E125ODE	Leyland Tiger TRCTL11/3LZ	Plaxton Derwent II	B54F	1987	MoD (87KF27), 1997
203	E672WWD	Leyland Tiger TRCTL11/3LZ	Plaxton Derwent II	B54F	1987	MoD (64KG06), 1997
204	E673WWD	Leyland Tiger TRCTL11/3LZ	Plaxton Derwent II	B54F	1987	MoD (87KF18), 1997
205	D576DPM	Leyland Tiger TRCTL11/3LZ	Plaxton Derwent II	B54F	1986	MoD (82KF20), 1997
206	D146KDE	Leyland Tiger TRCTL11/3LZ	Plaxton Derwent II	B54F	1987	MoD (82KF14), 1997
207	D578DPM	Leyland Tiger TRCTL11/3LZ	Plaxton Derwent II	B54F	1987	MoD (82KF37), 1997
208	E133ODE	Leyland Tiger TRCTL11/3LZ	Plaxton Derwent II	B54F	1987	MoD (87KF32), 1997
209	E137ODE	Leyland Tiger TRCTL11/3LZ	Plaxton Derwent II	B54F	1987	MoD (64KG03), 1997
210	E138ODE	Leyland Tiger TRCTL11/3LZ	Plaxton Derwent II	B54F	1987	MoD (87KF25), 1997
211	E139ODE	Leyland Tiger TRCTL11/3LZ	Plaxton Derwent II	B54F	1987	MoD (87KF24), 1997
212	E141ODE	Leyland Tiger TRCTL11/3LZ	Plaxton Derwent II	B54F	1987	MoD (87KF46), 1997
214	E144ODE	Leyland Tiger TRCTL11/3LZ	Plaxton Derwent II	B54F	1987	MoD (87KF20), 1997
215	E145ODE	Leyland Tiger TRCTL11/3LZ	Plaxton Derwent II	B71F	1987	MoD (87KF40), 1997
216	E149ODE	Leyland Tiger TRCTL11/3LZ	Plaxton Derwent II	B71F	1987	MoD (82KF35), 1997

Opposite: The availability of a large number of Leyland Tigers from the Ministry of Defence has allowed Silcox to replace many older buses, including the last double-decks. These arrived in left-hand drive form and have been converted by the company. These Tigers were followed by some Dennis Javelins with Wadham Stringer bodywork. The upper picture shows 131, K722UDE as it leaves Carmarthen on the long route to Haverfordwest. The lower picture shows 205, D576DPM and illustrates the finished conversion. *John Jones*

Silcox operates a network of services based in the adjacent towns of Pembroke and Pembroke Dock. M674CDE is one of a pair of Mercedes-Benz 709s converted for PCV duties by Mellor at Rochdale. It was photographed in Pembroke while working the Pembroke Dock to Monkton service. *John Jones*

217	A16WLS	Leyland Tiger TRCTL11/3LZ	Plaxton Derwent II	B71F	1986	MoD (82KF33), 1997
218	A14WLS	Leyland Tiger TRCTL11/3LZ	Plaxton Derwent II	B69F	1987	MoD (87KF19), 1998
219	A12WLS	Leyland Tiger TRCTL11/3LZ	Plaxton Derwent II	B69F	1987	MoD (87KF38), 1998
220	D577DPM	Leyland Tiger TRCTL11/3LZ	Plaxton Derwent II	B71F	1987	MoD (82KF35), 1998
221	NSV324	Leyland Tiger TRCTL11/3LZ	Plaxton Derwent II	B54F	1987	MoD (82KF41), 1998
222	A3WLS	Leyland Tiger TRCTL11/3LZ	Plaxton Derwent II	B54F	1987	MoD (87KF29), 1998
223	E183ODE	Leyland Tiger TRCTL11/3LZ	Plaxton Derwent II	B69F	1987	MoD (64KG04), 1999
224	A7WLS	Leyland Tiger TRCTL11/3LZ	Plaxton Derwent II	B54F	1987	MoD (87KF44), 1999
225	109CUF	Leyland Tiger TRCTL11/3LZ	Plaxton Derwent II	B54F	1987	MoD (87KF26), 1999
226	E194ODE	Leyland Tiger TRCTL11/3LZ	Plaxton Derwent II	B54F	1987	MoD (87KF39), 1999
227	A5WLS	Leyland Tiger TRCTL11/3LZ	Plaxton Derwent II	B54F	1987	MoD (87KF45), 1999
228	A15WLS	Leyland Tiger TRCTL11/3LZ	Plaxton Derwent II	B54F	1987	MoD (82KF15), 1999
229	GSK676	Leyland Leopard PSU5D/5L	Wadham Stringer Vanguard	B54F	1982	MoD (51AC03), 1999
230	K721UDE	Dennis Javelin	Wadham Stringer Vanguard	B40F	1993	MoD (15KL44), 1999
231	K722UDE	Dennis Javelin	Wadham Stringer Vanguard	B40F	1993	MoD (15KL51), 1999

Previous Registrations:

538OHU	AJD162T	A6WLS	G903WAY
804SHW	YBX608V	A11WLS	VAW527
817FKH	AFH182T	KSU409	WFH170S
9195PU	WFH166S	PVO624	LMA59P
A2WLS	E522MDE	VAW527	OKY54R
A4WLS	F866XJX		

Depot: Waterloo Garage, Pembroke Dock. **Outstations:** North End Car Park, Tenby and Milford Docks, Milford Haven
Livery: Red and cream (buses); cream, red and blue (coaches)

SILVER STAR

Seren Arian

Silver Star Coach Holidays Ltd, 13 Castle Square, Caernarfon, Gwynedd, LL55 2NF

JWU335J	Bristol RELL6G		Eastern Coach Works	BC50F	1971	Ashville College, Harrogate, 1987
NLJ525M	Bristol LH6L		Eastern Coach Works	B45F	1974	Alpine, Llandudno, 2000
GDZ3841	Leyland Leopard PSU3B/4R		Willowbrook Warrior(1988)	B51F	1975	Mayne of Manchester, 2000
MCA613P	Bristol LH6L		Eastern Coach Works	B43F	1975	Phillips, Holywell, 1998
MCA615P	Bristol LH6L		Eastern Coach Works	B43F	1975	Phillips, Holywell, 1998
OJD68R	Bristol LH6L		Eastern Coach Works	B39F	1977	Trimdon Motor Services, 1990
OJD87R	Bristol LH6L		Eastern Coach Works	B39F	1977	Trimdon Motor Services, 1990
WCC92V	Bedford YMT		Plaxton Supreme IV Exp	C53F	1980	
UTU665V	Leyland Leopard PSU5C/4R		Plaxton Supreme IV	C53F	1980	Jones of Flint, 1999
MAP342W	Leyland Leopard PSU3F/4R		Plaxton Supreme IV Exp	C53F	1981	Cresswell, Moira, 1999
J198PEY	Dennis Dart 9.8SDL3012		Plaxton Pointer	B40F	1992	
L913NWW	Volvo B10M-60		Van Hool Alizèe H	C48FT	1994	Wallace Arnold, 1997
N1EDW	Volvo B10M-62		Van Hool Alizèe HE	C49FT	1996	
N995BWJ	Volvo D10M-62		Van Hool Alizèe HE	C44FT	1996	Dave Parry, Cheslyn Hay, 1998
P553KCC	Dennis Dart SLF		Plaxton Pointer 2	N39F	1997	
T375JJC	Dennis Dart SLF		Plaxton Pointer 2	N38F	1999	
T255GON	Setra S315GT-HD		Setra	C48FT	1999	Dave Parry, Cheslyn Hay, 2000
V258DCC	Mercedes-Benz Vario O814		Plaxton Beaver 2	B31F	1999	

Previous Registrations:
GDZ3841   JVS928N   UTU665V   PGO342V, RDM378

Depot: Cibyn Industrial Estate, Caernarfon
Livery: Blue and cream (buses); green (coaches).

The interesting fleet of Silver Star operates from Caernarfon. Here, P553KCC, a Dennis Dart with Plaxton Pointer bodywork is seen heading north along Stryd Bangor on a tendered service that will take it onto the by-pass and out towards Rhosgadfan. *John Jones*

SIXTY-SIXTY

G D Handy, 5/6 Pentrebach Industrial Estate, Merthyr Tydfil, CF48 4BB

OTA645G	Bristol RELH6G	Eastern Coach Works	C45F	1969	Heritage MS, Merthyr Tydfil, 1998
JBZ8645	Volvo B58-56	Duple Dominant II	C49F	1979	Foster, Burgess Hill, 1995
WJI9360	Leyland Leopard PSU4E/4R	East Lancashire	B47F	1980	Dawes, Bassingbourne, 2000
DBV42W	Leyland Leopard PSU4E/4R	East Lancashire	B47F	1980	Stagecoach Ribble, 1998
DBV43W	Leyland Leopard PSU4E/4R	East Lancashire	B47F	1980	Stagecoach Ribble (B&P), 1998
HUI6006	DAF MB200DKTL600	Jonckheere Bermuda	C57F	1982	Venture Travel, Cardiff, 1994
NIJ6060	DAF SB3000DKV601	Van Hool Alizée	C51FT	1983	Lewis Meridian, 2000
TIB6060	Scania K112CRS	Plaxton Paramount 3500	C53F	1983	Thomas, Porth, 1997
LJI6060	Leyland Tiger TRCTL11/3R	Plaxton Paramount 3200	C53F	1983	Phillips, Penrhiwceiber, 1997
FBZ6060	DAF MB200DKFL600	Duple 340	C49FT	1986	Hanson Coach, Halifax, 1996
GUI6060	Leyland Tiger TRCTL11/3RZ	Duple 340	C50FT	1986	Venture Travel, Cardiff, 1996
OJI9477	LAG G355Z	LAG Panoramic	C49FT	1987	Byronis, Skewen, 2000
JIL3253	Mercedes-Benz L307D	Devon Conversions	M8	1987	Airways International, Cardiff, 1987
MJI6060	MAN 10.180 HOCL-R	Caetano Algarve 2	C35F	1991	Wickson, Walsall Wood, 1998
NIJ6060	DAF SB3000WS601	Van Hool Alizée	C49FT	1989	Lewis Meridian, Greenwich, 2000
PBZ6060	Mercedes-Benz 811D	UVG UrbanStar	BC29F	1996	Silverline, Merthyr Tydfil, 1997

Previous Registrations:

FBZ6060	C787MVH, LAZ5790	MJI6060	J515LRY
GUI6060	C518WBF, JIL3253	NIJ6060	F641OHD
HUI6060	WRK3X, IIB1825	OJI9477	D504YPB
JBZ8645	EWW231T	PBZ6060	N859PDW
JIL3253	E892PBO, GUI6060	TIB6060	B470YHT, 578DAF, B470YHT, PNK1M, TJI6709
LJI6060	FCK449Y, DSV520	WJI9360	DBV39W

Livery: White, red and silver (buses), white, purple and silver (coaches)

Although based in Merthyr Tydfil, the bus routes operated by Sixty-Sixty Silverline mostly serve the area between Swansea, Neath and Brecon. DBV42W is one of three East Lancashire-bodied Leopards originating with Burnley & Pendle. *John Jones*

STAGECOACH RED & WHITE

Red & White Services Ltd; The Valleys Bus Company Ltd; Aberdare Bus Company Ltd,
Rhondda Buses Ltd; Parfitts Motor Services Ltd; Eastern Valley Bus Co Ltd.
1 St Davidís Road, Cwmbran, Torfaen   NP44 1QX

150	M866LNY		Mercedes-Benz 711D		Plaxton Beaver	B27F	1995	Rhondda, 1997	
151	N151MTG		Mercedes-Benz 811D		UVG Citi Star	B31F	1995	Rhondda, 1997	
152-160			Mercedes-Benz 711D		UVG Citi Star	B27F	1995	Rhondda, 1997	
152	N152MTG	154	N154MTG	156	N156MTG	158	N158MTG	160	N160MTG
153	N153MTG	155	N155MTG	157	N157MTG	159	N159MTG		
161	P161TDW		Mercedes-Benz 709D		Plaxton Beaver	B27F	1996	Rhondda, 1997	
162	P162TDW		Mercedes-Benz 709D		Plaxton Beaver	B27F	1996	Rhondda, 1997	
163-171			Mercedes-Benz 711D		Plaxton Beaver	B27F	1996	Rhondda, 1997	
163	P163TNY	165	P165TNY	167	P167TNY	169	P169TNY	171	P171TNY
164	P164TNY	166	P166TNY	168	P168TNY	170	P170TNY		
185	N430WVR		Mercedes-Benz 709D		Alexander Sprint	B25F	1992	Stagecoach Manchester, 1999	
201	H401MRW		Mercedes-Benz 811D		Wright NimBus	B33F	1991	Stagecoach Midland Red, 1998	
208	J408PRW		Mercedes-Benz 811D		Wright NimBus	BC33F	1991	Stagecoach Midland Red, 1998	
214	J414PRW		Mercedes-Benz 811D		Wright NimBus	B33F	1991	Stagecoach Midland Red, 1998	
255w	K320FYG		Optare MetroRider		Optare	B29F	1993	Rhondda (Parfitts), 1997	
257w	L839MWT		Optare MetroRider		Optare	B31F	1993	Rhondda (Parfitts), 1997	
305-317			Mercedes-Benz 811D		Wright NimBus	B33F	1992		
305	J305UKG	309	K309YKG	312	K312YKG	314	K314YKG	316	K316YKG
306	J306UKG	310	K310YKG	313	K313YKG	315	K315YKG	317	K317YKG
307	J307UKG								
322	K322YKG		Mercedes-Benz 811D		Wright NimBus	B33F	1992		
323	K323YKG		Mercedes-Benz 811D		Wright NimBus	B33F	1992		
324	K324YKG		Mercedes-Benz 811D		Wright NimBus	B33F	1992		
325	K325YKG		Mercedes-Benz 811D		Wright NimBus	B33F	1992		
326	L326CHB		Mercedes-Benz 811D		Marshall C16	B33F	1993		
327	L327CHB		Mercedes-Benz 811D		Marshall C16	B33F	1993		
328	L328CHB		Mercedes-Benz 811D		Marshall C16	B33F	1993		
329	L329CHB		Mercedes-Benz 811D		Marshall C16	B33F	1993		
331	L331CHB		Mercedes-Benz 811D		Marshall C16	B33F	1993		
334-359			Mercedes-Benz 709D		Alexander Sprint	B25F	1994		
334w	L334FWO	339w	L339FWO	344	M344JBO	350	M350JBO	355	M355JBO
335w	L335FWO	340w	L340FWO	346	M346JBO	351	M351JBO	356	M356JBO
336w	L336FWO	341w	L341FWO	347	M347JBO	352	M352JBO	357	M357JBO
337	L337FWO	342w	L342FWO	348	M348JBO	353	M353JBO	358	M358JBO
338w	L338FWO	343w	L343FWO	349	M349JBO	354	M354JBO	359	M359JBO

361-371		Mercedes-Benz 709D		Alexander Sprint	B25F	1995		
361	M361LAX	364	M364LAX	366	M366LAX	368	M368LAX	370	M370LAX
362	M362LAX	365	M365LAX	367	M367LAX	369	M369LAX	371	M371LAX
363	M363LAX								

372-384		Mercedes-Benz 709D		Alexander Sprint	B25F	1996		
372	N372PNY	375	N375PNY	378	N378PNY	381	N381PNY	383	N383PNY
373	N373PNY	376	N376PNY	379	N379PNY	382	N382PNY	384	N384PNY
374	N374PNY	377	N377PNY	380	N380PNY				

431	G31TGW	Dennis Dart 8.5SDL3003	Carlyle Dartline	BC28F	1990	Stagecoach Selkent, 1998
436	G36VNX	Dennis Dart 8.5SDL3003	Carlyle Dartline	BC28F	1990	Stagecoach Selkent, 1998
438	G38TGW	Dennis Dart 8.5SDL3003	Carlyle Dartline	B28F	1990	Stagecoach Selkent, 1998
439	G39TGW	Dennis Dart 8.5SDL3003	Carlyle Dartline	B34F	1990	Stagecoach Selkent, 1998
440	G40TGW	Dennis Dart 8.5SDL3003	Carlyle Dartline	B28F	1990	Stagecoach Selkent, 1998

441-458		Dennis Dart 8.5SDL3015		Wright Handy-bus	B29F	1993		Stagecoach East London, 1998
441	NDZ3141	444	NDZ3144	449	NDZ3159	455	NDZ3155	457	NDZ3157
442	NDZ3142	445	NDZ3145	454	NDZ3154	456	NDZ3156	458	NDZ3158
443	NDZ3143								

459	JDZ2359	Dennis Dart 8.5SDL3003	Wright Handy-bus	B28F	1991	Stagecoach Selkent, 1998

463-470		Dennis Dart 8.5SDL3015		Wright Handy-bus	B29F	1993		Stagecoach East London, 1998-99
463	NDZ3133	465	NDZ3135	467	NDZ3137	469	NDZ3139	470	NDZ3140
464	NDZ3134	466	NDZ3136	468	NDZ3138				

550	N550MTG	Mercedes-Benz O405	Optare Prisma	B49F	1995	Rhondda, 1997
551	N551MTG	Mercedes-Benz O405	Optare Prisma	B49F	1995	Rhondda, 1997
554	P54XBO	Dennis Dart SLF	Wright Crusader	N43F	1997	Rhondda, 1997
556	P56XBO	Dennis Dart SLF	Marshall Capital C39	N43F	1997	Rhondda (Parfitts), 1997
557	P57XBO	Dennis Dart SLF	Marshall Capital C39	N43F	1997	Rhondda (Parfitts), 1997
558	P58XBO	Dennis Dart SLF	Marshall Capital C39	N43F	1997	Rhondda (Parfitts), 1997
559	P59VTG	Dennis Dart SLF	Marshall C37	N40F	1997	Rhondda, 1997
560	L414SFL	Dennis Dart 9.8SDL3054	Marshall C37	BC37F	1994	Rhondda, 1997
561	P61VTG	Dennis Dart SLF	Marshall C37	N40F	1997	Rhondda, 1997
562	N62MTG	Dennis Dart 9.8SDL3054	Plaxton Pointer	B40F	1995	Rhondda (Parfitts), 1997
563	N63MTG	Dennis Dart 9.8SDL3054	Plaxton Pointer	B40F	1995	Rhondda (Parfitts), 1997
564	M64HHB	Dennis Dart 9.8SDL3054	Wright Handy-bus	B39F	1995	Rhondda, 1997
565	M65HHB	Dennis Dart 9.8SDL3054	Wright Handy-bus	B39F	1995	Rhondda, 1997
566	M562JTG	Dennis Dart 9.8SDL3040	Plaxton Pointer	B43F	1994	Rhondda (Parfitts), 1997
567	M67HHB	Dennis Dart 9.8SDL3054	Wright Handy-bus	B39F	1995	Rhondda, 1997
568	M68HHB	Dennis Dart 9SDL3031	Marshall C36	B34F	1994	Rhondda, 1997
569	M69HHB	Dennis Dart 9SDL3031	Marshall C36	B34F	1994	Rhondda, 1997
570	M625KKG	Dennis Dart 9.8SDL3040	Plaxton Pointer	B43F	1994	Rhondda (Parfitts), 1997
583	L83CWO	Dennis Dart 9SDL3034	Plaxton Pointer	B35F	1993	Rhondda, 1997
584	L84CWO	Dennis Dart 9SDL3034	Plaxton Pointer	B35F	1993	Rhondda, 1997
585	L85CWO	Dennis Dart 9SDL3034	Plaxton Pointer	B35F	1993	Rhondda, 1997
586	L86CWO	Dennis Dart 9SDL3024	Wright Handy-bus	B35F	1993	Rhondda, 1997
587	L87CWO	Dennis Dart 9SDL3024	Wright Handy-bus	B35F	1993	Rhondda, 1997
588	L270EHB	Dennis Dart 9.8SDL3035	Plaxton Pointer	B43F	1994	Rhondda (Parfitts), 1997
589	L89CWO	Dennis Dart 9SDL3024	Wright Handy-bus	B35F	1993	Rhondda, 1997
590	K402EDT	Dennis Dart 9SDL3016	Northern Counties Paladin	B35F	1992	Rhondda, 1997
591	K91BNY	Dennis Dart 9SDL3011	Plaxton Pointer	B35F	1993	Rhondda, 1997
592	K92BNY	Dennis Dart 9SDL3011	Plaxton Pointer	B35F	1993	Rhondda, 1997
593	K93BNY	Dennis Dart 9SDL3011	Plaxton Pointer	B35F	1993	Rhondda, 1997

Opposite, top: **The Stagecoach Red & White fleet supports several operations including the Aberdare Bus Company and Rhondda Buses. Currently allocated to the Rhondda fleet is 554, P54XBO the only Dennis Dart within Stagecoach UK with a Wright Crusader body. It is seen on Oxford Street in Nantgarw, once the principal road from Cardiff to Llandudno until the town by-pass was opened.** *John Jones*

Opposite, bottom: **Two Mercedes-Benz O405 buses with Optare Prisma bodywork joined the Stagecoach Red & White fleet along with the business of Rhondda Buses. The Prisma body styling incorporates the standard O405 front and was part of an initiative by Mercedes-Benz to enter the UK bus market. Now in full corporate colours, 550, N550MTG, is seen in Pontypridd. The standard new single-deck bus for the Stagecoach group is the MAN 18.220 (Euro 2) and 18.230 (Euro 3) units which compete with Mercedes.** *John Jones*

Stagecoach, like all the major operators, allocate new vehicles for tenders and partnerships that include support for low-floor buses. As a result London Buses routes gain many new buses that allow mid-life vehicles to be allocated to provincial duties after refurbishment. Since 1998, Stagecoach Red and White have received Dennis Darts under this plan, including Wright-bodied 468, NDZ3138. It is currently based at Abergavenny and is seen on the town service late in 1999. *John Jones*

594	K94AAX	Dennis Dart 9SDL3011		Wright Handy-bus	B35F	1993	Rhondda, 1997	
595	K95AAX	Dennis Dart 9SDL3011		Wright Handy-bus	B35F	1993	Rhondda, 1997	
596	K96AAX	Dennis Dart 9SDL3016		Plaxton Pointer	B35F	1992	Rhondda, 1997	
597	K97XNY	Dennis Dart 9SDL3011		Plaxton Pointer(1995)	B35F	1992	Rhondda, 1997	
598	K98XNY	Dennis Dart 9.8SDL3017		Wright Handy-bus	B39F	1992	Rhondda, 1997	
599	J454JRH	Dennis Dart 9.8SDL3017		Plaxton Pointer	B40F	1991	Rhondda (Parfitts), 1997	
600	R706YUD	Dennis Dart SLF		Alexander ALX200	N37F	1998	Stagecoach Oxford, 1998	

601-627   Dennis Dart SLF   Alexander ALX200   N37F   1998

601	R601SWO	608	R608SWO	613	R613SWO	618	R618SWO	623	S623TDW
602	R602SWO	609	R609SWO	614	R614SWO	619	R619SWO	624	S624TDW
603	R603SWO	610	R610SWO	615	R615SWO	620	R620SWO	625	S625TDW
604	R604SWO	611	R611SWO	616	R616SWO	621	R621SWO	626	S626TDW
606	R606SWO	612	R612SWO	617	R617SWO	622	S622TDW	627	S627TDW
607	R607SWO								

681	J41GGB	Leyland Lynx LX2R11C15Z4S	Leyland Lynx 2	B51F	1991	Rhondda, 1997
682	J42GGB	Leyland Lynx LX2R11C15Z4S	Leyland Lynx 2	B51F	1991	Rhondda, 1997
683	F168SMT	Leyland Lynx LX112L10ZR1S	Leyland Lynx	B49F	1989	Stagecoach Cambus (V), 1999
684	F167SMT	Leyland Lynx LX112L10ZR1S	Leyland Lynx	B49F	1989	Stagecoach Cambus (V), 1999
685	F171SMT	Leyland Lynx LX112L10ZR1S	Leyland Lynx	B49F	1989	Stagecoach Cambus (V), 1999
686	F262WSD	Leyland Lynx LX112L10ZR1R(6HLXCT)	Lynx	B52F	1988	Western Buses (AA), 1998
691	E87KGV	Leyland Lynx LX112L10ZR1R	Leyland Lynx	B52F	1988	Rhondda, 1997
692	E62WDT	Leyland Lynx LX112TL11ZR1R	Leyland Lynx	B49F	1987	Rhondda, 1997
693	E63WDT	Leyland Lynx LX112TL11ZR1R	Leyland Lynx	B49F	1987	Rhondda, 1997
694	D109NDW	Leyland Lynx LX112TL11ZR1	Leyland Lynx	B48F	1987	Cynon Valley, 1992
695	E113RBO	Leyland Lynx LX112TL11ZR1	Leyland Lynx	B48F	1987	Cynon Valley, 1992
696	E114SDW	Leyland Lynx LX112TL11ZR1	Leyland Lynx	B40F	1907	Cynon Valley, 1992
697	E115SDW	Leyland Lynx LX112TL11ZR1	Leyland Lynx	B48F	1988	Cynon Valley, 1992
698	F74DCW	Leyland Lynx LX2R11C15Z4R	Leyland Lynx 2	B45F	1989	Cynon Valley, 1992

The English operations of Stagecoach Red and White were transferred to the management of Cheltenham and Gloucester from early 2000 along with the Ross-on-Wye depot and vehicles, including the Volvo Olympians. Only three Olympians remain in the fleet, all joining from Midland Red South in 1993. Shown leaving Newport for Underwood is 829, A549HAC. *John Jones*

701-708

Volvo B6-9.9M — Alexander Dash — B40F — 1994

701	L701FWO	703	L703FWO	705	L705FWO	707	L707FWO	708	L708FWO
702	L702FWO	704	L704FWO	706	L706FWO				

711	M71HHB	Volvo B6-9m	Plaxton Pointer	B35F	1994	Rhondda, 1997	
714	M74HHB	Volvo B6-9m	Plaxton Pointer	B35F	1994	Rhondda, 1997	
715	M75HHB	Volvo B6-9m	Plaxton Pointer	B35F	1994	Rhondda, 1997	
716	M76HHB	Volvo B6-9m	Plaxton Pointer	B35F	1994	Rhondda, 1997	
719	L79CWO	Volvo B6-9.9M	Plaxton Pointer	B40F	1994	Rhondda, 1997	
721	L81CWO	Volvo B6-9.9M	Plaxton Pointer	B40F	1994	Rhondda, 1997	
722	L82CWO	Volvo B6-9.9M	Plaxton Pointer	B40F	1994	Rhondda, 1997	
743	WDA2T	Volvo B10M-60	Plaxton Excalibur	C44FT	1992	Stagecoach Oxford, 1998	
744	A14RBL	Volvo Citybus B10M-50	East Lancashire (1995)	BC53F	1984	Rhondda, 1997	

750-770

Volvo B10M-55 — Alexander PS — BC48F — 1995

750	M750LAX	755	M755LAX	759	M759LAX	763	M763LAX	767	M767RAX
751	M751LAX	756	M756LAX	760	M760LAX	764	M764LAX	768	M768RAX
752	M752LAX	757	M757LAX	761	M761LAX	765	M765RAX	769	M769RAX
753	M753LAX	758	M758LAX	762	M762LAX	766	M766RAX	770	M770RAX
754	M754LAX								

771-784

Volvo B10M-62 — Plaxton PremiÈre Interurban BC51F — 1996-97

771	P771TTG	774	P774TTG	778	R778CDW	781	R781CDW	783	R783CDW
772	P772TTG	775	R775CDW	779	R779CDW	782	R782CDW	784	R784CDW
773	P773TTG	776	R776CDW	780	R780CDW				

The Welsh Bus Handbook

785-792 Volvo B10M-55   Alexander PS   BC48F   1998

785	R785DHB	788	R788DHB	790	R790DHB	791	R791DHB	792	R792DHB
787	R787DHB	789	R789DHB						

802	OHV702Y	Leyland Titan TNLXB2RR	Leyland	B44/27F	1983	East London, 1998
803	OHV719Y	Leyland Titan TNLXB2RR	Leyland	B44/27F	1983	East London, 1997
804	NUW619Y	Leyland Titan TNLXB2RR	Leyland	B44/27F	1982	East London, 1997
805	NUW651Y	Leyland Titan TNLXB2RR	Leyland	B44/27F	1982	East London, 1997
806	KYV542X	Leyland Titan TNLXB2RR	Leyland	B44/27F	1982	East London, 1997
807	NUW606Y	Leyland Titan TNLXB2RR	Leyland	B44/27F	1982	East London, 1997
808	NUW646Y	Leyland Titan TNLXB2RR	Leyland	B44/27F	1982	East London, 1997
809	A905SYE	Leyland Titan TNLXB2RR	Leyland	B44/29F	1983	East London, 1998
810	OHV699Y	Leyland Titan TNLXB2RR	Leyland	B44/27F	1983	East London, 1998
811	OHV686Y	Leyland Titan TNLXB2RR	Leyland	B44/27F	1983	East London, 1998
812	NUW662Y	Leyland Titan TNLXB2RR	Leyland	B44/27F	1982	East London, 1997
813	NUW665Y	Leyland Titan TNLXB2RR	Leyland	B44/27F	1982	East London, 1997
827	A541HAC	Leyland Olympian ONLXB/1R	Eastern Coach Works	B43/31F	1983	Midland Red South, 1993
828	A548HAC	Leyland Olympian ONLXB/1R	Eastern Coach Works	B43/31F	1983	Midland Red South, 1993
829	A549HAC	Leyland Olympian ONLXB/1R	Eastern Coach Works	B43/31F	1983	Midland Red South, 1993
912w	AAX489A	Leyland Tiger TRCTL11/3R	Plaxton Paramount 3200	C46F	1983	National Welsh, 1991
914	AAX516A	Leyland Tiger TRCTL11/3R	Plaxton Paramount 3200	C46F	1983	National Welsh, 1991
916w	CYJ492Y	Leyland Tiger TRCTL11/3R	Plaxton Paramount 3200	C50F	1983	Stagecoach South, 1994
926	EWR656Y	Leyland Tiger TRBTL11/2R	Duple Dominant	BC47F	1983	Rhondda, 1997
935w	A227MDD	Leyland Tiger TRCTL11/3R	Plaxton Paramount 3200	C51F	1984	Cheltenham & Gloucester, 1994

940-951 Dennis Javelin 11SDA2133   Plaxton Interurban   BC47F   1994

940	M940JBO	943	M943JBO	945	M945JBO	947	M947JBO	949	M949JBO
941	M941JBO	944	M944JBO	946	M946JBO	948	M948JBO	951	M951JBO
942	M942JBO								

955	M101CCD	Dennis Javelin 11SDL2133	Plaxton Interurban	BC47F	1994	Stagecoach South, 1996
956	M107CCD	Dennis Javelin 11SDL2133	Plaxton Interurban	BC47F	1994	Stagecoach South, 1996
957	L145BFV	Dennis Javelin 11SDL2133	Plaxton Interurban	BC47F	1993	Stagecoach Ribble (B&P), 1999
958	L151BFV	Dennis Javelin 11SDL2133	Plaxton Interurban	BC47F	1993	Stagecoach Ribble (B&P), 1999
959	L144BFV	Dennis Javelin 11SDL2133	Plaxton Interurban	BC47F	1993	Stagecoach Ribble (B&P), 2000
960	L153BFV	Dennis Javelin 11SDL2133	Plaxton Interurban	BC47F	1993	Stagecoach Ribble (B&P), 2000
962	M102CCD	Dennis Javelin 11SDL2133	Plaxton Interurban	BC47F	1994	Stagecoach Fife, 2000
963	M103CCD	Dennis Javelin 11SDL2133	Plaxton Interurban	BC47F	1995	Stagecoach Fife, 2000
964	M104CCD	Dennis Javelin 11SDL2133	Plaxton Interurban	BC47F	1995	Stagecoach Fife, 2000
965	L105SDY	Dennis Javelin 11SDL2133	Plaxton Interurban	BC47F	1994	Stagecoach Manchester, 2000
966	L149BFV	Dennis Javelin 11SDL2133	Plaxton Interurban	BC47F	1994	Stagecoach Ribble, 2000
967	L107SDY	Dennis Javelin 11SDL2133	Plaxton Interurban	BC47F	1994	Stagecoach Manchester, 2000

Ancillary Vehicles:-

RW16	E316HLO	Mercedes-Benz 307D	Pilcher Green	M12	1988	Rhondda, 1997
RW17	B101ETX	Dodge Commando G13	Wadham Stringer Vanguard TV		1984	MoD 1999 (99KM47)
RW18	D34PAX	Dodge Commando G13	Wadham Stringer Vanguard TV		1986	MoD 1999 ( )
RW19	B109ETX	Dodge Commando G13	Wadham Stringer Vanguard TV		1984	MoD 1999 ( )
RW22	F392DHL	Mercedes-Benz 709D	Reeve Burgess Beaver	B28F	1989	Rhondda, 1997

Previous Registrations:

A14RBL	B176FFS, WLT444, B660EGG	CYJ492Y	XUF531Y, 401DCD
AAX489A	SDW928Y	WDA2T	J420HDS, KSU462, J420HDS
AAX516A	SDW927Y		

The seven Volvo B10s delivered to Stagecoach Red and White in 1998 were part of the final order of non low-floor buses for the group. Five are allocated to Cwmbran for the Red and White services including 792, R792DHB seen here passing along St Mary Street in Cardiff. *John Jones*

Allocations:-

Aberdare (Cwmbach New Road, Cwmbach) - Red & White

Mercedes-Benz	208	214	307	310	312	314	322	326
	328	331						
Volvo B6	701	702	703	706	707	708	716	719
	721	722						
Lynx	683	684	685					

Brynmawr (Warwick Road) - Red & White

Mercedes-Benz	367	368	369	370	371	376	377	
Dart	449	466	600	606	608	609	610	
Volvo B6	704	705	711	714	715			
Volvo B10M PS	753							
Volvo Interurban	771	772	773	774	775	776	778	779
	780	781	782	783	784			
Leyland Lynx	694	695						
Javelin Interurban	951	960	962					
Tiger	926							

Caerphilly (Bedwas House Ind Est, Bedwas) - Red & White

Mercedes-Benz	151	158	159	160	161	162	169	170
	171	185						
Dart	443	444	445	567	586	587	607	611
	612	613	614	615	616	617	618	619
	620							
Lynx	693							

Chepstow (Bulwark Road) - Red & White

Mercedes-Benz	201	317	325	327	329	375		
Dart	563	566	570					
Javelin Interurban	940	941	942	943	944	945	946	947
	948	949						
Tiger	914							
Titan	803	804	805	807	808			
Olympian	827	828	829					

Cwmbran (St Davidís Road) - Red & White

Outstations - Abergavenny and Brecon

Mercedes-Benz	305	306	309	313	315	316	323	324
	337	346	347	348	349	350	351	352
	353	354	355	356	357	358	359	378
	379	380	381	382	383	384		
Dart	431	436	438	439	440	464	467	468
	469	596						
Volvo B10M PS	766	770	787	788	789	790	791	792
Lynx	696	697						
Titan	802	806	809	810	811	812	813	

The standard midibus for the Stagecoach group changed from the Volvo B6 to the Dennis Dart in the mid 1990s and bodywork has been supplied by both Plaxton and Alexander since the 1999 delivery. During 1998 a large number of the type with ALX200 bodywork were allocated to the Red and White fleet and these carry the *Lo-Liner* corporate branding for low-floor buses. Seen leaving Newport on commercial route 151 to Blackwood, 609, R609SWO, was based at the now closed Crosskeys depot. *John Jones*

Merthyr Tydfil (Merthyr Industrial Estate, Pant) - Red & White

Mercedes-Benz	344	361	362	363	364	365	366	372
	373	374						
Dart	454	455	456	458	463	465	470	562
	564	590	597	601	602	603	604	
Volvo B10M	744	750	751	752	754	755	756	757
	758	759	760	761	762	763	764	765
	767	768	769	785				

Porth (Aberrhondda Road) - Rhondda

Mercedes-Benz	150	152	153	154	155	156	157	163
	164	165	166	167	168			
Dart	441	442	457	459	554	559	560	561
	565	568	569	583	584	585	588	589
	591	592	593	594	595	598	599	621
	622	623	624	625	626	627		
Lynx	681	682	691	698				
Prisma	550	551						
Javelin	955	956	957	958	959	963	964	965
	966	967						
Volvo B10M	743							

Unallocated

Mercedes-Benz	334	335	336	338	339	340	341	
	342	343						
MetroRider	255	257						
Lynx	686	692						
Tiger	912	916	935					

The Dennis Javelin joined the Stagecoach fleet in 1994 to fulfill a need for inter-urban services buses. The Interurban body is a bus that uses the Plaxton Première frame, fitted with bus equipment and partitioning and minus many of the fitting associated with coaches. Restricted by their small doorways, they have been replaced in some fleets with Alexander PS buses, also with high-back seating and are now being concentrated at Red and White and Fife Buses. Originally new to the South fleet, 955, M101CCD is seen in Cardiff on a service originating in Pontypool. *John Jones*

SUMMERDALE

DG & BJL Davies and GR Jones, Summerdale Garage, Letterston, Pembrokeshire SA62 5UB

WGR144V	Ford R1014	Plaxton Supreme IV	C45F	1980	Bennett, Tamworth, 1994
VJU259X	Ford R1114	Plaxton Supreme VI Exp	C53F	1982	Ffoshelig Motors, Newchurch, 1987
OKY76X	Leyland Tiger TRCTL11/3R	Plaxton Supreme V	C46FT	1982	Kerricabs, Newport, 1994
B417CMC	Leyland Tiger TRCTL11/3R	Plaxton Paramount 3200	C53F	1985	Evans, Tregaron, 1997
E533UEJ	Leyland Tiger TRCTL11/3R	Duple 340	C55F	1987	Evans, Tregaron, 1998
YDE734	Volvo B10M-61	Van Hool Alizèe H	C47FT	1988	Rambler, Hastings, 1997
H965VWF	Mercedes-Benz 609D	Crystals	BC26F	1991	Clarkson, South Elmsall, 1996
H26HRK	Mercedes-Benz 408D	North West Coach Sales	M15	1990	MCH, Uxbridge, 1993
L469APJ	Mercedes-Benz 609D	Olympus	BC24F	1993	Jordan, Stourport, 1999

Previous Registrations:

E533UEJ	E771WSB, NKH819	L469APJ	L731BPL
H26HRK	H702ELX, MCH957	YDE734	AYU763(BE), F450WFX, XEL841, F507MAA, MDY397, F507MAA

Livery: Yellow and blue

Summerdale operate several tendered services in the Pembrokeshire area and commenced running route 345 in December 1998. This service links Mynachlog-Ddu with Fishguard on Thursdays. A hedgehog's view shows H965VWF, one of two Mercedes-Benz 609s in the fleet. *John Jones*

TANAT VALLEY

R E, P W & R M Morris, The Garage, Pentrefelin, Llangedwyn, Powys   SY10 9LE

#	Reg	Chassis	Body	Type	Year	History
1	D257YBB	Renault-Dodge S56	Robin Hood	BC19F	1987	Traction Motors, Smethwick, 1997
2	BRC140T	Leyland Leopard PSU3E/4R	Plaxton Supreme III Express	C49F	1979	Dalybus, Eccles, 1995
3	SCH148X	Leyland Leopard PSU3F/4R	Willowbrook 003	C53F	1982	Trent, 1992
4	HSD78V	Leyland Fleetline FE30AGR	Alexander AD	B44/31F	1980	Clydeside, 1995
5	D319DEF	Renault-Dodge S56	Northern Counties	B22F	1986	Midland, 1998
6	D150RAK	Renault-Dodge S56	Reeve Burgess	B25F	1987	Mainline, 1997
7	R649REP	Dennis Dart SLF	UVG UrbanStar	N40F	1998	
9	C958LWJ	MCW Metrobus DR102/53	MCW	BC42/28F	1986	Mainline, 1998
10	C960LWJ	MCW Metrobus DR102/53	MCW	BC42/28F	1986	Mainline, 1998
11	RNV413V	Leyland Leopard PSU3E/4R	Plaxton Supreme IV Exp	C53F	1979	Stagecoach Midland Red, 1999
12	XJI8356	Aüwaerter Neoplan N122/3	Aüwaerter Skyliner	C57/20CT	1986	Cannon, Garston, 1996
13	C446HLG	Bedford YNV Venturer	Duple Laser 2	C53F	1985	Alexcars, Cirencester, 1999
14	SJI1884	Volvo B10M-61	Duple Laser	C57F	1983	Evans, Tiverton Heath, 1998
15	OIB5647	Bova EL28/581	Duple Calypso	C53F	1984	Galloway, Mendlesham, 1990
16	A476NJK	Leyland Tiger TRCTL11/3R	Duple Laser	C53F	1984	Melvin, Aberdeen, 1999
17	B405UOD	Leyland Tiger TRCTL11/3RH	Duple Laser 2	C57F	1985	Smith, Carstairs, 1999
18	D734LAX	Bedford YNV Venturer	Duple 320	C57F	1986	Longmynd, Pontesbury, 1999
19	AKG1997A	Leyland Tiger TRCTL11/3R	Duple Laser	C49F	1984	Stagecoach Devon, 2000
20	KRN107T	Leyland Leopard PSU3E/4R	Duple Dominant II Express	C47F	1978	Kinch, Barrow-on-Soar, 1993
21	KRN111T	Leyland Leopard PSU3E/4R	Duple Dominant II Express	C47F	1979	Kinch, Barrow-on-Soar, 1993
22	G165XJF	Toyota Coaster HB31R	Caetano Optimo II	C19F	1990	Owen, Oswestry, 1999
23	C86NNV	Iveco-Fiat 79.14	Caetano Viana	C19F	1986	Jones, Llansilin, 1993

Tanat Valley operate commercial and tendered services from their bases at Pentrefelin and Llanrhaeadr using a variety of vehicles types. Pictured at the Pentrefelin base is the only Volvo product, a B10M with Duple Laser bodywork. *John Jones*

As the popularity for double-deck buses declines for commercial services the type are becoming confined to large urban areas. However, in some authorities, the type is still accepted for school transport contracts. Tanat Valley acquired two Metrobuses from Mainline in 1998 and their high-back seating has been retained. C960LWJ is seen on layover in Oswestry, a destination for several of the services operated. *John Jones*

24	D860LND	Renault-Dodge S56	Northern Counties	B20F	1986	MTL (Fareway), 1995
25	G624GOL	DAF 200	Leith	M16	1990	McLaughlin's, Penwortham, 1999
26	D71ASX	Renault-Dodge S56	Robin Hood	B25F	1987	Walker & Hutchinson, Pudsey, 1997
27	HSD84V	Leyland Fleetline FE30AGR	Alexander AD	B44/31F	1980	Clydeside, 1995
28	D38TKA	Freight Rover Sherpa	Dormobile	B16F	1987	Dumfries & Galloway RC, 1994
29	P115HCF	Dennis Javelin	Berkhof Axial 50	C53F	1997	Westbus, Hounslow, 1999
30	D421FEH	Freight Rover Sherpa	PMT Bursley	B20F	1986	Owen, Oswestry, 1992
31	CIB347	Hestair Duple SDA1512	Duple 425	C54FT	1987	Walton, Freckleton, 1999
32	BTX204T	Leyland Titan TNLXB1RF	Park Royal	BC43/29F	1979	Stagecoach Red & White, 1998
33	YSU939	Bova FHD12.280	Bova Futura	C49FT	1985	Watson, Sefton, 1999
35	A91YJR	Mercedes-Benz L608D	Reeve Burgess	BC19F	1983	Keir, Wallsend, 1999
36	HSD87V	Leyland Fleetline FE30AGR	Alexander AD	B44/31F	1980	Scutt, Owston Ferry, 1998
37	G652LYG	Iveco Daily 49.10	Th	B22F	1990	Leeds MB, 1999
38	TDK726S	Leyland Leopard PSU5B/4R	Plaxton Supreme III	C57F	1978	Jackson, Warrington, 2000
	H768JDD	Ford Transit VE6	Ford	M14	1991	private owner, 1998
	M74NUJ	LDV 400	LDV	M16	1995	private owner, 1999
	E148VGG	Toyota Coaster BB30R	Caetano Optimo	C19F	1987	Knight, Rock Ferry, 1999

Previous Registrations:

AKG197A	A225VWO	OIB5647	A323HFP, 2086PP, A481KRT
A476NJK	A808CCD, 418DCD	RNV413V	KUB546V, 4012VC
BTX204T	WDA5T	SJI1884	TNP615Y
C446HLG	C446CLG, ACH85A	TDK726S	TRY15S
CIB347	D108XSS, PSU626, D35BRS	YSU939	C260HGF

Depots: The Garage, Pentrefelin; Tanat Valley Garage, Llanrhaeadr ym Mochnant
Livery: Red and white or white

THOMAS BROS

G Thomas, Towy Garage, Llangadog, Carmarthenshire SA19 9LU

LAL746P	Leyland Leopard PSU3C/4R	Willowbrook Warrior (1988) B53F	1975	Nottingham, 1982
AEF878A	Leyland Leopard PSU3E/4R	Plaxton Viewmaster IV	C53F	1979	Gower Cs, Gorseinon, 1996
PRO439P	Bristol LHS6L	Plaxton Supreme IV	C33F	1980	Evans, Tregaron, 1991
NMV617W	Leyland Leopard PSU5D/5R	Plaxton Supreme IV	C53F	1981	Second City Travel, 1993
ABW82X	Leyland Leopard PSU3F/5R	Plaxton Supreme VI Exp	C53F	1982	Cheney, Banbury, 1987
AEF991Y	Leyland Tiger TRCTL11/2R	Plaxton Paramount 3200 E	C53F	1983	BTS, Borehamwood,
A17TBC	Leyland Tiger TRCTL11/3RH	Duple 340	C49FT	1986	Crosville, 1989
D631BPL	Dennis Lancet SDA525	Duple Dominant	B43F	1987	Dennis demonstrator, 1988
A18TBC	DAF MB230DKVL615	Plaxton Paramount 3500 III	C51FT	1987	Smith, Alcester, 1988
H16TBC	Ford Transit VE6	Zodiac	M14	1991	van, 1994
K461VVR	Volvo B10M-62	Van Hool Alizèe	C49FT	1993	Shearings, 2000
L439XFE	LDV 400	ALine	M16	1993	GS Hire, Humberside, 1997
L446XFE	LDV 400	ALine	M16	1993	GS Hire, Humberside, 1997
L454XFE	LDV 400	ALine	M16	1993	GS Hire, Humberside, 1997
L849THY	LDV 400	ALine	M16	1993	Whittal Williams, Abergavenny, 1997
L584MBW	LDV 400	ALine	M16	1993	Northfield School, Oxford, 1997
L905FWO	LDV 400	ALine	M16	1993	Whittal Williams, Abergavenny, 1997
L906FWO	LDV 400	ALine	M16	1993	Whittal Williams, Abergavenny, 1997
TPD80S	LDV 400	ALine	M16	1993	Weatherfield Hire, Cwmbran, 1997

Previous Registrations:

A17TBC	C69JTU	ABW82X	DFE361X, USU800	H16TBC	H407KOV
A18TBC	D129ACX	AEF878A	JTM104V, AEF667A	TPD80S	?

Depots: Rhosmaen Street, Llandeilo and Towy Garage, Llangadog
Livery: Cream and green; cream, green, and red (coaches)

D631BPL is a Dennis Lancet that spent its initial duties as a demonstrator. It is fitted with one of the last Duple bus bodies to be built and is seen preparing to leave Llandeilo on the Tuesday service to Lampeter through Llansawel. *John Jones*

THOMAS RHONDDA

W G Thomas & partners; J&I Thomas; Bus Depot, Aberrhondda Road, Porth,
Rhondda Cynon Taff CF39 0AG
TD & KD Thomas, Maesgwyn, Blanche Street, Williamstown, Rhondda Cynon
Taff CF40 1NG

Reg	Chassis	Body	Seats	Year	History
OEH604M	Bristol VRT/SL2/6LX	Eastern Coach Works	B43/31F	1974	PMT, 1990
NOC493R	Leyland Fleetline FE30AGR	MCW	B43/33F	1977	Atlas Bus, North Acton, 1994
FDN583S	Leyland Fleetline FE30AGR	Roe	B43/33F	1976	Dawlish Coaches, 1994
SDA509S	Leyland Fleetline FE30AGR	MCW	B43/33F	1977	West Midlands Travel, 1989
SDA532S	Leyland Fleetline FE30AGR	MCW	B43/33F	1977	West Midlands Travel, 1989
SDA631S	Leyland Fleetline FE30AGR	Park Royal	B43/33F	1977	West Midlands Travel, 1989
SDA659S	Leyland Fleetline FE30AGR	Park Royal	B43/33F	1978	Swanbrook, Cheltenham, 1995
TVP874S	Leyland Fleetline FE30AGR	MCW	B43/33F	1978	Roberts Coaches, Maerdy, 1998
CBV118S	Leyland Atlantean AN68A/1R	East Lancashire	B45/31F	1978	Warrington, 1998
CBV119S	Leyland Atlantean AN68A/1R	East Lancashire	B45/31F	1978	Warrington, 1998
CBV123S	Leyland Atlantean AN68A/1R	East Lancashire	B45/31F	1978	Warrington, 1998
ARC643T	Leyland Atlantean AN68A/1R	East Lancashire	B47/33D	1978	Dunn Line, Nottingham, 1997
ATV671T	Leyland Atlantean AN68A/1R	Northern Counties	B47/31D	1978	Dunn Line, Nottingham, 1997
WTG902T	Leyland Leopard PSU3E/4R	Plaxton Supreme III Exp	C51F	1978	Sunline, Radyr, 1997
CWU151T	Leyland Fleetline FE30AGR	Roe	B43/33F	1978	Yorkshire Rider, 1996
LFR125T	Leyland Atlantean AN68A/1R	East Lancashire	B45/31F	1979	Warrington, 1998
LFR126T	Leyland Atlantean AN68A/1R	East Lancashire	B45/31F	1979	Warrington, 1998
BTV653T	Leyland Atlantean AN68A/1R	East Lancashire	B47/33D	1979	Dunn Line, Nottingham, 1997
BRC679T	Leyland Atlantean AN68A/1R	Northern Counties	B45/31D	1979	Dunn Line, Nottingham, 1997
BEP973V	Bristol VRT/SL3/501	Eastern Coach Works	B43/31F	1980	Brewers, 1994
GEK12V	Leyland Atlantean AN68A/1R	East Lancashire	B45/31F	1980	Warrington, 1995
GEK14V	Leyland Atlantean AN68A/1R	East Lancashire	B45/31F	1980	Warrington, 1995
GEK15V	Leyland Atlantean AN68A/1R	East Lancashire	B45/31F	1980	Warrington, 1995
GEK16V	Leyland Atlantean AN68A/1R	East Lancashire	B45/31F	1980	Warrington, 1995
HFX422V	Ford R1114	Plaxton Supreme IV	C49F	1980	Sunline, Radyr, 1997
GSC633X	Leyland Atlantean AN68C/1R	Alexander AL	B45/30D	1981	Lothian Buses, 1999
GSC634X	Leyland Atlantean AN68C/1R	Alexander AL	B45/30D	1981	Lothian Buses, 1999
GSC638X	Leyland Atlantean AN68C/1R	Alexander AL	B45/30D	1981	Lothian Buses, 1999
GSC639X	Leyland Atlantean AN68C/1R	Alexander AL	B45/30D	1981	Lothian Buses, 1999
GSC643X	Leyland Atlantean AN68C/1R	Alexander AL	B45/30D	1981	Lothian Buses, 1999
GSC647X	Leyland Atlantean AN68C/1R	Alexander AL	B45/30D	1981	Lothian Buses, 2000
GSC651X	Leyland Atlantean AN68C/1R	Alexander AL	B45/30D	1981	Lothian Buses, 2000
GSC652X	Leyland Atlantean AN68C/1R	Alexander AL	B45/30D	1981	Lothian Buses, 2000
GSC657X	Leyland Atlantean AN68C/1R	Alexander AL	B45/30D	1981	Lothian Buses, 2000
GSC659X	Leyland Atlantean AN68C/1R	Alexander AL	B45/30D	1981	Lothian Buses, 2000
TDT1L	Ford R1014	Duple Dominant	B47F	1982	Isle of Wight CC, 1999
B828ETG	Scania K112CRS	Berkhof Esprite 350	C53F	1985	AJC, Leeds, 1995
WTA420	Scania K113CRB	Van Hool Alizèe	C51FT	1990	Bernard Kavanagh, Urlingford, 1997
H220GKK	Ford Transit VE6	Crystals	C16F	1991	
H818RWJ	Scania K113CRB	Plaxton Paramount 3500 III	C53F	1991	Acorn, Bristol, 1994
K331YDW	Mercedes-Benz 711D	Made-to-Measure	C24F	1992	
L334DTG	Mercedes-Benz 711D	Dormobile Routemaker	C25F	1993	
L337DTG	Scania K113CRB	Berkhof Excellence 2000HL	C51FT	1994	
M329RKG	Scania K113TRA	Berkhof Excellence 3000HD	C57/23DT	1994	
M330JHB	Ford Transit VE6	Crystals Challenger	BC20F	1995	
M933JHB	Volkswagen LT55	Advanced Vehicle Bodies	M15	1995	Apollo Club, Porthcawl

Opposite, top: **The Thomas Rhondda name comprises three operations and is seen here on R4WGT, a Bova Futura. The coach fleet largely comprises Scania and Bova products that are used mostly on shuttle services to Spain.** *John Jones*

Opposite, bottom: **Several Leyland Atlanteans from Lothian Buses have recently joined the Thomas Rhondda double-deck fleet and these have displaced nearly all of the remaining Bristols. An Atlantean that arrived from Warrington is East Lancashire-bodied CBV122S, which was new to Blackburn Transport.** *John Jones*

Carrying a modern livery style Thomas Coaches' WTA420 is a Van Hool Alizèe-bodied Scania. Having used the Swedish supplier for some years, recent deliveries have been of the integral Bova Futura model. During 2000 four new coaches from the Dutch manufacturer are due. *John Jones*

N945OBO	LDV 400	LDV	M16	1995	Meridian Services, Gloucester, 1999
P3WGT	Scania K113TRA	Berkhof Excellence 3000HD	C57/20DT	1996	
P2WGT	Scania K113CRB	Berkhof Axial 50	C51FT	1997	
P255YDW	Scania K113CRB	Berkhof Axial 50	C51FT	1997	
R12WGT	Mercedes-Benz Sprinter 614D	Onyx	BC24F	1998	
R4WGT	Bova FHD12.340	Bova Futura	C51FT	1998	
R5WGT	Bova FHD12.340	Bova Futura	C51FT	1998	
V6WGT	Scania K124IB6	Berkhof Excellence 3000HD	C57/19CT	1999	
WGT1	Ayats A3/BR1	Ayats Bravo	C57/16DT	1999	
W351UWO	Bova FHD12.370	Bova Futura	C51FT	2000	
W352UWO	Bova FHD12.370	Bova Futura	C51FT	2000	
W353UWO	Bova FHD12.370	Bova Futura	C51FT	2000	
W354UWO	Bova FHD12.370	Bova Futura	C51FT	2000	

Previous Registrations:

B828ETG	B413DHK, YSU985	P3WGT	YSU985
BEP973V	BEP973V, TDT1L	P255YDW	WGT1, M3WGT
HFX422V	HFX422V, PJI8364	TDT1L	RDL780X
M329RKG	WGT1	WTA420	G796FJX, 90KK2530

Depot: Aberrhondda Road, Porth.
Livery: White, orange and blue; white

TOWNLYNX

S A Lee, Coetia Llwyd, Northop Road, Holywell, Flintshire, CH8 8AE

ACW763R	Leyland National 11351A/1R		B49F	1977	Arriva North West, 1998
AYJ98T	Leyland National 11351A/1R		B52F	1979	Renown, Bexhill, 1996
D353JUM	Volkeswagen LT55	Optare City Pacer	BC25F	1986	Mullover, Bedford, 1996
D498RNM	Iveco Daily 49.10	Robin Hood City Nippy	B21F	1987	Ely, Woodston, 1998
E169XJO	Volkswagen LT55	Optare City Pacer	B25F	1987	Webster, Blisland, 1999
E858GNR	Volkswagen LT55	Optare City Pacer	B25F	1987	Amies, Shrewsbury, 1996
G32PSR	Iveco Daily 49.10	Robin Hood City Nippy	B23F	1987	Swiftlink, Harry Stoke, 1999
G40PSR	Iveco Daily 49.10	Phoenix	B23F	1987	Swiftlink, Harry Stoke, 1999

Livery: white, yellow and blue

Townlynx operates the frequent route 28 that links Flint with Mold. Arriva Cymru also operate the service. While the normal vehicles are minibuses, the Leyland Nationals are sometimes used as seen here when ACW763R was pictured in Mold. *John Jones*

VALE OF LLANGOLLEN

Vale of Llangollen Ltd, Hilbre, Well Street, Cefn Mawr, Wrexham LL14 3YD

TJI6309	Ailsa B55-10	Alexander AV	B44/31D	1976	Tayside, 1991
6400VT	Ailsa B55-10	Alexander AV	B44/31D	1977	Tayside, 1996
NAT746A	Ailsa B55-10	Alexander AV	B44/31D	1979	Tayside, 1995
1810VT	Ailsa B55-10	Alexander AV	B44/31D	1979	Tayside, 1995
2378VT	Ailsa B55-10	Alexander AV	B44/31D	1979	Tayside, 1995
467VT	Ailsa B55-10	Alexander AV	B44/31D	1979	Tayside, 1995
4384VT	Ailsa B55-10	Alexander AV	B44/31D	1980	Tayside, 1996
440VT	Ailsa B55-10	Alexander AV	B44/31D	1980	Tayside, 1997
1260VT	Ailsa B55-10	Alexander AV	B44/34F	1980	Tayside, 1997
6052VT	Ailsa B55-10	Alexander AV	B44/31D	1980	Tayside, 1996
3587VT	Volvo B55-10 Mk III	Alexander AV	B44/34F	1980	Tayside, 1997
7052VT	Volvo B55-10 Mk III	Alexander AV	B44/34F	1980	Tayside, 1997
9509VT	Volvo B55-10 Mk III	Alexander AV	B44/34F	1980	Tayside, 1997
2090VT	MCW Metrobus DR102/22	MCW	B43/30F	1981	Travel West Midlands, 1999
3810VT	MCW Metrobus DR102/22	MCW	B43/30F	1981	Travel West Midlands, 1999
LOA418X	MCW Metrobus DR102/22	MCW	B43/30F	1982	Travel West Midlands, 1999
6468VT	MCW Metrobus DR102/22	MCW	B43/30F	1982	Travel West Midlands, 1999
5958VT	Volvo B55-10 Mk III	Alexander AV	B44/37F	1984	Merseybus, 1996
8701VT	Volvo B55-10 Mk III	Alexander AV	B44/37F	1984	Merseybus, 1996
9975VT	Volvo B55-10 Mk III	Alexander AV	B44/37F	1984	Merseybus, 1996
7239VT	Volvo B10M-61	Plaxton Paramount 3500 III	C49FT	1987	Shamrock, Pontypridd, 1999
?	Volvo B10M-60	Jonckheere Deauville P599	C51FT	1990	Ellis, Wembley Park, 1998
VLT250	Volvo B10M-60	Jonckheere Deauville P599	C51F	1990	Budden's, Romsey, 1993
VLT177	Volvo B10M-60	Jonckheere Deauville P599	C51F	1990	McLean, Witney, 1994
?	Volvo B10M-60	Jonckheere Deauville P599	C51FT	1990	Ellis, Wembley Park, 1998
VLT293	Volvo B10M-60	Jonckheere Deauville P599	C51FT	1992	
VLT229	Volvo B10M-60	Jonckheere Deauville P599	C51FT	1992	
VLT483	Volvo B10M-60	Jonckheere Deauville P599	C51FT	1992	
VLT290	Volvo B10M-60	Jonckheere Deauville P599	C51FT	1992	
VLT191	Volvo B10M-60	Jonckheere Deauville 45	C51FT	1994	
VLT149	Volvo B10M-60	Jonckheere Deauville 45	C51FT	1994	
VLT22	Volvo B10M-60	Jonckheere Deauville 45	C51FT	1994	
VLT55	Volvo B10M-60	Jonckheere Deauville 45	C51FT	1994	
VLT935	Volvo B10M-62	Jonckheere Deauville 45	C51FT	1996	Classic, Annfield Plain, 1998
N2VLT	Volvo B10M-62	Jonckheere Deauville 45	C51FT	1996	
N3VLT	Volvo B10M-62	Jonckheere Deauville 45	C51FT	1996	
P3VLT	Volvo B10M-62	Jonckheere Mistral 50	C51FT	1997	
P5VLT	Volvo B10M-62	Jonckheere Mistral 50	C51FT	1997	
W2VLT	Volvo B10M-62	Jonckheere Mistral 50	C51FT	2000	
W5VLT	Volvo B10M-62	Jonckheere Mistral 50	C51FT	2000	

Previous Registrations:

440VT	CSL608V	9975VT	A157HLV
467VT	WTS267T	NAT746A	WTS256T, VLT483
1260VT	CSL609V	TJI6309	NSP339R, 8177VT
1810VT	WTS260T	VLT22	L5VLT
2090VT	LOA330X	VLT55	L6VLT
2378VT	WTS261T	VLT149	L4VLT
3587VT	DSP921V	VLT177	G165RBD, VLT55
3810VT	LOA370X	VLT191	L3VLT
4384VT	CSL606V	VLT229	J987GLG, VLT177
5958VT	A153HLV	VLT250	G146GLG, VLT293
6052VT	CSL616V	VLT280	
6400VT	SSN243S	VLT290	J459HCA, VLT250
6468VT	LOA435X	VLT293	J986GLG, VLT149
7052VT	DSP922V	VLT298	
7239VT	D875EEH, PNH182	VLT483	J458HCA, VLT191
8177VT	A370UNH, YRX481, TJI6309	VLT935	LSK871, M575DSJ
8701VT	A155HLV	?	G981LRP, 6468VT
9509VT	DSP927V	?	G142MNH, 3810VT

Livery: Sand, orange and blue

The Vale of Llangollen fleet contains many Alexander-bodied Volvo Ailsa buses mostly originating with Tayside Buses. Shown on school work in Wrexham here is 467VT. Many vehicles in this fleet carry VT and VLT index marks. *John Jones*

Vale of Llangollen provide coaches to several of the large tour companies, including Globus, whose colours they wear. Two Jonckheere Mistral coaches joined the fleet in 1997 and P5VLT is shown here. *Andrew Jarosz*

VOEL COACHES

Voel Coaches Ltd, Penisa Filling Station, Longacres Road, Dyserth,
Denbighshire LL18 6BP

Fleet No.	Chassis	Body	Seating	Year	Notes
JC9736	Guy Wolf NLW	Barnard	B21F	1949	Ex Hollis, Queensferry, 1982
VRP60S	Bristol VRT/SL3/6LXB	Alexander AL	B45/27D	1977	Ex Northampton, 1992
VVV63S	Bristol VRT/SL3/6LXB	Alexander AL	B45/27D	1977	Ex Northampton, 1992
HFM962T	Volvo B58-56	Plaxton Supreme III	C53F	1978	Ex Hanmer, Southsea, 1979
FVR264V	Leyland Atlantean AN68A/1R	Northern Counties	B43/32F	1979	GMS Buses, Manchester, 1996
MNC509W	Leyland Atlantean AN68A/1R	Northern Counties	B43/32F	1980	GMS Buses, Manchester, 1996
MNC525W	Leyland Atlantean AN68A/1R	Northern Counties	B43/32F	1980	GMS Buses, Manchester, 1996
GPA611V	Ford R1114	Duple Dominant II	C53F	1980	Ex Hodge, Sandhurst, 1984
GPA614V	Ford R1114	Duple Dominant II	C53F	1980	Ex Hodge, Sandhurst, 1984
7934VC	Volvo B58-61	Plaxton Supreme IV	C57F	1980	Ex Terry Shaw, Barnsley, 1983
6499VC	Volvo B10M-61	Van Hool Alizèe	C50FT	1984	
7488VC	Volvo B10M-61	Van Hool Alizèe	C50FT	1984	
XDM300	Volvo B10M-60	Van Hool Alizèe	C53F	1989	Clarkes of London, 1997
9155VC	Volvo B10M-60	Van Hool Alizèe	C53F	1989	Clarkes of London, 1997
776VC	Dennis Javelin	Berkhof Excellence 1000 L	C51FT	1994	Bicknell, Godalming, 1998
3377VC	Scania K113CRB	Van Hool Alizèe	C53FT	1995	
8868VC	Scania K113CRB	Van Hool Alizèe	C53FT	1995	
1760VC	Dennis Javelin	Berkhof Axial 50	C53F	1997	Q-Drive, Battersea, 1998
8214VC	Dennis Javelin	Berkhof Axial 50	C53F	1997	Q-Drive, Battersea, 1998
R766DUM	Volvo B9M	Van Hool Alizèe II	C30FT	1997	Dave Parry, Cheslyn Hay, 2000
R4MKD	Volvo B10M-62	Berkhof Axial 50	C53F	1998	
W	Mercedes-Benz O404	Hispano Vita	C FT	2000	
W	Mercedes-Benz O404	Hispano Vita	C FT	2000	

Previous Registrations:

776VC	M773GPB	7488VC	From new	8868VC	M3OVC	
1760VC	P883FMO	7934VC	HKY614W	9155VC	F168RJF	
3377VC	M2OVC	8214VC	B533BML	JC9736	From new	
6499VC	From new	XDM300	P882FMO			

Livery: Two-tone orange and white

Two Bristol VRs and five Leyland Atlanteans form the double-deck fleet of Voel coaches. Purchased from Northampton is VVV63S shown here. *John Jones*

WATTS

C P Watts, Old Post Garage, Bonvilston, Vale of Glamorgan CF5 6TQ

RUJ350R	Ford R1114	Plaxton Supreme III	C53F	1977	Venture Travel, Cardiff, 1990
XDG57S	Ford R1014	Plaxton Supreme III	C45F	1978	Stevens, Warmley, 1981
ERW265T	Ford R1114	Duple Dominant II Express	C53F	1979	Bebb, Llantwit Fardre, 1987
WTG342T	Bristol VRT/SL3/6LXB	Alexander AL	B44/31F	1978	Cardiff Bus, 1997
WTG353T	Bristol VRT/SL3/6LXB	Alexander AL	B44/31F	1979	Cardiff Bus, 1997
CWG692V	Leyland Atlantean AN68A/1R	Alexander AL	B45/29D	1979	Camm, Nottingham, 1993
DKG321V	Ford R1114	Plaxton Supreme IV	C53F	1979	Warner Fairfax, Tewkesbury, 1984
FUA394Y	Volvo B10M-61	Plaxton Paramount 3200	C53F	1983	Woodstones, Kidderminster, 1989
THL296Y	Volvo B10M-61	Duple Caribbean	C50F	1983	Shirley, Walsall, 1989
B568AHD	DAF SB2300DHTD585	Plaxton Paramount 3200	C53F	1985	Hurst & Leak, Goose Green, 1992
C280VFP	DAF MB200DKFL600	Plaxton Paramount 3200	C53F	1986	Bland, Stamford, 1990
E53MMT	Leyland Tiger TRCL10/3RZ	Duple 340	C53FT	1987	Classic, Annfield Plain, 1992
E42HLP	Mercedes-Benz 609D	Reeve Burgess Beaver	C19F	1988	EMMS, Nantgarw, 1993
E380MPX	Mercedes-Benz 811D	Robin Hood	C29F	1988	Wings, Uxbridge, 1991
F598BTG	Leyland Tiger TRCL10/3ARZM	Plaxton Paramount 3500 III	C51FT	1989	Hills of Tredegar, 1992
F149TEU	Mercedes-Benz 609D	Made-to-Measure	C24F	1989	
G54RTO	Volvo B10M-60	Duple 340	C55F	1990	Turner, Bristol, 1996
G55RTO	Volvo B10M-60	Duple 340	C55F	1990	Turner, Bristol, 1996
H185EJF	MAN 10-180 HOCL-R	Caetano Algarve II	C35F	1991	
J49SNY	Leyland Tiger TRCTL11/3ARZM	Plaxton Paramount 3200 III	C53F	1991	SE Wales Ambulance Trust, 1997
R733ECT	Mercedes-Benz Vario O814	Autobus Nouvelle	C33F	1997	
R70RAW	MAN 11.220 HOCL-R	Caetano Algarve 2	C35F	1998	
R73GNW	DAF DE33WSSB3000	Plaxton Première 320	C51F	1998	First Wessex, 1999
S576ACT	Mercedes-Benz Vario O814	Autobus Nouvelle	C29F	1998	

Depots: Old Post Garage, Bonvilston and Pentre Farm, Llantrithyd
Livery: Fawn, red and gold

Once dominated by Ford coaches, the Watts fleet now comprises a variety of types. R73GNW, shown here at its base, is a rear-engined DAF SB3000 with Plaxton Première 320 bodywork acquired during 1999.
John Jones

WILKINS TRAVEL

Wilkins Bros (Cymmer) Ltd, Eastern Avenue, Croeserw, Cymmer,
Neath & Port Talbot SA13 3PB

MCY85G	AEC Reliance 6U3ZR	Duple Dominant II(1981)	C53F	1969	Tenby Bus & Coach, 1991
HTG557K	Leyland Leopard PSU3B/4R	Plaxton Elite III Express	C53F	1972	Creamline, Tonmawr, 1987
SVO782R	AEC Reliance 6U2R	Plaxton Supreme III	C53F	1977	Kettlewell, Retford, 1992
WTG348T	Bristol VRT/SL3/6LXB	Alexander AL	B44/31F	1978	Cardiff Bus, 1999
WTG349T	Bristol VRT/SL3/6LXB	Alexander AL	B44/31F	1978	Cardiff Bus, 1999
WTG356T	Bristol VRT/SL3/6LXB	Alexander AL	B44/31F	1978	Cardiff Bus, 1999
WTG361T	Bristol VRT/SL3/6LXB	Alexander AL	B44/31F	1979	Cardiff Bus, 1999
WTG381T	Bristol VRT/SL3/6LXB	Alexander AL	B44/31F	1979	Cardiff Bus, 1999
ROU348S	Leyland Leopard PSU3E/4R	Plaxton Supreme III Express	C49F	1978	Cheltenham & Gloucester, 1987
MYD215V	Bedford YMT	Plaxton Supreme IV	C53F	1980	Lewis Coaches, Aberdare, 1994
KWB695W	Bedford YMT	Duple Dominant	B55F	1981	Grindle, Cinderford, 1999
EHW288W	Ford R1114	Duple Dominant II	C53F	1981	Turner, Bristol, 1986
SND303X	Leyland Leopard PSU5C/4R	Plaxton Supreme V	C53F	1981	Cheltenham & Gloucester, 1987
OHR492X	Bedford YMT	Duple Dominant II	C53F	1982	Grindle, Cinderford, 1999
KEC976X	Bedford YNT	Plaxton Supreme V	C53F	1982	Silver Badge, Windermere, 1983
RDT121X	Leyland Tiger TRCTL11/3R	Duple Dominant IV	C53F	1982	Pullman, Crofty, 1994

Wilkins Travel currently occupy the garage and workshops latterly used by Cream Line in the Pelenna valley outside Neath. Seen here is Dennis Javelin R580SWN which is fitted with a Marcopolo Explorer body and is the second of the type to join the fleet. *John Jones*

Pictured on school duties is Alexander-bodied Bristol VRWTG 349T. *John Jones*

OHV190Y	Ford R1114	Wadham Stringer Vanguard	B32F	1982	LB Southwark, 1994
OHV193Y	Ford R1114	Wadham Stringer Vanguard	B32F	1982	LB Southwark, 1994
OHV209Y	Ford R1114	Wadham Stringer Vanguard	B32F	1982	LB Southwark, 1994
NDW37X	Ford R1114	Duple Dominant IV Express	C51F	1983	Bebb, Llantwit Fardre, 1987
KIW3766	DAF MB200DKFL600	LAG Galaxy	C49FT	1986	
C768MVH	DAF MB230DKFL615	Duple 340	C57F	1986	Harris, Catshill, 1991
E51TYG	DAF MB230DKFL615	Duple 340	C53FT	1986	Castell Coaches, Trethomas, 1995
OIJ864	Leyland Royal Tiger RTC	Leyland Doyen	C53F	1988	West Riding, 1989
551FVW	Leyland Royal Tiger RTC	Leyland Doyen	C53F	1988	West Riding, 1989
G991OKJ	DAF MB230LT615	Caetano Algarve	C53F	1989	The King's Ferry, 1993
P974UKG	Iveco TurboDaily 59.12	UVG CitiStar	BC29F	1996	Phil Anslow, Pontypool, 1999
R641VNN	Dennis Javelin	Marcopolo Explorer	C57F	1997	
R580SWN	Dennis Javelin	Marcopolo Explorer	C57F	1998	
T896ATH	Volvo B10M-62	Berkhof Axial 50	C51FT	1999	
T899ATH	Volvo B10M-62	Berkhof Axial 50	C51FT	1999	
T520PYD	Bova FHD12.340	Bova Futura	C40FT	1999	
V418FCY	Bova FHD12.340	Bova Futura	C49FT	1999	

Previous Registrations:

551FVW	E51TYG		
E51TYG	D756KKG,551FVW	MCY85G	LWM475G, OIJ864
KIW3766	B73BCY	OIJ864	E50TYG

Depots: Il Heol Ty Gwyn, Tyle Teg, Maesteg and Johns Terrace, Tonmawr.
Livery: Cream and tan(buses); white, blue and grey (coaches).

The Welsh Bus Handbook

WILLIAMS BALA

Williams (Bala) Ltd, Bodolwyn Garage, Brenig Street, Bala, Gwynedd, LL23 7AH

NEL112P	Leyland Leopard PSU3C/4R	Plaxton Supreme III Exp	C53F	1976	Webber, Blisland, 2000
EGR704S	Bedford VAS5	Plaxton Supreme III	C29F	1978	Evans, Tregaron, 1997
RJI3380	Bedford YLQ	Duple Dominant II	C45F	1978	Lewis, Llanrhystud, 1997
RJI4080	Ford R1114	Plaxton Supreme IV	C53F	1980	Haydn's, Chirk, 1998
FWB494V	Bedford YLQ	Duple Dominant II	C45F	1980	Lewis, Llanrhystud, 1997
TDM769V	Leyland Leopard PSU3F/4R	Duple Dominant II	C53F	1980	Formby Coaches, 1991
LCW367W	Bedford YNT	Duple Dominant IV	C49F	1981	Evans, Tregaron, 1997
NDW140X	Leyland Tiger TRCTL11/2R	Plaxton Supreme V Express	C53F	1982	Formby Coaches, 1988
NMA746Y	Mercedes-Benz L508D	Devon Conversions	C19F	1983	Formby Coaches, 1988
PIL9377	Scania K112CRS	Jonckheere Bermuda P50	C51FT	1983	Vale of Llangollen, 1998
WIW3577	Scania K112CRS	Jonckheere Bermuda P50	C49FT	1983	Vale of Llangollen, 1998
DIW3778	Leyland Tiger TRCTL11/3R	Plaxton Paramount 3500	C49FT	1983	Dorking Coaches, 1994
WIB7183	Leyland Tiger TRCTL11/3R	Plaxton Paramount 3500	C50F	1983	Dorking Coaches, 1994
A36GJT	Leyland Tiger TRCTL11/3R	Plaxton Paramount 3200	C57F	1983	Lewis, Llanrhystud, 1997
FIL4135	Leyland Tiger TRCTL11/3R	Plaxton Paramount 3500 II	C49FT	1985	Travelmate, Wareham, 1995
C736FFJ	Ford Transit 190D	Carlyle	B16F	1986	Webber, Blisland, 2000
E795CCA	Mercedes-Benz 709D	PMT	C25F	1988	Bryn Melyn, Llangollen, 1993
NIL9777	Volvo B10M-60	Plaxton Paramount 3500 III	C53F	1989	Vale of Llangollen, 1997

Previous Registrations:

DIW3778	BAJ634Y	RJI3380	VRY287S, 6962WF
FIL4135	B406CMC	RJI4080	WTU351W
LCW367W	HHG916W, 1359UP	WIB7183	GRH1Y, RHE194,WWE222Y
NIL9777	F994KFM, 9975VT, 7052VT, F439LTU, 3810VT	WIW3577	DLX41Y, SEL219, XUJ357Y, IIL1347
PIL9377	DLX43Y, HIL7988, 7239VT		

Livery: White, red and yellow

The five Leyland Tiger coaches in the Williams Bala fleet play a major role and all have Plaxton bodywork. Showing the early Paramount styling is WIB7183 which, when new, was the flagship in the East Yorkshire fleet as GRH1Y. *Malcolm Flynn*

WILLIAMS

Williams Motors (Cwmdu) Ltd, Rich Way, The Watton, Brecon, Powys, LD3 7EA.

TPJ270S	Bedford YMT	Plaxton Supreme III	C53F	1977	Hardings, Betchworth, 1995
CRW510T	Bedford YMT	Plaxton Supreme IV	C53F	1978	Evans, Tregaron, 1995
NAB848T	Bedford YLQ	Plaxton Supreme IV	C45F	1979	Yarranton, Eardiston, 1984
FCT703V	Bedford YMT	Plaxton Supreme IV	C53F	1980	Tourmaster, Crowland, 1998
GFO775X	Bedford YMQ	Duple Dominant II	C45F	1981	
299DMW	Mercedes-Benz 0303/15R	Mercedes-Benz	C49F	1982	Redwing, Camberwell, 1987
226DMW	Mercedes-Benz 0303/15RHP	Mercedes-Benz	C49F	1982	Redwing, Camberwell, 1987
GWO1L	Mercedes Benz 0303/15R	Mercedes Benz	C51FT	1983	Luckett, Fareham, 1992
6654HA	Kässbohrer Setra S215HR	Kässbohrer Rational	C49F	1985	Sutherland, Edinburgh, 1996
WSU259	Kässbohrer Setra S215HD	Kässbohrer	C53F	1986	Landtourers, Farnham, 1993
YSU903	Kässbohrer Setra S215HD	Kässbohrer	C53F	1986	Landtourers, Farnham, 1993
D119NUS	Mercedes-Benz L608D	Alexander AM	B20F	1986	First Aberdeen (Mair), 1997
E222WMB	Mercedes-Benz 307D	Advanced Vehicle Bodies	M12	1987	Safeway, Batley, 1996
F687UCR	Dennis Javelin 12SDA1907	Plaxton Paramount 3200 III	C53F	1988	Titchen, Benfleet, 1997
F704PAY	Mercedes Benz 0303/15R	Mercedes Benz	C53F	1989	Redwing, Camberwell, 2000
F706PAY	Mercedes Benz 0303/15R	Mercedes Benz	C53F	1989	Redwing, Camberwell, 2000
IIL8518	Mercedes-Benz 811D	Reeve Burgess Beaver	BC33F	1989	British Telecom, Goonhilly, 1997
F483OCN	Mercedes-Benz 408D	G & M Coachworks	M16	1989	Marks, Plymouth, 1996
F700JNU	Ford Transit VE6	Ford	M14	1989	Coxís Taxi Services, Belper, 1994
HEU350	Kässbohrer Setra S215HDI	Kässbohrer Tornado	C49FT	1989	Angelaa, Bursledon, 1996
G529FHB	Leyland-DAF 200	Leyland-DAF	M8	1990	
G663SCJ	Leyland-DAF 200	Leyland-DAF	M8	1990	

The Williams fleet now contains three Bova Futura coaches. Shown in the latest application of the livery is M259BGF, which arrived during the summer of 1999. It is seen outside the City Hall in Cardiff. This vehicle is an example of the less-common low-height Futura. *John Jones*

G818UPX	Mercedes-Benz 308D	Devon Conversions	M8	1990	Lewis, Llanrhystyd, 1994
H160NBF	Ford Transit VE6	Premier	M8	1991	van, 1994
IIL8521	Toyota Coaster HDB30R	Caetano Optimo II	C21F	1991	Taylor's, Sutton Scotney, 1996
PBZ9057	Mercedes-Benz 709D	Olympus	BC25F	1991	Bradshaw, Heywood, 1998
8914RU	Mercedes-Benz OH1628L	Jonckheere Deauville P50	C55F	1992	Redwing, Camberwell, 1998
J7BBC	Bova FHM12.290	Bova Futura	C53F	1992	Biss Bros, Bishops Stortford, 1998
J8BBC	Bova FHM12.290	Bova Futura	C53F	1992	Biss Bros, Bishops Stortford, 1998
K729CPY	Ford Transit VE6	Ford	M8	1993	Oxfordshire CC, 2000
L958HDH	Leyland-DAF 400	Leyland-DAF	M16	1993	LB Hillingdon, 1996
L417OYB	Ford Transit VE6	Ford	M8	1994	crewbus, 1997
M259BGF	Bova FLD12.270	Bova Futura	C53F	1994	Q-Drive, Battersea, 1999
M846BTC	LDV 400	LDV	M16	1994	Oxfordshire CC, 2000
M703HDF	LDV 200	LDV	M8	1994	private owner, 1998
M457OOA	Ford Transit VE6	Ford	M8	1995	KR Motors, Awsworth, 1998
H2DWD	Ford Transit VE6	Aztec	M11	1995	Travel House, Swansea, 1999
H14DWD	Ford Transit VE6	Aztec	M12	1995	Travel House, Swansea, 1999
5583HA	EOS E180Z	EOS 90	C49FT	1995	Whyte & Urquhart, Newmachar, 1997
M5JLW	MAN 18.370HOCL-R	Caetano Algarve II	C49FT	1995	
N100TCC	Setra S250	Setra Special	C53F	1996	Skills, Nottingham, 2000
N5DMW	MAN 11.190HOCL-R	Caetano Algarve II	C35F	1996	
P5DMW	MAN 18.370HOCL-R	Caetano Algarve II	C49FT	1996	
R543ACV	LDV Pilot	LDV	M8	1997	crewbus, 1997
T525KEP	Mercedes-Benz 814D	Olympus	BC19F	1999	van, 1999

Previous Registrations:

226DMW	PUL94Y, ALJ664A	IIL8518	F875XCV
299DMW	PUL80Y, ALJ587A	IIL8521	J234HVK
5583HA	M552SSA	MIB552	-
6654HA	49SIP, B388RJU	PBZ9057	H825HEM
GWO1L	PUL93Y ALJ805A	WSU259	C209UPC
HEU350	F27YBO, RIB6581, F699UOR	YSU903	C210UPC, YSU904

Depots: Rich Way, Brecon; Canal Road, Brecon and Crescent Garage, Cwmdu
Livery: Cream, orange and brown

Integral coaches by Mercedes-Benz have only been imported into the UK in relatively small numbers. While the latest O404 model is just entering service, the durability of the earlier O303 can be evidenced by 299DMW, one of five operated by Williams, the earliest dating back to 1982.
John Jones

Index to vehicles

Reg	Operator	Reg	Operator	Reg	Operator	Reg	Operator	Reg	Operator
7CCH	K M P	7074DK	Cross Gates	A512VKG	Cardiff Bus	ATH180T	Meyers
34BCG	Clynnog & Trefor	7239VT	Vale of Llangollen	A541HAC	Stagecoach R&W	ATH352V	Merlyn's
93FYB	Ken Hopkins	7289DD	Richards Bros	A548HAC	Stagecoach R&W	ATV671T	Thomas Rhondda
99KMH	Ken Hopkins	7488VC	Voel Coaches	A549HAC	Stagecoach R&W	AUJ746T	James Brothers
102UTF	Goodsir	7660DD	First Cymru	A576NWX	Arriva Cymru	AUP351W	G M
109CUF	Silcox	7934VC	Voel Coaches	A616WEP	Hawkes	AUP371W	G M
151WYB	Clynnog & Trefor	8098DD	First Cymru	A675HNB	First Cymru	AVK143V	Howells
164EWN	James Brothers	8124DD	First Cymru	A688HNB	First Cymru	AVK162V	Mansel David
210HKT	Edwards Coaches	817FKH	Silcox	A694HNB	First Cymru	AVK172V	Arthur Thomas
226DMW	Williams	8214VC	Voel Coaches	A698AWB	Alpine	AWN813V	First Cymru
241KRO	Ellis Travel	8443PH	Express Motors	A702HVT	Mid Wales	AYG849S	Express Motors
250DBX	Midway Motors	8701VT	Vale of Llangollen	A703HVT	Mid Wales	AYJ98T	Townlynx
278TNY	First Cymru	8853DD	First Cymru	A705HVT	Mid Wales	B27PAJ	East End
279NDE	Bysiau cwm Taf	8868VC	Voel Coaches	A706HVT	Mid Wales	B29PAJ	East End
297EYR	Goodsir	8914RU	Williams	A708LNC	Diamond Glantawe	B44MRF	Berwyn
299DMW	Williams	9155VC	Voel Coaches	A734JAY	Edwards Bros	B101ETX	Stagecoach R&W
329UWL	James Brothers	9195PU	Silcox	A748NNA	First Cymru	B102KPF	Arriva Cymru
367ARV	Arvonia	9509VT	Vale of Llangollen	A774WHB	I B T	B109ETX	Stagecoach R&W
431DWN	Brian Isaac	9616DD	First Cymru	A801LEY	Alpine	B124PEL	First Cymru
440VT	Vale of Llangollen	963CDE	Jones Login	A901SYE	Shamrock	B176WYV	Alpine
467VT	Vale of Llangollen	9975VT	Vale of Llangollen	A905SYE	Stagecoach R&W	B186BLG	Arriva Cymru
490ENU	Lewis Whitland	A2WLS	Silcox	A930SYE	Shamrock	B191BLG	Arriva Cymru
521WDE	Jones Login	A4WLS	Silcox	A942TYA	Alpine	B192BLG	Arriva Cymru
526FDE	Jones Login	A5WLS	Silcox	A945MDH	Browns of Builth	B193BLG	Arriva Cymru
526NDE	Edwards Bros	A6WLS	Silcox	A946MDH	Browns of Builth	B194BLG	Arriva Cymru
529FN	Cross Gates	A7KMP	K M P	A967YSX	Cardiff Bus	B196BLG	Arriva Cymru
538OHU	Silcox	A7ORJ	Jones Llanfaethlu	A968YSX	Cardiff Bus	B218JPH	W E Jones & Son
540CCY	Brian Isaac	A7WLS	Silcox	A969YSX	Cardiff Bus	B219YUH	Newport Transport
551FVW	Wilkins Travel	A8ORJ	Jones Llanfaethlu	A970YSX	Cardiff Bus	B220YUH	Newport Transport
552OHU	GHA Coaches	A8WEJ	W E Jones & Son	A971YSX	Cardiff Bus	B221OJU	Edwards Coaches
560DFM	Eagles & Crawford	A9ORJ	Jones Llanfaethlu	A972YSX	Cardiff Bus	B221YUH	Newport Transport
572RKJ	Owens Motors	A11WLS	Silcox	A973SYE	Shamrock	B222YUH	Newport Transport
604JPU	Express Motors	A12WLS	Silcox	A973YSX	Cardiff Bus	B223YUH	Newport Transport
668VDE	Edwards Bros	A14RBL	Stagecoach R&W	A974YSX	Cardiff Bus	B224YUH	Newport Transport
6697RU	K M P	A14WLS	Silcox	AAE654V	First Cymru	B225YUH	Newport Transport
691DDE	Alpine	A15RBL	GHA Coaches	AAL423A	Porthcawl Omnibus	B226YUH	Newport Transport
708EYG	Goodsir	A15WLS	Silcox	AAL516A	First Cymru	B290KPF	Meyers
723CTH	Hawkes	A16WLS	Silcox	AAX450A	First Cymru	B405UOD	Tanat Valley
772URB	K M P	A17TBC	Thomas Bros	AAX466A	First Cymru	B417CMC	Summerdale
776VC	Voel Coaches	A18TBC	Thomas Bros	AAX489A	Stagecoach R&W	B440VOW	Ellis Travel
791VT	Vale of Llangollen	A36GJT	Williams Bala	AAX515A	First Cymru	B513LFP	Arriva Cymru
804SHW	Silcox	A3WLS	Silcox	AAX516A	Stagecoach R&W	B567NCC	Alpine
834TDE	Jones Login	A42SMA	Arriva Cymru	AAX529A	First Cymru	B568AHD	Watts
898FCY	Hawkes	A44KLF	James Brothers	AAZ9102		Berwyn	B634BEP	Gwyn Williams
948RJO	First Cymru	A80RGE	Express Motors	ABW82X	Thomas Bros	B679EWE	Phillips
978HHT	Edwards Coaches	A91YJR	Tanat Valley	ACW763R	Townlynx	B828ETG	Thomas Rhondda
997EAY	Cerbydau Carreglefn	A103OUG	Arriva Cymru	ACY178A	First Cymru	B890AJX	Edwards Coaches
1200VT	Vale of Llangollen	A104OUG	Arriva Cymru	ADE612V	Richards Bros	BAU178T	Clynnog & Trefor
1760VC	Voel Coaches	A114TRP	Mid Wales	ADU327X	First Cymru	BAZ7052	D & G Coaches
1810VT	Vale of Llangollen	A115UDE	First Cymru	AEF32Y	Edwards Coaches	BBM62A	E Jones & Sons
1862HX	Alpine	A122GSA	P & O Lloyd	AEF221Y	Arriva Cymru	BBR738S	Richards Bros
1885FM	Midway Motors	A126GSA	P & O Lloyd	AEF222Y	Arriva Cymru	BBX190V	Richards Bros
1923DD	First Cymru	A130SNH	Llynfi Coaches	AEF224Y	Arriva Cymru	BBX915V	Silcox
2039NU	Shuttle	A132FDC	GHA Coaches	AEF229Y	Arriva Cymru	BCS867T	P & O Lloyd
2090VT	Vale of Llangollen	A151HLV	Cardiff Bus	AEF819A	Bridgend Bus	BDE140V	Silcox
2358DD	First Cymru	A152HLV	Cardiff Bus	AEF868A	Pied Bull Coaches	BDE143V	Silcox
2375RU	Shuttle	A154HLV	Cardiff Bus	AEF878A	Thomas Bros	BDE792V	Jones Login
2378VT	Vale of Llangollen	A156HLV	Cardiff Bus	AEF991Y	Thomas Bros	BEP969V	K M P
2405DD	First Cymru	A158HLV	Cardiff Bus	AEY365	Jones Llanfaethlu	BEP973V	Thomas Rhondda
3338DD	First Cymru	A159HLV	Cardiff Bus	AFY180X	Edwards Coaches	BEP976V	First Cymru
3377VC	Voel Coaches	A160HLV	Cardiff Bus	AGM450L	Newport Transport	BEP978V	First Cymru
3432RE	Edwards Bros	A161HLV	Cardiff Bus	AHU512V	Eagles & Crawford	BEP980V	First Cymru
3475DD	First Cymru	A162HLV	Cardiff Bus	AJA144B	Arriva Cymru	BEP981V	First Cymru
3587VT	Vale of Llangollen	A163HLV	Cardiff Bus	AKG197A	Tanat Valley	BEP984V	First Cymru
3810VT	Vale of Llangollen	A227MDD	Stagecoach R&W	AKG219A	First Cymru	BEY7W	Alpine
4384VT	Vale of Llangollen	A228LRU	Edwards Coaches	AKK174T	G M	BFJ209T	Clynnog & Trefor
4858DW	Gwyn Williams	A233GNR	Bysiau cwm Taf	AKK176T	Mansel David	BKE850T	Clynnog & Trefor
5182PO	P & O Lloyd	A260VWN	Cerbydau Cenarth	ANA182Y	First Cymru	BLZ3144	Ken Hopkins
5210DD	First Cymru	A279ROW	GHA Coaches	ANA189Y	First Cymru	BMA520W	Alpine
5373PO	P & O Lloyd	A302XWF	Jones Llanfaethlu	ANA582Y	Diamond Glantawe	BMA521W	Eagles & Crawford
5519DD	First Cymru	A345VEP	Jones Llanfaethlu	ANA589Y	Diamond Glantawe	BMA522W	Arriva Cymru
5583HA	Williams	A428VNY	Cardiff Bus	ANA596Y	Diamond Glantawe	BNT667T	Bryn Melyn
5652MT	Gwyn Williams	A429VNY	Cardiff Bus	ANA604Y	Diamond Glantawe	BPA342K	Edwards Coaches
5958VT	Vale of Llangollen	A430VNY	Cardiff Bus	ANA608Y	Brian Isaac	BPT927S	Alpine
6052VT	Vale of Llangollen	A431VNY	Cardiff Bus	ANA624Y	First Cymru	BPT928S	Alpine
6400VT	Vale of Llangollen	A432VNY	Cardiff Bus	ANA630Y	First Cymru	BRC140T	Tanat Valley
6468VT	Vale of Llangollen	A433VNY	Cardiff Bus	ANA651Y	Brian Isaac	BRC679T	Thomas Rhondda
6499VC	Voel Coaches	A434VNY	Cardiff Bus	ANA653Y	Brian Isaac	BRC838T	Alpine
6654HA	Williams	A435VNY	Cardiff Bus	APM116T	Mansel David	BRC840T	Alpine
6689DP	GHA Coaches	A436VNY	Cardiff Bus	APT807W	Jones Llanfaethlu	BTU364S	GHA Coaches
6690DD	First Cymru	A447PFO	Bridgend Bus	APT818W	Jones Llanfaethlu	BTV651T	Edwards Coaches
6709PO	P & O Lloyd	A476NJK	Tanat Valley	APT820W	GHA Coaches	BTV653T	Thomas Rhondda
6738UN	James Brothers	A482GFF	Lewy y Llan	ARC643T	Thomas Rhondda	BTX204T	Tanat Valley
7052VT	Vale of Llangollen	A511LPP	Browns of Builth	ATA556L	Ellis Travel	BUH238V	Pencoed Travel

Registration	Operator	Registration	Operator	Registration	Operator	Registration	Operator	Registration	Operator
BVJ771V	Lewis y Llan	CWG692V	Watts	DFB680W	Coastal Continental	E304VEP	First Cymru		
BVR87T	Ferris Holidays	CWR506Y	Arriva Cymru	DIW3778	Williams Bala	E305VEP	First Cymru		
BWJ68T	GHA Coaches	CWR507Y	Arriva Cymru	DJN25X	Arriva Cymru	E306VEP	First Cymru		
BXI637	Gwyn Williams	CWR508Y	Arriva Cymru	DKG321V	Watts	E316ACC	Nefyn Coaches		
C7EJS	E Jones & Sons	CWR509Y	Arriva Cymru	DTT496T	Richards Bros	E316HLO	Stagecoach R&W		
C23MAK	Mid Wales	CWR510Y	Arriva Cymru	DWY148T	Alpine	E321OPR	Lewis Whitland		
C41GKG	I B T	CWR512Y	Arriva Cymru	E36RBO	Richards Bros	E321TTX	Edwards Coaches		
C42GKG	I B T	CWR513Y	Arriva Cymru	E37EVW	Arriva Cymru	E329EVH	Browns of Builth		
C43GKG	I B T	CWR522Y	Arriva Cymru	E41MMT	East End	E330OMG	James Brothers		
C86NNV	Tanat Valley	CWR523Y	Arriva Cymru	E42HLP	Watts	E333MDE	Edwards Bros		
C124LHS	Jones Llanfaethlu	CWR527Y	Arriva Cymru	E45RDW	Lewis y Llan	E333NBX	Gwyn Williams		
C135SPB	East End	CWU151T	Thomas Rhondda	E45UKL	Arriva Cymru	E348UOH	Longs		
C195WJT	I B T	CYJ492Y	Stagecoach R&W	E49WEM	Arriva Cymru	E380MPX	Watts		
C207HTH	First Cymru	D28KKP	Arriva Cymru	E51TYG	Wilkins Travel	E442YAO	Midway Motors		
C208GTU	Arriva Cymru	D34PAX	Stagecoach R&W	E53MMT	Watts	E448AFT	GHA Coaches		
C209GTU	Arriva Cymru	D38TKA	Tanat Valley	E62WDT	Stagecoach R&W	E533UEJ	Summerdale		
C210GTU	Arriva Cymru	D44MBO	I B T	E63WDT	Stagecoach R&W	E566JFR	Express Motors		
C211GTU	Arriva Cymru	D46MBO	I B T	E87KGV	Stagecoach R&W	E591NBX	Gwyn Williams		
C212GTU	Arriva Cymru	D71ASX	Tanat Valley	E98DMA	D Jones & Son	E596NBX	Gwyn Williams		
C220EKJ	Arriva Cymru	D82VCC	Arriva Cymru	E98LLP	Hawkes	E601NBX	Gwyn Williams		
C221EKJ	Arriva Cymru	D90ALX	Cross Gates	E102DJR	Nefyn Coaches	E628WWD	Silcox		
C257UAJ	Arriva Cymru	D92VCC	Bryn Melyn	E103JNH	Arvonia	E634YWL	Gwyn Williams		
C258UAJ	Arriva Cymru	D109NDW	Stagecoach R&W	E113RBO	Stagecoach R&W	E642VFY	Arriva Cymru		
C280VFP	Watts	D114DRV	Clynnog & Trefor	E114SDW	Stagecoach R&W	E657RVP	Express Motors		
C284AOR	Pied Bull Coaches	D119NUS	Williams	E115SDW	Stagecoach R&W	E669ECJ	Gwyn Williams		
C285EHU	Hawkes	D129VRP	Mid Wales	E118MHN	Eagles & Crawford	E672WWD	Silcox		
C312KTH	First Cymru	D132WCC	Howells	E125ODE	Stagecoach R&W	E673WWD	Silcox		
C315DVU	Pied Bull Coaches	D140HML	Mid Wales	E126AAL	John's Travel	E695UNE	Mid Wales		
C324LDT	D & G Coaches	D141NON	Longs	E129RDW	Bridgend Bus	E700YNS	Eagles & Crawford		
C327PEW	Express Motors	D146KDE	Silcox	E133ODE	Silcox	E712UHB	Owens Motors		
C327UFP	Shamrock	D150RAK	Tanat Valley	E133YUD	Browns of Builth	E716BDM	Bysiau cwm Taf		
C331MLG	Shamrock	D154VRP	Arriva Cymru	E134YUD	Browns of Builth	E737EVJ	Browns of Builth		
C353SVV	Jones Llanfaethlu	D166VRP	Jones Llanfaethlu	E137ODE	Silcox	E753JAY	James Brothers		
C406WCJ	Mansel David	D177VRP	Mid Wales	E138ODE	Silcox	E756HJF	Eagles & Crawford		
C420WCJ	Mansel David	D204FBK	Hawkes	E139ODE	Silcox	E762HJF	Mansel David		
C446HLG	Tanat Valley	D219SKD	D & G Coaches	E141ODE	Silcox	E788MDE	Richards Bros		
C469BHY	Bridgend Bus	D228VCD	Clynnog & Trefor	E144ODE	Silcox	E795CCA	Williams Bala		
C472LKU	E Jones & Sons	D244VNL	John's Travel	E145ODE	Silcox	E807FRY	Shamrock		
C488JCY	Mansel David	D257WEY	Alpine	E147TBO	Browns of Builth	E807WEP	Gwyn Williams		
C499FAX	Henley's	D257YBB	Tanat Valley	E148VGG	Tanat Valley	E830ATT	Cardiff Bus		
C566GWO	Cardiff Bus	D272MDB	Berwyn	E149ODE	Silcox	E858GNR	Townlynx		
C598HTX	Edwards Coaches	D317UTU	Henley's	E149TBO	Browns of Builth	E885MYP	Edwards Bros		
C659HTX	Howells	D319DEF	Tanat Valley	E151AGG	Berwyn	E940THB	Hawkes		
C736FFJ	Williams Bala	D338PGO	Ken Hopkins	E169XJO	Townlynx	ECS875V	Howells		
C745TJF	James Brothers	D353JUM	Townlynx	E183ODE	Silcox	ECS884V	Alpine		
C768MVH	Wilkins Travel	D372UVL	James Brothers	E185UKG	Cross Gates	ECT912	Jones Llanfaethlu		
C810GFM	Henley's	D387SGS	Gwyn Williams	E192UKG	Bridgend Bus	ECY988V	First Cymru		
C818FMC	Ken Hopkins	D409TFT	Gwyn Williams	E194ODE	Silcox	ECY989V	First Cymru		
C830XCJ	Phillips	D421FEH	Tanat Valley	E206BOD	First Cymru	ECY990V	First Cymru		
C881KAV	Howells	D441BCJ	Browns of Builth	E209KCK	Hawkes	EDT917V	K M P		
C882KAV	Howells	D443UHC	Arriva Cymru	E210HRY	Hawkes	EGR704S	Williams Bala		
C901FCY	First Cymru	D44AVJ	Richards Bros	E215FLD	Cross Gates	EHW288W	Wilkins Travel		
C902FCY	First Cymru	D458CKV	Gwyn Williams	E217FLD	Cross Gates	EJR123W	Howells		
C903FCY	First Cymru	D498RNM	Townlynx	E222WMB	Williams	EKA228Y	Express Motors		
C904FCY	First Cymru	D509MJA	Llithfaen Motors	E226VOH	Bridgend Bus	ENY26V	Gwyn Williams		
C905FCY	First Cymru	D509OTA	Burrows	E227FLD	Jones Llanfaethlu	EPH215V	Pencoed Travel		
C906FCY	First Cymru	D523GBX	Browns of Builth	E233FLD	Jones Llanfaethlu	ERU390V	Arthur Thomas		
C907FCY	First Cymru	D568EWS	Mansel David	E238MBX	Richards Bros	ERW265T	Watts		
C926PFL	Howells	D574EWS	Gavenny Bus	E246RBE	Eagles & Crawford	ESU294	Clynnog & Trefor		
C934VLB	Jones Llanfaethlu	D576DPM	Silcox	E256TUB	Arriva Cymru	ETH176V	Hawkes		
C944LOJ	Cerbydau Cenarth	D577DPM	Silcox	E258TUB	Arriva Cymru	EWE206V	GHA Coaches		
C958LWJ	Tanat Valley	D578DPM	Silcox	E262REP	Browns of Builth	EWM630Y	Shuttle		
C960LWJ	Tanat Valley	D583EWS	Gavenny Bus	E262TUB	Arriva Cymru	EWN992W	First Cymru		
CBV118S	Thomas Rhondda	D603MKH	Silcox	E267BRG	John's Travel	EWN994W	First Cymru		
CBV119S	Thomas Rhondda	D631BPL	Thomas Bros	E272BRG	John's Travel	EWN995W	First Cymru		
CBV123S	Thomas Rhondda	D640NOE	Bridgend Bus	E274NVN	Hawkes	EWR656Y	Stagecoach R&W		
CCC596	Alpine	D642DRT	George Edwards	E278HDL	Clynnog & Trefor	EWS744W	First Cymru		
CEF230Y	Arriva Cymru	D683NCV	Browns of Builth	E279TTH	First Cymru	EWT207Y	Phil Anslow		
CEF232Y	Arriva Cymru	D68VDV	Berwyn	E280HDL	Clynnog & Trefor	EWT209Y	Phil Anslow		
CEJ939Y	Llithfaen Motors	D734LAX	Tanat Valley	E280TTH	First Cymru	EWV515	Berwyn		
CIB347	Tanat Valley	D858FCJ	Browns of Builth	E281TTH	First Cymru	EWW945Y	First Cymru		
CIB7866	GHA Coaches	D860LND	Tanat Valley	E282TTH	First Cymru	EWX213Y	Phillips		
CJH117V	Clynnog & Trefor	D879UFJ	Bridgend Bus	E287UCY	First Cymru	EWX215Y	Phil Anslow		
CJJ679W	Clynnog & Trefor	D914BFO	Browns of Builth	E289VEP	First Cymru	EWX531Y	Arriva Cymru		
CKC928X	Shuttle	D929NDB	Gavenny Bus	E290VEP	First Cymru	EXI1726	Express Motors		
CKM137Y	Alpine	D948UDY	GHA Coaches	E291VEP	First Cymru	EXI790	Express Motors		
CLZ4965	Ken Hopkins	D955UDY	Jones Llanfaethlu	E292VEP	First Cymru	EYP30V	Hawkes		
CNH602T	Clynnog & Trefor	D958WJH	Gwyn Williams	E293VEP	First Cymru	F21TMP	James Brothers		
CNP316B	Jones Llanfaethlu	D967NCY	Hawkes	E294VEP	First Cymru	F24CWO	Merlynls		
CPT737S	Alpine	D969PJA	Gavenny Bus	E295VEP	First Cymru	F41YHB	Newport Transport		
CRL918V	Owens Motors	D983OEJ	Richards Bros	E296VEP	First Cymru	F42DJC	Alpine		
CRW510T	Williams	D985ARE	Shamrock	E297VEP	First Cymru	F42YHB	Newport Transport		
CTX382X	Bridgend Bus	DAY1T	Express Motors	E298VEP	First Cymru	F43DJC	Alpine		
CTX384V	Longs	DBV42W	Sixty-Sixty	E299VEP	First Cymru	F43YHB	Newport Transport		
CTX386V	Longs	DBX548W	Sixty-Sixty	E300VEP	First Cymru	F44YHB	Newport Transport		
CTX391V	Coastal Continental	DCA525X	GHA Coaches	E301VEP	First Cymru	F45YHB	Newport Transport		
CTX392X	Bridgend Bus	DCA528	Eagles & Crawford	E302BWL	Bysiau cwm Taf	F46GNS	I B T		
CTX393X	Bridgend Bus	DEM821Y	Arriva Cymru	E302VEP	First Cymru	F46YHB	Newport Transport		
CTX395X	Bridgend Bus	DEM821Y	Cardiff Bus	E303VEP	First Cymru	F62AVV	Alpine		
CUP759V	Coastal Continental	DEM822Y	Cardiff Bus	E304BWL	Cerbydau Carreglefn	F62XRP	Berwyn		

Reg	Operator	Reg	Operator	Reg	Operator	Reg	Operator
F66FKW	Arriva Cymru	F321AWN	First Cymru	F852LHS	I B T	G113PGT	Arriva Cymru
F68LNU	Shuttle	F322AWN	First Cymru	F854YJX	Pullman Coaches	G115PGT	Gwyn Williams
F70LAL	GHA Coaches	F322EJO	Shuttle	F866PAC	Clynnog & Trefor	G116JBO	Berwyn
F74DCW	Stagecoach R&W	F323DCY	First Cymru	F876RDE	Richards Bros	G117OGA	Express Motors
F94KDS	I B T	F324DCY	First Cymru	F898LCJ	Mansel David	G119PGT	Richards Bros
F99CEP	First Cymru	F325DCY	First Cymru	F916TTP	Alpine	G120TJA	Arriva Cymru
F100CEP	First Cymru	F326DCY	First Cymru	F918YWY	Shamrock	G121GOJ	Ellis Travel
F107NRT	GHA Coaches	F327DCY	First Cymru	F921MTM	Shuttle	G121KUB	Pullman Coaches
F107YWO	John's Travel	F329FCY	First Cymru	F924YWY	Pullman Coaches	G134CLF	Jones Llanfaethlu
F112AHB	Bridgend Bus	F330FCY	First Cymru	F947CUA	Jones Llanfaethlu	G142JCC	Alpine
F113AHB	Bridgend Bus	F331FCY	First Cymru	F951BMS	Shuttle	G151FJC	Arriva Cymru
F114YVP	Berwyn	F332FCY	First Cymru	F961XWM	Bridgend Bus	G152FJC	Arriva Cymru
F117YVP	Merlyn's	F333FCY	First Cymru	F962XWM	Bridgend Bus	G160YRE	Arriva Cymru
F130YVP	Shuttle	F334FCY	First Cymru	F963XWM	Bridgend Bus	G161YRE	Arriva Cymru
F131YVP	Shuttle	F334FWW	Richards Bros	F964XWM	Bridgend Bus	G162YRE	Arriva Cymru
F133UDE	Richards Bros	F335FCY	First Cymru	F982EDS	Shuttle	G163YRE	Arriva Cymru
F134DEP	First Cymru	F336FCY	First Cymru	F991UME	Arriva Cymru	G165XJF	Tanat Valley
F135DEP	First Cymru	F337FCY	First Cymru	F995DRN	GHA Coaches	G166HWO	Cardiff Bus
F136LJO	Richards Bros	F338FCY	First Cymru	FAA356W	Clynnog & Trefor	G167HWO	Cardiff Bus
F137LJO	Richards Bros	F338XOV	John's Travel	FBV490W	Edwards Coaches	G169FJC	Arriva Cymru
F138LJO	Richards Bros	F339FCY	First Cymru	FBV499W	Edwards Coaches	G170FJC	Arriva Cymru
F149TEU	Watts	F340FCY	First Cymru	FBV509W	Express Motors	G171FJC	Arriva Cymru
F150TRY	Shuttle	F341FCY	First Cymru	FBV511W	Express Motors	G172FJC	Arriva Cymru
F152AWO	Llynfi Coaches	F342FCY	First Cymru	FBX560W	Llithfaen Motors	G173FJC	Arriva Cymru
F153AWO	Llynfi Coaches	F343FCY	First Cymru	FBZ1473	M & H Travel	G174FJC	Arriva Cymru
F154AWO	Llynfi Coaches	F345ONO	Oare's	FBZ6060	Sixty-Sixty	G175FJC	Arriva Cymru
F155AWO	Llynfi Coaches	F349TSX	I B T	FCT703V	Williams	G176FJC	Arriva Cymru
F167SMT	Stagecoach R&W	F356TSX	Express Motors	FDE362T	Hawkes	G177FJC	Arriva Cymru
F168SMT	Stagecoach R&W	F360SPD	Brian Isaac	FDN583S	Thomas Rhondda	G183PAO	GHA Coaches
F171SMT	Stagecoach R&W	F360URU	Newport Transport	FEK1F	First Cymru	G194CLF	Jones Llanfaethlu
F201OPD	Bryn Melyn	F361SPD	Brian Isaac	FFI 11V	Edwards Coaches	G216EOA	Nefyn Coaches
F207EFK	Midway Motors	F368RPO	Ellis Travel	FFP200V	Midway Motors	G222EOA	Express Motors
F208EWN	Edwards Coaches	F383MUT	Edwards Bros	FFR168S	GHA Coaches	G229FJC	Arriva Cymru
F210DCC	Alpine	F392DHL	Stagecoach R&W	FFR172S	GHA Coaches	G230FJC	Arriva Cymru
F210DCC	Alpine	F405KOD	Cardiff Bus	FFW508T	Richards Bros	G232FJC	Arriva Cymru
F211DCC	Arriva Cymru	F407OSR	James Brothers	FIL3825	Oareis	G233EOA	Brian Isaac
F212DCC	Arriva Cymru	F408KOD	Cardiff Bus	FIL4135	Williams Bala	G233FJC	Arriva Cymru
F213DCC	Arriva Cymru	F424EJC	Arriva Cymru	FIL4161	Alpine	G234FJC	Arriva Cymru
F214DCC	Arriva Cymru	F425EJC	Arriva Cymru	FIL7131	First Cymru	G235FJC	Arriva Cymru
F215DCC	Arriva Cymru	F426EJC	Arriva Cymru	FIL7485	GHA Coaches	G236FJC	Arriva Cymru
F216DCC	Arriva Cymru	F426ENB	James Brothers	FIL8275	Phil Anslow	G237EOA	Brian Isaac
F217DCC	Arriva Cymru	F427EJC	Arriva Cymru	FJC239	Cerbydau Carreglefn	G237FJC	Arriva Cymru
F218DCC	Arriva Cymru	F427RRY	Shuttle	FRJ243D	Edwards Coaches	G238FJC	Arriva Cymru
F219DCC	Arriva Cymru	F428EJC	Arriva Cymru	FRP909T	Clynnog & Trefor	G239FJC	Arriva Cymru
F220DCC	Arriva Cymru	F428EMB	Bridgend Bus	FTU376T	Alpine	G240FJC	Arriva Cymru
F221DCC	Arriva Cymru	F428JRJ	Browns of Builth	FTU386T	Alpine	G241GCC	Arriva Cymru
F222DCC	Arriva Cymru	F463EAX	Gavenny Bus	FUA394Y	Watts	G242GCC	Arriva Cymru
F223DCC	Arriva Cymru	F480SBX	Longs	FUJ900V	Edwards Coaches	G243GCC	Arriva Cymru
F229FSU	First Cymru	F481WFA	Meyers	FVR264V	Voel Coaches	G249HUH	Cardiff Bus
F231CNY	Cardiff Bus	F482WFX	Richards Bros	FWA499V	Pencoed Travel	G250HUH	Cardiff Bus
F232CNY	Cardiff Bus	F483OCN	Williams	FWB494V	Williams Bala	G251HUH	Cardiff Bus
F233CNY	Cardiff Bus	F531NRD	Brian Isaac	FYA201T	Browns of Builth	G252HUH	Cardiff Bus
F234CNY	Cardiff Bus	F535NRD	Brian Isaac	FYJ994V	Gwyn Williams	G253HUH	Cardiff Bus
F235CNY	Cardiff Bus	F544JRO	John's Travel	G31TGW	Stagecoach R&W	G254HUH	Cardiff Bus
F236CNY	Cardiff Bus	F546EJA	First Cymru	G32PSR	Townlynx	G255HUH	Cardiff Bus
F237CNY	Cardiff Bus	F566ABV	Richards Bros	G34VME	Arriva Cymru	G256EHD	George Edwards
F238CNY	Cardiff Bus	F567ABV	Edwards Bros	G35VME	Arriva Cymru	G256HUH	Cardiff Bus
F239CNY	Cardiff Bus	F598BTG	Watts	G36VME	Arriva Cymru	G257HUH	Cardiff Bus
F240CNY	Cardiff Bus	F601AWN	First Cymru	G36VNV	Stagecoach R&W	G258EHD	Eagles & Crawford
F241CNY	Cardiff Bus	F602HEC	James Brothers	G38TGW	Stagecoach R&W	G258HUH	Cardiff Bus
F242CNY	Cardiff Bus	F603AWN	First Cymru	G38YHJ	Arriva Cymru	G259HUH	Cardiff Bus
F242OFP	Berwyn	F604AWN	First Cymru	G39TGW	Stagecoach R&W	G261EHD	George Edwards
F243CNY	Cardiff Bus	F606AWN	First Cymru	G39VME	Arriva Cymru	G278HDW	Pied Bull Coaches
F244CNY	Cardiff Bus	F607AWN	First Cymru	G39YHJ	Arriva Cymru	G278MWU	Howells
F245CNY	Cardiff Bus	F608AWN	First Cymru	G40HDW	Gavenny Bus	G279MWU	Howells
F246CNY	Cardiff Bus	F609XMS	Stagecoach R&W	G40PSR	Townlynx	G300LEP	Gwyn Williams
F247CNY	Cardiff Bus	F612RBX	First Cymru	G40TGW	Stagecoach R&W	G304YBX	First Cymru
F248CNY	Cardiff Bus	F614XMS	GHA Coaches	G40YHJ	Arriva Cymru	G307VNB	Browns of Builth
F262WSD	Stagecoach R&W	F618XWY	First Cymru	G41VME	Arriva Cymru	G311DPA	Arriva Cymru
F276AWW	Arriva Cymru	F651SRK	Howells	G46TGW	Glyn Williams	G312DPA	Arriva Cymru
F289AWW	Arriva Cymru	F671DBO	Shamrock	G47FKG	Newport Transport	G313DPA	Arriva Cymru
F290AWW	Arriva Cymru	F687UCR	Williams	G48FKG	Newport Transport	G314DPA	Arriva Cymru
F293AWW	Arriva Cymru	F700JNU	Williams	G49FKG	Newport Transport	G315DPA	Arriva Cymru
F300GNS	First Cymru	F701KMA	Arriva Cymru	G50FKG	Newport Transport	G316DPA	Arriva Cymru
F302MNK	Arriva Cymru	F702KMA	Arriva Cymru	G51FKG	Newport Transport	G324NNW	Arriva Cymru
F303MNK	Arriva Cymru	F704KMA	Arriva Cymru	G51OUB	First Cymru	G333LCP	James Brothers
F304AWW	Arriva Cymru	F704PAY	Williams	G52FKG	Newport Transport	G344GEP	First Cymru
F307AWN	First Cymru	F706PAY	Williams	G53KTX	Newport Transport	G345GEP	First Cymru
F308AWN	First Cymru	F712FDV	First Cymru	G54RTO	Watts	G346GEP	First Cymru
F309AWN	First Cymru	F713FDV	First Cymru	G55KTX	Newport Transport	G347GEP	First Cymru
F310AWN	First Cymru	F714FDV	Cardiff Bus	G56KTX	Newport Transport	G348JTH	First Cymru
F311AWN	First Cymru	F721FDV	First Cymru	G57KTX	Newport Transport	G349JTH	First Cymru
F312AWN	First Cymru	F723TLW	Berwyn	G58KTX	Newport Transport	G350JTH	First Cymru
F313AWN	First Cymru	F724FDV	GHA Coaches	G60RGG	Nefyn Coaches	G351JTH	First Cymru
F314AWN	First Cymru	F725USF	GHA Coaches	G76PKR	Arriva Cymru	G352JTH	First Cymru
F315AWN	First Cymru	F727FDV	First Cymru	G97KUB	Shamrock	G353JTH	First Cymru
F316AWN	First Cymru	F749FDV	First Cymru	G98SKR	Brian Isaac	G354JTH	First Cymru
F317AWN	First Cymru	F757GUS	Shuttle	G99PCK	Shuttle	G355JTH	First Cymru
F319AWN	First Cymru	F790GNA	James Brothers	G102KUB	Shamrock	G356JTH	First Cymru
F320AWN	First Cymru	F808TMD	D & G Coaches	G112PGT	Richards Bros	G357JTH	First Cymru

Reg	Operator	Reg	Operator	Reg	Operator	Reg	Operator
G358JTH	First Cymru	GIW2269	Gwyn Williams	H376OTH	First Cymru	HSD78V	Tanat Valley
G359JTH	First Cymru	GKE441Y	Cerbydau Cenarth	H377OTH	First Cymru	HSD84V	Tanat Valley
G360JTH	First Cymru	GMB382T	Express Motors	H378OTH	First Cymru	HSD87V	Tanat Valley
G361JTH	First Cymru	GMB392T	Alpine	H379OTH	First Cymru	HSU548	Clynnog & Trefor
G365JTH	First Cymru	GMB649T	Express Motors	H380OTH	First Cymru	HTG557K	Wilkins Travel
G366JTH	First Cymru	GMS305S	I B T	H381OTH	First Cymru	HUA606Y	First Cymru
G367MEP	First Cymru	GNT435V	Bryn Melyn	H382TTH	First Cymru	HUI4199	Oare's
G368MEP	First Cymru	GPA611V	Voel Coaches	H384XVJ	Williams	HUI4958	Ken Hopkins
G369MEP	First Cymru	GPA614V	Voel Coaches	H390GAV	Llynfi Coaches	HUI6060	Sixty-Sixty
G370MEP	First Cymru	GPA625V	Richards Bros	H399CJF	Browns of Builth	HUI8123	East End
G371MEP	First Cymru	GRF712V	Alpine	H401MRW	Stagecoach R&W	HUP763T	East End
G372MEP	First Cymru	GRY626N	Mansel David	H402MRW	Stagecoach R&W	HUP768T	Alpine
G373MEP	First Cymru	GSC630X	Ken Hopkins	H426KPA	I B T	HVC9V	Richards Bros
G416WFP	Edwards Coaches	GSC633X	Thomas Rhondda	H428KPD	I B T	IIL3481	I B T
G439GJC	Oare's	GSC634X	Thomas Rhondda	H429KPD	I B T	IIL6443	I B T
G464VPG	Mid Wales	GSC638X	Thomas Rhondda	H446YKH	Clynnog & Trefor	IIL6541	Ken Hopkins
G490RVR	Berwyn	GSC639X	Thomas Rhondda	H448YKH	Clynnog & Trefor	IIL7331	I B T
G511VYE	Glyn Williams	GSC640X	Ken Hopkins	H466LEY	Goodsir	IIL8518	Williams
G514VYE	Glyn Williams	GSC643X	Thomas Rhondda	H492OHB	Shamrock	IIL8521	Williams
G517VYE	Glyn Williams	GSC645X	Ken Hopkins	H493OHB	Shamrock	IIL9168	Arriva Cymru
G529FHB	Williams	GSC647X	Thomas Rhondda	H494OHB	Shamrock	IIL9169	Arriva Cymru
G554RVR	Berwyn	GSC651X	Thomas Rhondda	H544KSG	Berwyn	IUI2173	Merlyn's
G555HTH	Gwyn Williams	GSC652X	Thomas Rhondda	H557XNN	Meyers	J7BBC	Williams
G55RTO	Watts	GSC657X	Thomas Rhondda	H604UWR	Cerbydau Carreglefn	J8BBC	Williams
G577PRM	GHA Coaches	GSC659X	Thomas Rhondda	H681YGO	Silcox	J34UTG	M & H Travel
G584RNC	Shamrock	GSK676	Silcox	H687UHH	Shamrock	J40MCL	Merlyn's
G601KTX	Cardiff Bus	GSU368	Goodsir	H688UHH	Shamrock	J41GGB	Stagecoach R&W
G602KTX	Cardiff Bus	GSU388	First Cymru	H689UHH	Shamrock	J42GGB	Stagecoach R&W
G603KTX	Cardiff Bus	GSV494	Lewis Whitland	H689YGO	Silcox	J47UFL	Pullman Coaches
G604KTX	Cardiff Bus	GTG779W	Henley's	H690UHH	Bridgend Bus	J49SNY	Watts
G605KTX	Cardiff Bus	GTO300V	P & O Lloyd	H704FDE	Richards Bros	J64PDE	Richards Bros
G606KTX	Cardiff Bus	GUI6060	Sixty-Sixty	H713WGK	Howells	J96NJT	Newport Transport
G607KTX	Cardiff Bus	GVJ522X	James Brothers	H733HWK	Arriva Cymru	J97NJT	Newport Transport
G609JET	Express Motors	GWE617V	Shamrock	H736EDE	Silcox	J100OMP	Browns of Builth
G624GOL	Tanat Valley	GWE618V	Shamrock	H741TWB	Nefyn Coaches	J113LKO	Brian Isaac
G63SNN	First Cymru	GWO1L	Williams	H742TWB	Henley's	J114LKO	Brian Isaac
G652LYG	Tanat Valley	H2DWD	Williams	H743EDE	Silcox	J114NJT	Phil Anslow
G663SCJ	Williams	H9CCH	Jones Llanfaethlu	H754DTM	Shuttle	J115NJT	Phil Anslow
G684AAD	Edwards Bros	H14DWD	Williams	H754EDE	Silcox	J124AHH	GHA Coaches
G729WJU	Phillips	H16TBC	Thomas Bros	H768JDD	Tanat Valley	J145UCY	Llynfi Coaches
G732ETX	Cerbydau Cenarth	H20DBW	Gwyn Williams	H782GTA	First Cymru	J149UCY	Llynfi Coaches
G761HJC	Alpine	H26HRK	Summerdale	H787NUH	Shamrock	J176WAX	Cardiff Bus
G762HJC	Alpine	H28MJN	Arriva Cymru	H788GTA	First Cymru	J177WAX	Cardiff Bus
G767RVJ	Browns of Builth	H29MJN	Arriva Cymru	H788NUH	Shamrock	J178WAX	Cardiff Bus
G777WFC	Browns of Builth	H34PAJ	Arriva Cymru	H818RWJ	Thomas Rhondda	J179WAX	Cardiff Bus
G818UPX	Williams	H49NDU	Cardiff Bus	H825ERV	First Cymru	J180WAX	Cardiff Bus
G837LWR	Richards Bros	H59PNY	Newport Transport	H835DNE	Howells	J181WAX	Cardiff Bus
G841CLV	Bridgend Bus	H61PNY	Newport Transport	H852OWN	First Cymru	J182WAX	Cardiff Bus
G841PNW	First Cymru	H61WNN	First Cymru	H853OWN	First Cymru	J189BWJ	Longs
G844UDV	GHA Coaches	H62PNY	Newport Transport	H859NOC	Brian Isaac	J198PEY	Silver Star
G847VAY	Shamrock	H63PNY	Newport Transport	H881EBX	First Cymru	J221HDS	Arvonia
G869YBX	Cerbydau Cenarth	H64PNY	Newport Transport	H920OOJ	Browns of Builth	J248SOC	Berwyn
G908UPP	Hawkes	H78CFV	GHA Coaches	H930EBX	Gwyn Williams	J261UDW	Cardiff Bus
G913KWF	Clynnog & Trefor	H127YGG	Oare's	H931DRJ	Richards Bros	J262UDW	Cardiff Bus
G978KJX	Richards Bros	H130LPU	Arriva Cymru	H942DRJ	Mid Wales	J263UDW	Cardiff Bus
G991OKJ	Wilkins Travel	H149NOJ	Arriva Cymru	H943DRJ	Mid Wales	J264UDW	Cardiff Bus
GBX484W	Jones Login	H158HDE	Richards Bros	H964LEY	Jones Llanfaethlu	J265UDW	Cardiff Bus
GCC572	Cerbydau Carreglefn	H160NBF	Williams	H965VWF	Summerdale	J266UDW	Cardiff Bus
GDE148X	Jones Login	H160PNY	Newport Transport	H990FTT	First Cymru	J267UDW	Cardiff Bus
GDE371W	First Cymru	H168DJU	Eagles & Crawford	H992FTT	First Cymru	J268UDW	Cardiff Bus
GDZ3841	Silver Star	H168OTG	Longs	H993FTT	First Cymru	J269UDW	Cardiff Bus
GDZ886	Gwyn Williams	H169OTG	Browns of Builth	H994FTT	First Cymru	J270UDW	Cardiff Bus
GEK12V	Thomas Rhondda	H170OTG	Longs	H995FTT	First Cymru	J271UDW	Cardiff Bus
GEK14V	Thomas Rhondda	H171OTG	Cardiff Bus	H996FTT	First Cymru	J272UWO	Cardiff Bus
GEK15V	Thomas Rhondda	H172GTA	First Cymru	HBD166N	East End	J273UWO	Cardiff Bus
GEK16V	Thomas Rhondda	H172RBO	Cardiff Bus	HBD919T	GHA Coaches	J274UWO	Cardiff Bus
GEY371	Cerbydau Carreglefn	H173GTA	First Cymru	HBX971X	Richards Bros	J275UWO	Cardiff Bus
GEY389Y	Arriva Cymru	H173RBO	Cardiff Bus	HDL410N	East End	J276UWO	Cardiff Bus
GFO775X	Williams	H174GTA	First Cymru	HEN867N	Alpine	J277UWO	Cardiff Bus
GGM110W	Bryn Melyn	H174RBO	Cardiff Bus	HEU350	Williams	J278UWO	Cardiff Bus
GHC521N	Edwards Coaches	H175ANE	Oare's	HFM962T	Voel Coaches	J279UWO	Cardiff Bus
GHV48N	Howells	H175GTA	First Cymru	HFX422V	Thomas Rhondda	J281UWO	Cardiff Bus
GIL2339	Longs	H175RBO	Cardiff Bus	HHH371V	Glyn Williams	J282UWO	Cardiff Bus
GIL2987	Longs	H177GTA	First Cymru	HIL5659	M & H Travel	J284UWO	Cardiff Bus
GIL3127	Edwards Coaches	H178GTA	First Cymru	HIL5698	Oare's	J285UWO	Cardiff Bus
GIL3217	Longs	H179EJU	Mid Wales	HIL7540	Pencoed Travel	J286UWO	Cardiff Bus
GIL3276	Midway Motors	H179GTA	First Cymru	HIL7542	Pencoed Travel	J291RNE	James Brothers
GIL4128	Longs	H185EJF	Watts	HIL7592	Arriva Cymru	J292TTX	Edwards Coaches
GIL4450	Longs	H202CRH	Bryn Melyn	HIL7593	Arriva Cymru	J296NNB	Arriva Cymru
GIL4527	Longs	H220GKK	Thomas Rhondda	HIL7642	Oare's	J297NNB	Arriva Cymru
GIL5102	Longs	H227GDE	Silcox	HIL8914	Diamond Glantawe	J305UKG	Stagecoach R&W
GIL5103	Longs	H254PAJ	Arriva Cymru	HJB460W	Alpine	J306UKG	Stagecoach R&W
GIL5149	Longs	H272LJC	Lewis y Llan	HJB462W	Gwyn Williams	J307UKG	Stagecoach R&W
GIL6240	Hawkes	H273LJC	Lewis y Llan	HJB463W	Alpine	J375WWK	First Cymru
GIL6241	Hawkes	H326DTR	First Cymru	HJI548	Brian Isaac	J378MBX	Merlyn's
GIL6324	Longs	H332FEJ	Richards Bros	HJI2859	Brian Isaac	J387ODE	Silcox
GIL7045	Longs	H366NCY	Llynfi Coaches	HJP479V	Hawkes	J400CCH	Diamond Glantawe
GIL7827	Longs	H368NDW	Shamrock	HMA564T	K M P	J408PRW	Stagecoach R&W
GIL8494	Pencoed Travel	H374OTH	First Cymru	HPB674N	Richards Bros	J414PRW	Stagecoach R&W
GIL9220	Longs	H375OTH	First Cymru	HRP674N	Ellis Travel	J447UUK	Mid Wales

Reg	Operator	Reg	Operator	Reg	Operator	Reg	Operator
J454JRH	Stagecoach R&W	K107YTX	Newport Transport	KFM191T	P & O Lloyd	L234BUT	Lewis Whitland
J500CCH	Diamond Glantawe	K108YTX	Newport Transport	KIB1767	I B T	L270EHB	Stagecoach R&W
J580VTH	First Cymru	K109YTX	Newport Transport	KIW3766	Wilkins Travel	L287ETG	Cardiff Bus
J581VTH	First Cymru	K115TCP	Ferris Holidays	KMA395T	Alpine	L288ETG	Cardiff Bus
J582VTH	First Cymru	K155CRE	Arriva Cymru	KMA396T	Alpine	L289ETG	Cardiff Bus
J587SOG	Gavenny Bus	K156BRF	Arriva Cymru	KMA397T	Alpine	L290ETG	Cardiff Bus
J608VDW	Cardiff Bus	K157BRF	Arriva Cymru	KPJ249W	P & O Lloyd	L291ETG	Cardiff Bus
J609VDW	Cardiff Bus	K183YDW	Cardiff Bus	KPJ251W	P & O Lloyd	L292ETG	Cardiff Bus
J610VDW	Cardiff Bus	K184YDW	Cardiff Bus	KPJ280W	P & O Lloyd	L293ETG	Cardiff Bus
J654UHN	Arriva Cymru	K185YDW	Cardiff Bus	KRN107T	Tanat Valley	L326CHB	Stagecoach R&W
J655UHN	Arriva Cymru	K186YDW	Cardiff Bus	KRN111T	Tanat Valley	L327CHB	Stagecoach R&W
J781KHD	Pullman Coaches	K187YDW	Cardiff Bus	KSD108W	Ferris Holidays	L328CHB	Stagecoach R&W
J782KHD	Pullman Coaches	K197XEL	Phil Anslow	KSD113W	Ferris Holidays	L329CHB	Stagecoach R&W
J792KHD	Pullman Coaches	K205OHS	Phil Anslow	KSU409	Silcox	L331CHB	Stagecoach R&W
J854PUD	D Jones & Son	K206OHS	Phil Anslow	KSV361	Clynnog & Trefor	L334DTG	Thomas Rhondda
J886PNC	Brian Isaac	K309YKG	Stagecoach R&W	KUB550V	Express Motors	L334FWO	Stagecoach R&W
J901MAF	First Cymru	K310YKG	Stagecoach R&W	KUC144P	Howells	L335FWO	Stagecoach R&W
J912PEY	Bryn Melyn	K312YKG	Stagecoach R&W	KUC237P	Howells	L336FWO	Stagecoach R&W
J916WVC	First Cymru	K313YKG	Stagecoach R&W	KUI1350	Ken Hopkins	L337DTG	Thomas Rhondda
J918HGD	Cerbydau Cenarth	K314YKG	Stagecoach R&W	KUI1371	Bysiau cwm Taf	L337FWO	Stagecoach R&W
J986UCY	Longs	K315YKG	Stagecoach R&W	KUI1372	Bysiau Ffoshelig	L338FWO	Stagecoach R&W
JAK211W	East End	K316YKG	Stagecoach R&W	KUX221W	Alpine	L339FWO	Stagecoach R&W
JAZ9864	Alpine	K317YKG	Stagecoach R&W	KUY442X	Bysiau Ffoshelig	L340FWO	Stagecoach R&W
JBD972Y	Edwards Coaches	K319YKG	Stagecoach R&W	KWB695W	Wilkins Travel	L341FWO	Stagecoach R&W
JBZ4492	Cerbydau Cenarth	K320FYG	Stagecoach R&W	KYU88X	Berwyn	L342FWO	Stagecoach R&W
JBZ6925	Henley's	K320YKG	Stagecoach R&W	KYV452X	Gwyn Williams	L343FWO	Stagecoach R&W
JBZ6926	Mansel David	K321YKG	Stagecoach R&W	KYV542X	Stagecoach R&W	L361ANR	Shamrock
JBZ8645	Sixty-Sixty	K322YKG	Stagecoach R&W	L2ARV	Arvonia	L362ANR	Shamrock
JC2772	Alpine	K323YKG	Stagecoach R&W	L4USE	I B T	L364GTH	First Cymru
JC9736	Voel Coaches	K324YKG	Stagecoach R&W	L6BMS	First Cymru	L370XBX	Shamrock
JDZ2359	Stagecoach R&W	K325YKG	Stagecoach R&W	L8BMS	First Cymru	L380PAS	Meyers
JEU803X	Midway Motors	K331YDW	Thomas Rhondda	L14BMS	First Cymru	L407XMR	George Edwards
JEY554Y	Alpine	K336RCN	Phil Anslow	L35OKV	Arriva Cymru	L414SFL	Stagecoach R&W
JIL2037	Eagles & Crawford	K337RCN	Phil Anslow	L36OKV	Arriva Cymru	L417OYB	Williams
JIL2284	Porthcawl Omnibus	K355NWM	Cerbydau Cenarth	L37OKV	Arriva Cymru	L421CPB	Arriva Cymru
JIL2433	Bysiau Ffoshelig	K365TJF	Shamrock	L38DBC	Shamrock	L422CPB	Arriva Cymru
JIL3253	Sixty-Sixty	K366TJF	Shamrock	L38OKV	Arriva Cymru	L423CPB	Arriva Cymru
JIL6904	Mansel David	K367TJF	D Jones & Son	L51CNY	Phil Anslow	L425CPB	Arriva Cymru
JIL7167	Edwards Coaches	K401BAX	First Cymru	L65ORB	M & H Travel	L427CPB	Arriva Cymru
JIL7652	Ken Hopkins	K402BAX	First Cymru	L68EKG	Newport Transport	L428CPC	Arriva Cymru
JKO63N	Richards Bros	K402EDT	Stagecoach R&W	L69EKG	Newport Transport	L438FPA	Arriva Cymru
JKO64N	Richards Bros	K403BAX	First Cymru	L71EKG	Newport Transport	L439FPA	Arriva Cymru
JMB404T	Clynnog & Trefor	K404BAX	First Cymru	L73EKG	Newport Transport	L439XFE	Thomas Bros
JMB406T	Alpine	K405BAX	First Cymru	L77KMP	K M P	L446XFE	Thomas Bros
JNJ365V	Hawkes	K406BAX	First Cymru	L79CWO	Stagecoach R&W	L454XFE	Thomas Bros
JPL105K	Alpine	K407BAX	First Cymru	L81CWO	Stagecoach R&W	L466THY	Williams
JSA103V	I B T	K408BAX	First Cymru	L82CWO	Stagecoach R&W	L466XNR	Shamrock
JSA104V	I B T	K409BAX	First Cymru	L83CWO	Stagecoach R&W	L467XNR	Shamrock
JSJ426W	Hawkes	K410BAX	First Cymru	L84CWO	Stagecoach R&W	L469APJ	Summerdale
JTD390P	Arriva Cymru	K451VAY	Shamrock	L85CWO	Stagecoach R&W	L485XDE	Richards Bros
JTD395P	Arriva Cymru	K461VVR	Thomas Bros	L86CWO	Stagecoach R&W	L495XNR	Bryn Melyn
JTL804V	Arriva Cymru	K530RJX	Richards Bros	L87CWO	Stagecoach R&W	L500BWN	Brian Isaac
JIM114V	Richards Bros	K542OGA	Arriva Cymru	L89CWO	Stagecoach R&W	L501HCY	First Cymru
JTU596T	K M P	K586MHY	Shamrock	L92GAX	Ferris Holidays	L502HCY	First Cymru
JTU597T	Goodsir	K588MHY	Shamrock	L94GAX	Ferris Holidays	L500IICY	First Cymru
JUH228W	Merlynís	K589TRY	Shamrock	L101GBO	Cardiff Bus	L504HCY	First Cymru
JUH229W	Bysiau Ffoshelig	K590TRY	Shamrock	L102GBO	Cardiff Bus	L505HCY	First Cymru
JUI1720	Bysiau Ffoshelig	K649RDE	Jones Login	L103GBO	Cardiff Bus	L506GEP	First Cymru
JUI4435	Ken Hopkins	K650RDE	Jones Login	L104GBO	Cardiff Bus	L506HCY	First Cymru
JUX65V	Cross Gates	K651TDE	Silcox	L105GBO	Cardiff Bus	L507HCY	First Cymru
JVJ511Y	Browns of Builth	K659NGB	GHA Coaches	L105SDY	Stagecoach R&W	L508HCY	First Cymru
JWE247W	Brian Isaac	K701UTT	First Cymru	L106GBO	Cardiff Bus	L509HCY	First Cymru
JWE248W	Brian Isaac	K704UTT	First Cymru	L107SDY	Stagecoach R&W	L510HCY	First Cymru
JWU335J	Silver Star	K705UTT	First Cymru	L144BFV	Stagecoach R&W	L511HCY	First Cymru
JWW226N	Ellis Travel	K706UTT	First Cymru	L145BFV	Stagecoach R&W	L512HCY	First Cymru
JYG432V	Oare's	K707UTT	First Cymru	L149BFV	Stagecoach R&W	L513HCY	First Cymru
K3MCT	Merlyn's	K708UTT	First Cymru	L151BFV	Stagecoach R&W	L514HCY	First Cymru
K6BUS	D Jones & Son	K709UTT	First Cymru	L151FRJ	Arriva Cymru	L515HCY	First Cymru
K7KMP	K M P	K712UTT	First Cymru	L152FRJ	Arriva Cymru	L516HCY	First Cymru
K10BMS	First Cymru	K715UTT	First Cymru	L153BFV	Stagecoach R&W	L517HCY	First Cymru
K11BMS	First Cymru	K716UTT	First Cymru	L153FRJ	Arriva Cymru	L518HCY	First Cymru
K12BMS	First Cymru	K721UDE	Silcox	L154FRJ	Arriva Cymru	L519HCY	First Cymru
K27EWC	Arriva Cymru	K722UDE	Silcox	L170EKG	Newport Transport	L520HCY	First Cymru
K27GVC	James Brothers	K726DWN	Silcox	L172EKG	Newport Transport	L521HCY	First Cymru
K61BAX	Phil Anslow	K729CPY	Williams	L188DDW	Cardiff Bus	L522HCY	First Cymru
K75TBX	Brian Isaac	K744ECY	Longs	L189DDW	Cardiff Bus	L523HCY	First Cymru
K82BWN	First Cymru	K777GSM	Burrows	L190DDW	Cardiff Bus	L524HCY	First Cymru
K91BNY	Stagecoach R&W	K780UDE	Silcox	L191DDW	Cardiff Bus	L525JEP	First Cymru
K92BNY	Stagecoach R&W	K805SCC	Nefyn Coaches	L192DDW	Cardiff Bus	L526JEP	First Cymru
K93BNY	Stagecoach R&W	K902PLM	Cross Gates	L193DDW	Cardiff Bus	L527JEP	First Cymru
K94AAX	Stagecoach R&W	K928AEP	Shamrock	L194DDW	Cardiff Bus	L528JEP	First Cymru
K95AAX	Stagecoach R&W	K929AEP	Shamrock	L195DDW	Cardiff Bus	L529JEP	First Cymru
K96AAX	Stagecoach R&W	K981KGY	Arriva Cymru	L196DDW	Cardiff Bus	L530JEP	First Cymru
K97RGA	Phil Anslow	K982KGY	Arriva Cymru	L197DDW	Cardiff Bus	L531JEP	First Cymru
K97XNY	Stagecoach R&W	K983KGY	Arriva Cymru	L218AAB	First Cymru	L532JEP	First Cymru
K98XNY	Stagecoach R&W	KAD353V	Arthur Thomas	L219AAB	First Cymru	L533JEP	First Cymru
K104YTX	Newport Transport	KAZ6917	M & H Travel	L21RPX	Williams	L534JEP	First Cymru
K105YTX	Newport Transport	KBC1V	Porthcawl Omnibus	L220AAB	First Cymru	L535JEP	First Cymru
K106UFP	Cross Gates	KDL121W	Gwyn Williams	L220JAW	Owens Motors	L536JEP	First Cymru
K106YTX	Newport Transport	KEC976X	Wilkins Travel	L231BUT	Lewis Whitland	L536XNR	Shamrock

Reg	Operator	Reg	Operator	Reg	Operator	Reg	Operator
L537EHD	George Edwards	LIL9407	Edwards Coaches	M201RHB	Henley's	M750LAX	Stagecoach R&W
L537JEP	First Cymru	LIL9924	Bysiau Ffoshelig	M242JHB	Glyn Williams	M751LAX	Stagecoach R&W
L538JEP	First Cymru	LIL9971	Jones Login	M243JHB	Glyn Williams	M752LAX	Stagecoach R&W
L538XUT	First Cymru	LIL9972	Shamrock	M244JHB	Glyn Williams	M753LAX	Stagecoach R&W
L539JEP	First Cymru	LIL9973	Jones Login	M252CDE	First Cymru	M754LAX	Stagecoach R&W
L540JEP	First Cymru	LIL9974	Jones Login	M252KNR	Shamrock	M755LAX	Stagecoach R&W
L541JEP	First Cymru	LIL9975	Phil Anslow	M253CDE	First Cymru	M756LAX	Stagecoach R&W
L542JEP	First Cymru	LJA611P	Edwards Coaches	M254CDE	First Cymru	M757LAX	Stagecoach R&W
L543JEP	First Cymru	LJI6060	Sixty-Sixty	M255CDE	First Cymru	M758LAX	Stagecoach R&W
L544JEP	First Cymru	LJN648P	First Cymru	M256CDE	First Cymru	M759LAX	Stagecoach R&W
L544XUT	Ferris Holidays	LMS151W	Coastal Continental	M257CDE	First Cymru	M760LAX	Stagecoach R&W
L545JEP	First Cymru	LNV335	Porthcawl Omnibus	M258CDE	First Cymru	M761LAX	Stagecoach R&W
L546JEP	First Cymru	LOA418X	Vale of Llangollen	M259BGF	Williams	M762JCU	Oare's
L547JEP	First Cymru	LOI6690	First Cymru	M298XSF	Bysiau cwm Taf	M762LAX	Stagecoach R&W
L548JEP	First Cymru	LPJ323P	Bysiau cwm Taf	M303KRY	Ferris Holidays	M763LAX	Stagecoach R&W
L549JEP	First Cymru	LRB200W	Glyn Williams	M329RKG	Thomas Rhondda	M764LAX	Stagecoach R&W
L550JEP	First Cymru	LRB216W	Glyn Williams	M330JHB	Thomas Rhondda	M765RAX	Stagecoach R&W
L552XNR	Shamrock	LSU379V	First Cymru	M344JBO	Stagecoach R&W	M766RAX	Stagecoach R&W
L553XNR	Shamrock	LVO801W	Richards Bros	M346JBO	Stagecoach R&W	M767RAX	Stagecoach R&W
L584MBW	Thomas Bros	LVS433P	Richards Bros	M347JBO	Stagecoach R&W	M768RAX	Stagecoach R&W
L601FKG	First Cymru	LWG533W	Porthcawl Omnibus	M348JBO	Stagecoach R&W	M769RAX	Stagecoach R&W
L602FKG	First Cymru	LWN790X	Porthcawl Omnibus	M349JBO	Stagecoach R&W	M770RAX	Stagecoach R&W
L603FKG	First Cymru	M1GWT	Glyn Williams	M350JBO	Stagecoach R&W	M777GSM	Shuttle
L604FKG	First Cymru	M2ARV	Arvonia	M351JBO	Stagecoach R&W	M777KMP	K M P
L605FKG	First Cymru	M5JLW	Williams	M352JBO	Stagecoach R&W	M794MTH	Cross Gates
L606FKG	First Cymru	M7KMP	K M P	M353JBO	Stagecoach R&W	M798DDE	Richards Bros
L607FKG	First Cymru	M10CAE	Caelloi	M354JBO	Stagecoach R&W	M829PHN	Nefyn Coaches
L608FKG	First Cymru	M16SMC	Silcox	M355JBO	Stagecoach R&W	M846BTC	Williams
L638DNA	Arriva Cymru	M17SMC	Silcox	M356JBO	Stagecoach R&W	M847RCP	Arriva Cymru
L646DNA	Arriva Cymru	M18SMC	Silcox	M357JBO	Stagecoach R&W	M849RCP	Arriva Cymru
L701FWO	Stagecoach R&W	M28TWJ	Mid Wales	M358JBO	Stagecoach R&W	M851JHB	Shamrock
L702FWO	Stagecoach R&W	M31KUT	Shamrock	M359JBO	Stagecoach R&W	M852JHB	Shamrock
L703FWO	Stagecoach R&W	M36LHP	Brian Isaac	M361CDE	Silcox	M866LNY	Stagecoach R&W
L704FWO	Stagecoach R&W	M38LHP	Brian Isaac	M361LAX	Stagecoach R&W	M884WAK	Pullman Coaches
L705FWO	Stagecoach R&W	M64HHB	Stagecoach R&W	M362LAX	Stagecoach R&W	M892MDT	Ferris Holidays
L706FWO	Stagecoach R&W	M65HHB	Stagecoach R&W	M363LAX	Stagecoach R&W	M933JHB	Thomas Rhondda
L707FWO	Stagecoach R&W	M65KTG	Newport Transport	M364LAX	Stagecoach R&W	M940CDE	Edwards Bros
L708FWO	Stagecoach R&W	M67HHB	Stagecoach R&W	M365LAX	Stagecoach R&W	M940JBO	Stagecoach R&W
L715WCC	Arriva Cymru	M67KTG	Newport Transport	M366LAX	Stagecoach R&W	M941JBO	Stagecoach R&W
L716WCC	Arriva Cymru	M68HHB	Stagecoach R&W	M367LAX	Stagecoach R&W	M942JBO	Stagecoach R&W
L717WCC	Arriva Cymru	M69HHB	Stagecoach R&W	M368CDE	Silcox	M943JBO	Stagecoach R&W
L775GNM	Shamrock	M74KTG	Newport Transport	M368LAX	Stagecoach R&W	M943UDT	Arriva Cymru
L816HCY	First Cymru	M74NUJ	Tanat Valley	M369LAX	Stagecoach R&W	M944JBO	Stagecoach R&W
L817HCY	First Cymru	M75KTG	Newport Transport	M370LAX	Stagecoach R&W	M945JBO	Stagecoach R&W
L818HCY	First Cymru	M76KTG	Newport Transport	M371LAX	Stagecoach R&W	M945LYR	Arriva Cymru
L819HCY	First Cymru	M77KMP	K M P	M378BJC	Berwyn	M946JBO	Stagecoach R&W
L820HCY	First Cymru	M91JHB	Phil Anslow	M385KVR	Arriva Cymru	M947JBO	Stagecoach R&W
L821HCY	First Cymru	M92JHB	Phil Anslow	M392MWN	Diamond Glantawe	M948JBO	Stagecoach R&W
L822HCY	First Cymru	M93JHB	Phil Anslow	M394KVR	Arriva Cymru	M949JBO	Stagecoach R&W
L823HCY	First Cymru	M101CCD	Stagecoach R&W	M411BEY	Arriva Cymru	M951JBO	Stagecoach R&W
L824HCY	First Cymru	M102CCD	Stagecoach R&W	M412BEY	Arriva Cymru	M982KKG	Shamrock
L825HCY	First Cymru	M103CCD	Stagecoach R&W	M413BEY	Arriva Cymru	M983KKG	Shamrock
L839MWT	Stagecoach R&W	M104CCD	Stagecoach R&W	M425JNY	Shamrock	M984KKG	Shamrock
L840MWT	Stagecoach R&W	M105OCY	Diamond Glantawe	M426JNY	Shamrock	M985KKG	Shamrock
L844JCY	First Cymru	M107CCD	Stagecoach R&W	M455HPG	Arriva Cymru	M986KKG	Shamrock
L849MWX	Berwyn	M107JHB	Cardiff Bus	M456HPG	Arriva Cymru	M987KKG	Shamrock
L849THY	Thomas Bros	M107NEP	First Cymru	M457HPG	Arriva Cymru	M997CYS	First Cymru
L905FWP	Thomas Bros	M108JHB	Cardiff Bus	M457OOA	Williams	MAP340W	I B T
L906FWP	Thomas Bros	M108NEP	First Cymru	M458JPA	Arriva Cymru	MAP342W	Silver Star
L913NWW	Silver Star	M109JHB	Cardiff Bus	M459DDE	Jones Login	MAU615P	Lewis y Llan
L914UGA	Phil Anslow	M109PWN	First Cymru	M460DDE	Jones Login	MAX334X	Mid Wales
L924SCR	Jones Llanfaethlu	M110KBO	Cardiff Bus	M466MPM	Arriva Cymru	MBX447	Alpine
L927UGA	Phil Anslow	M110PWN	First Cymru	M467MPM	Arriva Cymru	MCA613P	Silver Star
L928UGA	Phil Anslow	M111PWN	First Cymru	M498DDE	Mansel David	MCA615P	Silver Star
L957JGSI	Shamrock	M112KBO	Cardiff Bus	M515ACC	Alpine	MCH351W	Cerbydau Carreglefn
L958HDH	Williams	M113KBO	Cardiff Bus	M536OJH	Mansel David	MCH352W	Richards Bros
L963NWW	E Jones & Sons	M114KBO	Cardiff Bus	M542JHB	Edwards Coaches	MCO253H	G M
L975CVD	Jones Login	M115KBO	Cardiff Bus	M562JTG	Stagecoach R&W	MCY85G	Wilkins Travel
LAL746P	Thomas Bros	M116KBO	Cardiff Bus	M568BVL	Mid Wales	MCY111X	Edwards Coaches
LAZ3830	Owens Motors	M117KBO	Cardiff Bus	M589CDE	Jones Login	MCY839X	Diamond Glantawe
LBZ2577	Brian Isaac	M118KBO	Cardiff Bus	M591CDE	Richards Bros	MDS691P	Express Motors
LCC542P	M & H Travel	M119KBO	Cardiff Bus	M625KKG	Stagecoach R&W	MEY395	Arriva Cymru
LCW367W	Williams Bala	M120KBO	Cardiff Bus	M637BEY	K M P	MFV30T	D & G Coaches
LDE547P	Richards Bros	M121KBO	Cardiff Bus	M647UCT	Bysiau cwm Taf	MFV34T	D & G Coaches
LFJ874W	Clynnog & Trefor	M122KBO	Cardiff Bus	M662UCT	Ferris Holidays	MFV34T	Henley's
LFR125T	Thomas Rhondda	M123KBO	Cardiff Bus	M674CDE	Silcox	MFV37T	Henley's
LFR126T	Thomas Rhondda	M124KBO	Cardiff Bus	M680DDE	Richards Bros	MHJ729V	Glyn Williams
LFR129T	Edwards Coaches	M125KBO	Cardiff Bus	M703HDF	Williams	MHJ732V	Glyn Williams
LFR862X	Arthur Thomas	M126KBO	Cardiff Bus	M710HBC	Shamrock	MHL98	Jones Llanfaethlu
LFR864X	Arthur Thomas	M127KBO	Cardiff Bus	M711HBC	Shamrock	MHL100	Jones Llanfaethlu
LHG445T	Ferris Holidays	M128KBO	Cardiff Bus	M711YJC	Arriva Cymru	MHX530P	Silcox
LHT729P	Coastal Continental	M129KBO	Cardiff Bus	M712YJC	Arriva Cymru	MIB284	G M
LIB1181	Ken Hopkins	M130KBO	Cardiff Bus	M713YJC	Arriva Cymru	MIB657	First Cymru
LIJ6832	Pied Bull Coaches	M131KBO	Cardiff Bus	M714YJC	Arriva Cymru	MIL2407	Edwards Coaches
LIL3934	I B T	M132KBO	Cardiff Bus	M720LTG	Edwards Coaches	MIL6317	Midway Motors
LIL5069	First Cymru	M133KBO	Cardiff Bus	M737JKG	Shamrock	MIL6782	Shamrock
LIL5070	First Cymru	M134SKY	Phil Anslow	M738JKG	Shamrock	MIL6783	Bridgend Bus
LIL5071	First Cymru	M135SKY	Phil Anslow	M740DDE	Richards Bros	MIL6897	Shamrock
LIL5845	I B T	M166KTG	Newport Transport	M742LTG	Thomas Rhondda	MIL7104	P & O Lloyd
LIL7332	Pencoed Travel	M197CDE	Richards Bros	M745KDD	Williams	MIL9466	G M

Reg	Operator	Reg	Operator	Reg	Operator	Reg	Operator
MJI6060	Sixty-Sixty	N372PNY	Stagecoach R&W	N990FWT	Pullman Coaches	NSV324	Silcox
MKH87A	GHA Coaches	N373PNY	Stagecoach R&W	N993CCC	Arriva Cymru	NUW606Y	Stagecoach R&W
MKH487A	First Cymru	N374PNY	Stagecoach R&W	N994CCC	Arriva Cymru	NUW619Y	Stagecoach R&W
MKH678A	Edwards Coaches	N375PNY	Stagecoach R&W	N995BWJ	Silver Star	NUW646Y	Stagecoach R&W
MKH690A	Edwards Coaches	N376PNY	Stagecoach R&W	N995CCC	Arriva Cymru	NUW651Y	Stagecoach R&W
MKH730A	Edwards Coaches	N377PNY	Stagecoach R&W	N996CCC	Arriva Cymru	NUW662Y	Stagecoach R&W
MKH824A	Edwards Coaches	N378PNY	Stagecoach R&W	N996KUS	Arriva Cymru	NUW665Y	Stagecoach R&W
MNC509W	Voel Coaches	N379PNY	Stagecoach R&W	N997CCC	Arriva Cymru	NWG990X	Mansel David
MNC525W	Voel Coaches	N380PNY	Stagecoach R&W	NAB848T	Williams	NWO731	Cerbydau Cenarth
MNM26V	Cerbydau Cenarth	N381PNY	Stagecoach R&W	NAE887L	Gwyn Williams	NWS288R	Goodsir
MPH679W	Thomas Rhondda	N382PNY	Stagecoach R&W	NAT746A	Vale of Llangollen	OAO530R	Mid Wales
MRJ102W	Edwards Coaches	N383PNY	Stagecoach R&W	NDE86R	Silcox	OBR771T	Alpine
MSF679T	Owens Motors	N384PNY	Stagecoach R&W	NDE481Y	Richards Bros	OBR772R	Jones Llanfaethlu
MUE313V	Hawkes	N389KDE	Jones Login	NDL654R	Alpine	OBX345R	Richards Bros
MUT253V	Diamond Glantawe	N390KDE	Jones Login	NDW37X	Wilkins Travel	OBX346R	Richards Bros
MUT254V	Diamond Glantawe	N418EJC	Caelloi	NDW140X	Williams Bala	OCO120S	P & O Lloyd
MUT255V	Diamond Glantawe	N419UWN	Phil Anslow	NDW401X	Cardiff Bus	OCU420R	Coastal Continental
MUT261V	Diamond Glantawe	N430WVR	Stagecoach R&W	NDW402X	Cardiff Bus	ODJ583W	Mansel David
MUT262V	Diamond Glantawe	N461OTX	Shamrock	NDW403X	Cardiff Bus	OEH604M	Thomas Rhondda
MUT263V	Diamond Glantawe	N462OTX	Shamrock	NDW404X	Cardiff Bus	OGE9Y	I B T
MVC12P	Cerbydau Carreglefn	N463OTX	Shamrock	NDW405X	Cardiff Bus	OHR492X	Wilkins Travel
MYD215V	Wilkins Travel	N468SPA	Arriva Cymru	NDW406X	Cardiff Bus	OHV190Y	Wilkins Travel
N1EDW	Silver Star	N470SPA	Arriva Cymru	NDW407X	Cardiff Bus	OHV193Y	Wilkins Travel
N2ARV	Arvonia	N511PNY	Shamrock	NDW408X	Cardiff Bus	OHV199Y	Howells
N2GHA	GHA Coaches	N512PNY	Shamrock	NDW409X	Cardiff Bus	OHV209Y	Wilkins Travel
N2PCL	Pullman Coaches	N513PNY	Shamrock	NDW410X	Cardiff Bus	OHV686Y	Stagecoach R&W
N2VLT	Vale of Llangollen	N523DCC	Arriva Cymru	NDW411X	Cardiff Bus	OHV693Y	Shamrock
N3ALP	Alpine	N550MTG	Stagecoach R&W	NDW412X	Cardiff Bus	OHV699Y	Stagecoach R&W
N3GHA	GHA Coaches	N551MTG	Stagecoach R&W	NDW413X	Cardiff Bus	OHV702Y	Stagecoach R&W
N3VLT	Vale of Llangollen	N551UCY	First Cymru	NDW414X	Cardiff Bus	OHV719Y	Stagecoach R&W
N4ALP	Alpine	N552UCY	First Cymru	NDW415X	Cardiff Bus	OHV764Y	Shamrock
N5DMW	Williams	N553UCY	First Cymru	NDW416X	Cardiff Bus	OHV775Y	Shamrock
N7EJS	E Jones & Sons	N554UCY	First Cymru	NDW417X	Cardiff Bus	OHV783Y	Gwyn Williams
N10CGC	Cross Gates	N555UCY	First Cymru	NDW418X	Cardiff Bus	OIB3520	Lewis Whitland
N23OBO	Cardiff Bus	N556UCY	First Cymru	NDZ3133	Stagecoach R&W	OIB5647	Tanat Valley
N24FWU	Arriva Cymru	N557UCY	First Cymru	NDZ3134	Stagecoach R&W	OIB5880	G M
N24OBO	Cardiff Bus	N558UCY	First Cymru	NDZ3135	Stagecoach R&W	OIB7631	G M
N25FWU	Arriva Cymru	N559UCY	First Cymru	NDZ3136	Stagecoach R&W	OIB7915	G M
N25OBO	Cardiff Bus	N561UCY	First Cymru	NDZ3137	Stagecoach R&W	OIJ864	Wilkins Travel
N26OBO	Cardiff Bus	N562UCY	First Cymru	NDZ3138	Stagecoach R&W	OIL3796	First Cymru
N27OBO	Cardiff Bus	N563UCY	First Cymru	NDZ3139	Stagecoach R&W	OIL4470	Longs
N28OBO	Cardiff Bus	N564UCY	First Cymru	NDZ3140	Stagecoach R&W	OIL4471	Longs
N29OBO	Cardiff Bus	N565UCY	First Cymru	NDZ3141	Stagecoach R&W	OIL4472	Longs
N50RDE	Edwards Bros	N566UCY	First Cymru	NDZ3142	Stagecoach R&W	OIL4473	Longs
N62MTG	Stagecoach R&W	N567UCY	First Cymru	NDZ3143	Stagecoach R&W	OIL4474	Longs
N63MTG	Stagecoach R&W	N568UCY	First Cymru	NDZ3144	Stagecoach R&W	OIL5271	Longs
N71HHB	Stagecoach R&W	N571OUH	I B T	NDZ3145	Stagecoach R&W	OIL5274	Longs
N74HHB	Stagecoach R&W	N572OUH	I B T	NDZ3154	Stagecoach R&W	OIL5276	Longs
N74WSB	Shamrock	N573OUH	I B T	NDZ3155	Stagecoach R&W	OJC496	Express Motors
N75HHB	Stagecoach R&W	N595DWY	Ferris Holidays	NDZ3156	Stagecoach R&W	OJD196R	Howells
N76HHB	Stagecoach R&W	N609MHB	First Cymru	NDZ3157	Stagecoach R&W	OJD234R	Howells
N78PDW	Newport Transport	N610MHB	First Cymru	NDZ3158	Stagecoach R&W	OJD239R	Howells
N79PDW	Newport Transport	N611MHB	First Cymru	NDZ3159	Stagecoach R&W	OJD68R	Silver Star
N81PDW	Newport Transport	N612MHB	First Cymru	NEL112P	Williams Bala	OJD87R	Silver Star
N82PDW	Newport Transport	N613MHB	First Cymru	NEY819	Arriva Cymru	OJI0400	Cerbydau Cenarth
N83PDW	Newport Transport	N614MHB	First Cymru	NGL371	Midway Motors	OJI9477	Sixty-Sixty
N100TCC	Williams	N615BCF	Ferris Holidays	NIJ6060	Sixty-Sixty	OJV121S	W E Jones & Son
N112EWJ	First Cymru	N615MHB	First Cymru	NIL2454	First Cymru	OKG292R	Coastal Continental
N113VWN	First Cymru	N616MHB	First Cymru	NIL2455	First Cymru	OKW525R	P & O Lloyd
N114VWN	First Cymru	N617MHB	First Cymru	NIL2456	First Cymru	OKY76X	Summerdale
N115VWN	First Cymru	N618MHB	First Cymru	NIL3278	Midway Motors	OLG601V	Phillips
N118TCN	M & H Travel	N620TTH	Diamond Glantawe	NIL3279	W E Jones & Son	OMA503V	Hawkes
N121YLS	Shamrock	N671TPF	Arriva Cymru	NIL3945	Burrows	ONF25P	W E Jones & Son
N122YLS	Shamrock	N681YAV	Cross Gates	NIL3946	Burrows	OPL77W	Lewis Whitland
N134PTG	Cardiff Bus	N682AOJ	Edwards Bros	NIL7708	Edwards Bros	ORU236G	Edwards Coaches
N135PTG	Cardiff Bus	N711AHP	Llynfi Coaches	NIL8646	Phil Anslow	OTA645G	Sixty-Sixty
N136PTG	Cardiff Bus	N714CYC	Diamond Glantawe	NIL8647	Phil Anslow	OUT11W	First Cymru
N137PTG	Cardiff Bus	N715CYC	Diamond Glantawe	NIL8649	Phil Anslow	OVL494	Express Motors
N138PTG	Cardiff Bus	N716CYC	Diamond Glantawe	NIL8653	Phil Anslow	OVV847R	East End
N139PTG	Cardiff Bus	N716SOP	Owens Motors	NIL8654	Phil Anslow	OWE856R	Alpine
N140PTG	Cardiff Bus	N717CYC	Diamond Glantawe	NIL8655	Phil Anslow	OWW905P	Berwyn
N141PTG	Cardiff Bus	N718DJC	Arriva Cymru	NIL8656	Phil Anslow	P2ARV	Arvonia
N142PTG	Cardiff Bus	N719DJC	Arriva Cymru	NIL8657	GHA Coaches	P2WAL	George Edwards
N143PTG	Cardiff Bus	N737NDD	Berwyn	NIL8658	GHA Coaches	P2WGT	Thomas Rhondda
N143XEG	Shamrock	N753VCY	Pullman Coaches	NIL9692	Ken Hopkins	P3VLT	Vale of Llangollen
N144XEG	Shamrock	N755NAY	Shamrock	NIL9777	Williams Bala	P3WGT	Thomas Rhondda
N145XEG	Shamrock	N776CJC	K M P	NIW2232	Lewis y Llan	P5ALP	Alpine
N151MTG	Stagecoach R&W	N777KMP	K M P	NIW6519	Berwyn	P5DMW	Williams
N152MTG	Stagecoach R&W	N77KMP	K M P	NJC393	Cerbydau Carreglefn	P5PCL	Pullman Coaches
N153MTG	Stagecoach R&W	N785ORY	Midway Motors	NJI5235	Owens Motors	P5VLT	Vale of Llangollen
N154MTG	Stagecoach R&W	N827XRD	Ferris Holidays	NJX206W	Edwards Coaches	P10CAE	Caelloi
N155MTG	Stagecoach R&W	N848FDT	K M P	NKE306P	Richards Bros	P10GWS	Gwyn Williams
N156MTG	Stagecoach R&W	N854PDW	Shamrock	NLJ506N	Silver Star	P26TTX	Ferris Holidays
N157MTG	Stagecoach R&W	N855PDW	Shamrock	NMA746Y	Williams Bala	P27TTX	Ferris Holidays
N158MTG	Stagecoach R&W	N856PDW	Shamrock	NMV617W	Thomas Bros	P54XBO	Stagecoach R&W
N159MTG	Stagecoach R&W	N857PDW	Shamrock	NOC493R	Thomas Rhondda	P56XBO	Stagecoach R&W
N160MTG	Stagecoach R&W	N919ETH	Oare's	NRG170M	Edwards Coaches	P57XBO	Stagecoach R&W
N180PDW	Newport Transport	N937WJL	E Jones & Sons	NRN397PJ	Edwards Coaches	P58XBO	Stagecoach R&W
N289DWY	Shamrock	N945OBO	Thomas Rhondda	NRO266V	Edwards Coaches	P59VTG	Stagecoach R&W
N313VWN	Brian Isaac	N960LDE	Richards Bros	NSG216M	W E Jones & Son	P61VTG	Stagecoach R&W

Registration	Operator	Registration	Operator	Registration	Operator	Registration	Operator
P91VDW	Newport Transport	P970UKG	Phil Anslow	R237AEY	Arriva Cymru	R721EWV	Midway Motors
P92VDW	Newport Transport	P971SDE	Edwards Bros	R238AEY	Arriva Cymru	R733ECT	Watts
P93VDW	Newport Transport	P971UKG	Phil Anslow	R239AEY	Arriva Cymru	R749XPO	Shamrock
P94VDW	Newport Transport	P974UKG	Wilkins Travel	R294RJM	Shuttle	R751XPO	Shamrock
P96TTX	Llynfi Coaches	PAZ4945	Phillips	R407AOR	Glyn Williams	R752XPO	Shamrock
P97SDE	Richards Bros	PBZ6060	Sixty-Sixty	R408AOR	Glyn Williams	R766DUM	Voel Coaches
P97TTX	Llynfi Coaches	PBZ9057	Williams	R409HKG	Glyn Williams	R775CDW	Stagecoach R&W
P98VGD	Shamrock	PCA419V	Alpine	R410HTG	Glyn Williams	R776CDW	Stagecoach R&W
P115HCF	Tanat Valley	PCA421V	Alpine	R421AOR	Glyn Williams	R778CDW	Stagecoach R&W
P122DMS	Shamrock	PCA425V	Alpine	R422AOR	Glyn Williams	R779CDW	Stagecoach R&W
P161TDW	Stagecoach R&W	PDW484	Newport Transport	R424AOR	Glyn Williams	R780CDW	Stagecoach R&W
P162TDW	Stagecoach R&W	PDW99H	Edwards Coaches	R481EDW	First Cymru	R781CDW	Stagecoach R&W
P163TNY	Stagecoach R&W	PHB309R	I B T	R482EDW	First Cymru	R782CDW	Stagecoach R&W
P164TNY	Stagecoach R&W	PHB310R	I B T	R483EDW	First Cymru	R783CDW	Stagecoach R&W
P165TNY	Stagecoach R&W	PIB2734	Ellis Travel	R484EDW	First Cymru	R784CDW	Stagecoach R&W
P166TNY	Stagecoach R&W	PIL2142	Ken Hopkins	R485EDW	First Cymru	R785DHB	Stagecoach R&W
P167TNY	Stagecoach R&W	PIL2488	Bridgend Bus	R486EDW	First Cymru	R787DHB	Stagecoach R&W
P168TNY	Stagecoach R&W	PIL2489	Bridgend Bus	R486UCC	Arriva Cymru	R788DHB	Stagecoach R&W
P169TNY	Stagecoach R&W	PIL2841	Phil Anslow	R487EDW	First Cymru	R789DHB	Stagecoach R&W
P170TNY	Stagecoach R&W	PIL2859	Phil Anslow	R487UCC	Arriva Cymru	R790DHB	Stagecoach R&W
P171TNY	Stagecoach R&W	PIL2861	Phil Anslow	R488EDW	First Cymru	R791DHB	Stagecoach R&W
P176ANR	Shamrock	PIL2862	Phil Anslow	R489EDW	First Cymru	R792DHB	Stagecoach R&W
P177ANR	Shamrock	PIL3563	Bridgend Bus	R490EDW	First Cymru	R792DUB	Arriva Cymru
P177VDW	Newport Transport	PIL4059	P & O Lloyd	R519RGM	Ferris Holidays	R793DUB	Arriva Cymru
P182NAK	I B T	PIL6350	I B T	R521UCC	Arriva Cymru	R794DUB	Arriva Cymru
P190VDW	Newport Transport	PIL7240	I B T	R522UCC	Arriva Cymru	R795DUB	Arriva Cymru
P220OLC	Shuttle	PIL9377	Williams Bala	R530HDE	Silcox	R796DUB	Arriva Cymru
P224WBV	Shamrock	PIW4792	Burrows	R531HDE	Silcox	R797DUB	Arriva Cymru
P225WBV	Shamrock	PJC630S	Alpine	R532HDE	Silcox	R798DUB	Arriva Cymru
P255YDW	Thomas Rhondda	PJI6076	Owens Motors	R543ACV	Williams	R799DUB	Arriva Cymru
P260SDE	Richards Bros	PJI7756	P & O Lloyd	R546GDE	Jones Login	R801YJC	Arriva Cymru
P337CEP	Diamond Glantawe	PKG702Y	Henley's	R580SWN	Wilkins Travel	R802YJC	Arriva Cymru
P338CEP	Diamond Glantawe	PNA963W	James Brothers	R581SWN	First Cymru	R803YJC	Arriva Cymru
P339CEP	Diamond Glantawe	POI6312	P & O Lloyd	R582SWN	First Cymru	R804YJC	Arriva Cymru
P423PBP	Glyn Williams	PPE658R	Jones Llanfaethlu	R583SWN	First Cymru	R805YJC	Arriva Cymru
P501HEG	Shuttle	PPH473R	Burrows	R584SWN	First Cymru	R807YJC	Arriva Cymru
P502HEG	Shuttle	PPT910	Cross Gates	R585SWN	First Cymru	R808YJC	Arriva Cymru
P503HEG	Shuttle	PRN117T	Phillips	R586SWN	First Cymru	R809YJC	Arriva Cymru
P504HEG	Shuttle	PRO439W	Thomas Bros	R587SWN	First Cymru	R810YJC	Arriva Cymru
P553KCC	Silver Star	PRR449R	Midway Motors	R588SWN	First Cymru	R811YJC	Arriva Cymru
P569BTH	First Cymru	PSC58Y	Mansel David	R589SWN	First Cymru	R812YJC	Arriva Cymru
P570BTH	First Cymru	PSN916Y	Pencoed Travel	R590SWN	First Cymru	R813YJC	Arriva Cymru
P571BTH	First Cymru	PSO178W	Phil Anslow	R591SWN	First Cymru	R814YJC	Arriva Cymru
P572BTH	First Cymru	PSU626	First Cymru	R592SWN	First Cymru	R815YJC	Arriva Cymru
P573BTH	First Cymru	PSX180Y	Arthur Thomas	R593SWN	First Cymru	R816YJC	Arriva Cymru
P574BTH	First Cymru	PSX184Y	Arthur Thomas	R594SWN	First Cymru	R817YJC	Arriva Cymru
P575BTH	First Cymru	PTD668S	Hawkes	R595SWN	First Cymru	R818YJC	Arriva Cymru
P575GCF	Shamrock	PUF586R	Alpine	R596SWN	First Cymru	R819YJC	Arriva Cymru
P576BTH	First Cymru	PUO852S	Mid Wales	R597SWN	First Cymru	R821YJC	Arriva Cymru
P576GCF	Shamrock	PVO624	Silcox	R598SWN	First Cymru	R870MRD	Ferris Holidays
P577BTH	First Cymru	PWL939W	Edwards Coaches	R599SWN	First Cymru	R871MRD	Ferris Holidays
P578BTH	First Cymru	R1EMS	Express Motors	R601SWO	Stagecoach R&W	R915GBX	Lewis Whitland
P579BTH	First Cymru	R2ARV	Arvonia	R602SWO	Stagecoach R&W	R916ULA	Shamrock
P580BTH	First Cymru	R3PCL	Pullman Coaches	R603SWO	Stagecoach R&W	R921ULA	Shamrock
P619VDW	First Cymru	R4MKD	Voel Coaches	R604SWO	Stagecoach R&W	R925PTF	Ferris Holidays
P620VDW	First Cymru	R4WGT	Thomas Rhondda	R606SWO	Stagecoach R&W	R962FYS	D & G Coaches
P621VDW	First Cymru	R5GHA	GHA Coaches	R607SWO	Stagecoach R&W	R979PRD	I B T
P633KTF	Shamrock	R5WGT	Thomas Rhondda	R607USP	Edwards Bros	R997FNW	Pullman Coaches
P634KTF	Shamrock	R6ALP	Alpine	R608SWO	Stagecoach R&W	RAZ9859	Bysiau Ffoshelig
P658KEY	Arriva Cymru	R10ARE	Oare's	R609SWO	Stagecoach R&W	RBO202	Richards Bros
P669KRD	Ferris Holidays	R12CBC	Berwyn	R610SWO	Stagecoach R&W	RBO284	Richards Bros
P680LWA	Bysiau cwm Taf	R12WGT	Thomas Rhondda	R611SWO	Stagecoach R&W	RBO350	Richards Bros
P688HND	Bysiau cwm Taf	R42EDW	Bebb	R612SWO	Stagecoach R&W	RBO509Y	Cardiff Bus
P688KCC	Arriva Cymru	R43EDW	Bebb	R613SWO	Stagecoach R&W	RBZ3428	D & G Coaches
P690CWN	Pullman Coaches	R70RAW	Watts	R614SWO	Stagecoach R&W	RCW649X	Edwards Bros
P721JYA	Diamond Glantawe	R73GNW	Watts	R615SWO	Stagecoach R&W	RDC106R	Jones Llanfaethlu
P722JYA	Diamond Glantawe	R86BDW	Newport Transport	R616SWO	Stagecoach R&W	RDT121X	Wilkins Travel
P723JYA	Diamond Glantawe	R87BDW	Newport Transport	R617BWO	Phil Anslow	REG900W	Johnis Travel
P724JYA	Diamond Glantawe	R89BDW	Newport Transport	R617SWO	Stagecoach R&W	RGS99R	Richards Bros
P731FCY	First Cymru	R89GWO	Bebb	R618SWO	Stagecoach R&W	RIL1027	I B T
P742RDE	Jones Login	R91GWO	Bebb	R619SWO	Stagecoach R&W	RIL1067	P & O Lloyd
P742UWW	Shamrock	R113PMO	Ferris Holidays	R620SWO	Stagecoach R&W	RIL1072	P & O Lloyd
P743RDE	Bysiau cwm Taf	R157RJH	Ferris Holidays	R621SWO	Stagecoach R&W	RIL3744	M & H Travel
P771TTG	Stagecoach R&W	R160LDE	Jones Login	R624CTX	Phil Anslow	RIL3747	Porthcawl Omnibus
P772TTG	Stagecoach R&W	R161LDE	Jones Login	R630VYB	Edwards Coaches	RIL6494	Ken Hopkins
P773TTG	Stagecoach R&W	R162LDE	Jones Login	R631EYS	Shamrock	RIW4037	E Jones & Sons
P774TTG	Stagecoach R&W	R175VWN	First Cymru	R631VYB	Edwards Coaches	RJE40S	Clynnog & Trefor
P779WDE	Silcox	R176VWN	First Cymru	R632VNN	Llynfi Coaches	RJI2713	Owens Motors
P780WDE	Silcox	R177VWN	First Cymru	R641VNN	Wilkins Travel	RJI3380	Williams Bala
P783BJU	Henley's	R178VWN	First Cymru	R649REP	Tanat Valley	RJI4080	Williams Bala
P808WWO	Ferris Holidays	R180EOT	Shamrock	R669UCC	Bryn Melyn	RJI4378	M & H Travel
P869GEY	Ellis Travel	R183EOT	Shamrock	R703TRV	Shamrock	RJI5712	Eagles & Crawford
P895FMO	Shamrock	R184EBX	Shamrock	R704TRV	Shamrock	RKG419Y	Cardiff Bus
P896FMO	Shamrock	R184EOT	Shamrock	R705TRV	Shamrock	RKG420Y	Cardiff Bus
P897FMO	Shamrock	R188BDW	Newport Transport	R706TRV	Shamrock	RKG421Y	Cardiff Bus
P898FMO	Shamrock	R190TKU	Shamrock	R706YUD	Stagecoach R&W	RKG422Y	Cardiff Bus
P901PWW	Richards Bros	R233AEY	Arriva Cymru	R707TRV	Shamrock	RKG423Y	Cardiff Bus
P902PWW	Richards Bros	R234AEY	Arriva Cymru	R708TRV	Shamrock	RKG424Y	Cardiff Bus
P916DEJ	Richards Bros	R235AEY	Arriva Cymru	R713TRV	Shamrock	RKG425Y	Cardiff Bus
P969UKG	Phil Anslow	R236AEY	Arriva Cymru	R720TRV	Shamrock	RKG426Y	Cardiff Bus

Reg	Operator	Reg	Operator	Reg	Operator	Reg	Operator
RKG427Y	Cardiff Bus	S499CDE	Edwards Bros	T11AGO	Nefyn Coaches	T687BWN	Brian Isaac
RLG429V	Arriva Cymru	S558MCC	Arriva Cymru	T38PTG	Phil Anslow	T896ATH	Wilkins Travel
RMA435V	Eagles & Crawford	S559MCC	Arriva Cymru	T56JKG	Phil Anslow	T899ATH	Wilkins Travel
RMA442V	Alpine	S576ACT	Watts	T57JKG	Phil Anslow	T931KNW	Owens Motors
RNV413V	Tanat Valley	S622TDW	Stagecoach R&W	T58JKG	Phil Anslow	T941RDE	Richards Bros
ROK452M	Coastal Continental	S623TDW	Stagecoach R&W	T72JCC	K M P	T943BWO	Shamrock
ROK459M	Coastal Continental	S624TDW	Stagecoach R&W	T73JBO	Bebb	T944BWO	Shamrock
ROU348S	Wilkins Travel	S625TDW	Stagecoach R&W	T73JKG	Ferris Holidays	T961ACC	Nefyn Coaches
RPC59X	Lewis Whitland	S626TDW	Stagecoach R&W	T74JBO	Bebb	TAZ5539	Howells
RPR715R	East End	S627TDW	Stagecoach R&W	T74JKG	Ferris Holidays	TAZ5541	Howells
RPR751K	Mansel David	S752XYA	Diamond Glantawe	T75JBO	Bebb	TAZ5542	Howells
RRP861R	East End	S775BLG	Richards Bros	T75JKG	Ferris Holidays	TAZ5543	Howells
RRS225X	Phil Anslow	S787NRV	Glyn Williams	T76JBO	Bebb	TAZ9653	Hawkes
RSG821V	Glyn Williams	S788NRV	Glyn Williams	T76JKG	Ferris Holidays	TAZ9658	Hawkes
RUH12Y	Newport Transport	S794JTH	Pullman Coaches	T91JBA	Phillips	TBD278G	Express Motors
RUH17Y	Newport Transport	S810MCC	Clynnog & Trefor	T101XDE	First Cymru	TBD284G	Express Motors
RUJ350R	Watts	S822MCC	Arriva Cymru	T102XDE	First Cymru	TBX713	Alpine
RVO839X	Richards Bros	S823MCC	Arriva Cymru	T103XDE	First Cymru	TCC2T	Alpine
RWA860R	Alpine	S824MCC	Arriva Cymru	T120JBC	I B T	TDE701S	Clynnog & Trefor
RWA861R	Alpine	S825MCC	Arriva Cymru	T141RDE	Silcox	TDK726S	Tanat Valley
RWN727Y	Merlyn's	S846SNY	Glyn Williams	T142RDE	Silcox	TDM769V	Williams Bala
RXO828	Express Motors	S848RJC	Arriva Cymru	T143RDE	Silcox	TDT1L	Thomas Rhondda
RYX492	Cross Gates	S865AEJ	Cerbydau Cenarth	T144DAX	Cardiff Bus	TDT863S	Alpine
S1EMS	Express Motors	S895SNY	Shamrock	T145DAX	Cardiff Bus	TDW315J	Edwards Coaches
S6GHA	GHA Coaches	S896SNY	Shamrock	T146DAX	Cardiff Bus	TGG739R	First Cymru
S6PCL	Pullman Coaches	S908JCC	Bryn Melyn	T147DAX	Cardiff Bus	THL296Y	Watts
S12CBC	Berwyn	SAS858T	Alpine	T148DAX	Cardiff Bus	TIB4587	Ellis Travel
S36UBO	Bebb	SBZ1621	Cross Gates	T149DAX	Cardiff Bus	TIB4921	Oare's
S45UBO	Bebb	SCD693X	Lewis Whitland	T150DAX	Cardiff Bus	TIB5002	Berwyn
S46UBO	Bebb	SCH148X	Tanat Valley	T158PNY	Shamrock	TIB5909	Burrows
S47UBO	Bebb	SCN273S	Howells	T159PNY	Shamrock	TIB5912	Burrows
S48UBO	Bebb	SCN283S	Edwards Coaches	T160PNY	Shamrock	TIB6060	Sixty-Sixty
S49UBO	Bebb	SDA509S	Thomas Rhondda	T161PNY	Shamrock	TIB9157	Alpine
S51UBO	Bebb	SDA532S	Thomas Rhondda	T162PNY	Shamrock	TJI1698	Hawkes
S52UBO	Bebb	SDA631S	Thomas Rhondda	T163PNY	Shamrock	TJI4123	Phil Anslow
S53UBO	Bebb	SDA659S	Thomas Rhondda	T164PNY	Shamrock	TJI4124	Phil Anslow
S58BTX	Shamrock	SDA778S	W E Jones & Son	T255GON	Silver Star	TJI4700	Pullman Coaches
S62UBO	Bebb	SEL247H	W E Jones & Son	T303PNY	Shamrock	TJI5404	Merlyn's
S63UBO	Bebb	SFD254W	Merlyn's	T304PNY	Shamrock	TJI5405	Merlyn's
S64UBO	Bebb	SFF756T	James Brothers	T305PNY	Shamrock	TJI6309	Vale of Llangollen
S65UBO	Bebb	SGR778V	Berwyn	T310SEJ	Cerbydau Cenarth	TKM109X	Alpine
S67UBO	Bebb	SGR779V	GHA Coaches	T375JJC	Silver Star	TKM110X	Alpine
S68UBO	Bebb	SGR792V	GHA Coaches	T491SKG	Shamrock	TMA254V	Clynnog & Trefor
S69UBO	Bebb	SHO628P	First Cymru	T492SKG	Shamrock	TND128X	Hawkes
S71UBO	Bebb	SHP693R	Llynfi Coaches	T493SKG	Shamrock	TNR812X	Arriva Cymru
S72UBO	Bebb	SIB4631	Oareis	T510RDE	Richards Bros	TPD80S	Thomas Bros
S91UEY	Jones Llanfaethlu	SIB6740	I B T	T520PYD	Wilkins Travel	TPD119X	Arriva Cymru
S92UBO	Bebb	SIB7356	Cross Gates	T525KEP	Williams	TPD122X	Arriva Cymru
S110TDW	Newport Transport	SIL1392	M & H Travel	T560JJC	Arriva Cymru	TPD126X	Arriva Cymru
S112TDW	Newport Transport	SIL2243	Owens Motors	T561JJC	Arriva Cymru	TPJ270S	Williams
S113TDW	Newport Transport	SIL4275	Ken Hopkins	T562JJC	Arriva Cymru	TPL166S	Gwyn Williams
S114TDW	Newport Transport	SJI1884	Tanat Valley	T563JJC	Arriva Cymru	TPU73R	P & O Lloyd
S115TDW	Newport Transport	SJI2154	Gwyn Williams	T564JJC	Arriva Cymru	TPX332P	Richards Bros
C116RKG	First Cymru	SJI2155	Gwyn Williams	T565JJC	Arriva Cymru	TRM15S	Clynnog & Trefor
S116TDW	Newport Transport	SJI2156	Gwyn Williams	T500JJO	Arriva Cymru	TRN476V	Edwards Coaches
S117TDW	Newport Transport	SJI2449	Edwards Coaches	T567JJC	Arriva Cymru	TRT95M	Edwards Coaches
S118TDW	Newport Transport	SKG895S	Mansel David	T568JJC	Arriva Cymru	TSO20X	Express Motors
S135UEY	Cerbydau Carreglefn	SLO514R	W E Jones & Son	T569JJC	Arriva Cymru	TTA650X	D Jones & Son
S211TDW	Newport Transport	SMS125P	Alpine	T570JJC	Arriva Cymru	TUA161W	Owens Motors
S224BDE	Silcox	SMU919N	W E Jones & Son	T582SKG	Phil Anslow	TVP874S	Thomas Rhondda
S301SHB	Cardiff Bus	SND135X	First Cymru	T583SKG	Phil Anslow	TWJ340Y	Express Motors
S302SHB	Cardiff Bus	SND293X	Edwards Coaches	T584SKG	Phil Anslow	TWJ342Y	Express Motors
S303SHB	Cardiff Bus	SND295X	Edwards Coaches	T585SKG	Phil Anslow	TWR465W	East End
S304SHB	Cardiff Bus	SND297X	Cerbydau Cenarth	T586SKG	Phil Anslow	TXA114K	Arriva Cymru
S305SHB	Cardiff Bus	SND303X	Wilkins Travel	T587SKG	Phil Anslow	TXI2425	Pencoed Travel
S306SHB	Cardiff Bus	SND429X	Diamond Glantawe	T588SKG	Phil Anslow	TXI8754	Oare's
S307SHB	Cardiff Bus	SND435X	Edwards Coaches	T589SKG	Phil Anslow	UAR587W	First Cymru
S308SHB	Cardiff Bus	SND462X	Diamond Glantawe	T590SKG	Phil Anslow	UAR598W	First Cymru
S309SHB	Cardiff Bus	SND487X	Diamond Glantawe	T601DAX	Glyn Williams	UAS68T	Alpine
S310SHB	Cardiff Bus	SND505X	Diamond Glantawe	T601JCC	Express Motors	UBZ3360	Ellis Travel
S311SHB	Cardiff Bus	SND513X	Diamond Glantawe	T602DAX	Glyn Williams	UBZ3362	GHA Coaches
S312SHB	Cardiff Bus	SND519X	Diamond Glantawe	T603DAX	Glyn Williams	UCK277	Lewis y Llan
S313SHB	Cardiff Bus	SNJ684R	Ellis Travel	T604DAX	Glyn Williams	UCS186S	Ferris Holidays
S314SHB	Cardiff Bus	SNS823W	Hawkes	T606SBX	Pullman Coaches	UDE351T	Jones Login
S315SHB	Cardiff Bus	SOI196	Edwards Coaches	T622SEJ	First Cymru	UDM449V	GHA Coaches
S316DLG	Lewis y Llan	SRJ751R	Pencoed Travel	T623SEJ	First Cymru	UDM451V	Bryn Melyn
S316SHB	Cardiff Bus	SSN250S	Ferris Holidays	T624SEJ	First Cymru	UDT183S	Pencoed Travel
S317SHB	Cardiff Bus	SSU632	Clynnog & Trefor	T625SEJ	First Cymru	UET680S	Lewis y Llan
S318SHB	Cardiff Bus	STD179L	Edwards Coaches	T626SEJ	First Cymru	UEY441T	Cerbydau Carreglefn
S319SHB	Cardiff Bus	STJ847L	East End	T627SEJ	First Cymru	UEY454T	Goodsir
S320SHB	Cardiff Bus	STK131T	Edwards Coaches	T628SEJ	First Cymru	UFT919T	Bridgend Bus
S377MCC	K M P	SVO782R	Wilkins Travel	T629SEJ	First Cymru	UHW10T	G M
S403JUA	George Edwards	SWH376T	Goodsir	T630SEJ	First Cymru	UJN430Y	Arriva Cymru
S426MCC	Arriva Cymru	T4PCL	Pullman Coaches	T631SEJ	First Cymru	UKE416H	G M
S427MCC	Arriva Cymru	T5TAF	Bysiau cwm Taf	T632SEJ	First Cymru	UKG474S	D & G Coaches
S428MCC	Arriva Cymru	T7ALP	Alpine	T633SEJ	First Cymru	UKH170W	W E Jones & Son
S429MCC	Arriva Cymru	T7KMP	K M P	T634SEJ	First Cymru	ULJ252J	Edwards Coaches
S490BBX	Gwyn Williams	T9MCL	Merlyn's	T635SEJ	First Cymru	ULJ253J	Edwards Coaches
S490MCC	Caelloi	T10CAE	Caelloi	T636SEJ	First Cymru	ULJ260J	Edwards Coaches
S496MCC	Express Motors	T10MCL	Merlyn's	T637SEJ	First Cymru	ULJ264J	Edwards Coaches

Reg	Operator	Reg	Operator	Reg	Operator	Reg	Operator	Reg	Operator
ULS668T	Hawkes	V629KWR	Shamrock	W891MDT	Ferris Holidays	WTU467W	Arriva Cymru
UOI4323	First Cymru	V630EEJ	Cerbydau Cenarth	WAO644Y	Diamond Glantawe	WTU473W	East End
URF660S	Clynnog & Trefor	V670LWT	Pullman Coaches	WAO646Y	Cross Gates	WTU478W	Arriva Cymru
URF677S	Alpine	V703LWT	Pullman Coaches	WAZ4435	M & H Travel	WTU499W	Alpine
URN153V	G M	V705LWT	Pullman Coaches	WBC940X	I B T	WWL532T	Cerbydau Cenarth
USE633R	Jones Llanfaethlu	V979FAV	Llynfi Coaches	WBD875S	Goodsir	WWP834V	Lewis Whitland
USU192	Clynnog & Trefor	V980FAV	Llynfi Coaches	WBD876S	Berwyn	WWY905L	Jones Llanfaethlu
UTU665V	Silver Star	VAH278X	GHA Coaches	WBN981L	Edwards Coaches	WYM675	Ken Hopkins
UTU691V	Eagles & Crawford	VAH279X	GHA Coaches	WBR336R	Williams	XBN196	Ken Hopkins
V2FOS	Bysiau Ffoshelig	VAW527	Silcox	WBX871T	Silcox	XBO117T	Mansel David
V6WGT	Thomas Rhondda	VBA164S	G M	WCC92V	Silver Star	XBX467T	Jones Login
V7GHA	GHA Coaches	VBA168S	G M	WDA2T	Stagecoach R&W	XBZ4111	Edwards Coaches
V7PCL	Pullman Coaches	VBG91V	Phil Anslow	WDA913T	Porthcawl Omnibus	XDG57S	Watts
V8GHA	GHA Coaches	VBM948W	Mansel David	WDA923T	Goodsir	XDL304	Ellis Travel
V8PCL	Pullman Coaches	VBX144	Lewis Whitland	WDA926T	Phillips	XDM300	Voel Coaches
V9PCL	Pullman Coaches	VCY401	Gwyn Williams	WDA966T	Coastal Continental	XDV604S	Clynnog & Trefor
V12DJS	D Jones & Son	VDH244S	First Cymru	WDA969T	P & O Lloyd	XFM203	Newport Transport
V32HAX	Bebb	VEC170R	Mansel David	WDA977T	Porthcawl Omnibus	XFU128V	P & O Lloyd
V34HAX	Bebb	VEX296X	East End	WDA981T	Alpine	XFU130V	P & O Lloyd
V35HAX	Bebb	VEX299X	GHA Coaches	WDC219Y	Arriva Cymru	XGR445V	Bryn Melyn
V35HTG	Newport Transport	VIA8311	Ellis Travel	WDC220Y	Arriva Cymru	XHK234X	First Cymru
V36HTG	Newport Transport	VJU259X	Summerdale	WDM352R	Alpine	XHR104	Edwards Coaches
V37HTG	Newport Transport	VKN835X	Porthcawl Omnibus	WDZ4138	Express Motors	XIB3942	Henley's
V37KWO	Bebb	VKN837X	Porthcawl Omnibus	WEB409T	Mansel David	XJA515L	Edwards Coaches
V38HTG	Newport Transport	VLT22	Vale of Llangollen	WFU468V	P & O Lloyd	XJI4840	Ken Hopkins
V39HTG	Newport Transport	VLT55	Vale of Llangollen	WGR144V	Summerdale	XJI8356	Tanat Valley
V54HAX	Bebb	VLT149	Vale of Llangollen	WGT1	Thomas Rhondda	XJI9612	Johnis Travel
V56KWO	Bebb	VLT177	Vale of Llangollen	WHN468	East End	XJJ660V	Clynnog & Trefor
V57KWO	Bebb	VLT191	Vale of Llangollen	WIB1701	GHA Coaches	XNK200X	Midway Motors
V58KWO	Bebb	VLT229	Vale of Llangollen	WIB7183	Williams Bala	XNN890Y	Richards Bros
V59KWO	Bebb	VLT250	Vale of Llangollen	WIW3577	Williams Bala	XNV885S	Berwyn
V78JKG	Bebb	VLT290	Vale of Llangollen	WJI1414	Cerbydau Cenarth	XPG166T	Edwards Coaches
V79JKG	Bebb	VLT293	Vale of Llangollen	WJI1726	I B T	XPG194T	P & O Lloyd
V81JKG	Bebb	VLT483	Vale of Llangollen	WJI8931	Cerbydau Cenarth	XRU281K	Edwards Coaches
V107LVH	M & H Travel	VLT935	Vale of Llangollen	WJI8932	Cerbydau Cenarth	XSJ664T	Alpine
V116LVH	Shamrock	VNB157L	Edwards Coaches	WJI8945	Ken Hopkins	XSU653	Clynnog & Trefor
V117LVH	Shamrock	VNB173L	Edwards Coaches	WJI9360	Sixty-Sixty	XTB5T	Alpine
V140HTG	Newport Transport	VNH156W	East End	WJX478V	Merlynis	XTB6T	Alpine
V151JKG	Cardiff Bus	VRP39S	Express Motors	WKE69S	G M	XTB8T	Alpine
V152JKG	Cardiff Bus	VRP60S	Voel Coaches	WKG602	W E Jones & Son	XTB9T	Alpine
V153JKG	Cardiff Bus	VTD720T	Alpine	WKO125S	Burrows	XTB11T	Alpine
V154JKG	Cardiff Bus	VUP745R	Richards Bros	WLG999W	James Brothers	XTE229V	Porthcawl Omnibus
V155JKG	Cardiff Bus	VUP850	Alpine	WND477	Alpine	XUA76X	Phil Anslow
V156JKG	Cardiff Bus	VVV63S	Voel Coaches	WOI3003	Brian Isaac	XVS913	Jones Llanfaethlu
V157JKG	Cardiff Bus	W2ARV	Arvonia	WOI3004	Brian Isaac	XWS541V	Mansel David
V158JKG	Cardiff Bus	W9ALP	Alpine	WPJ8S	W E Jones & Son	XXI7360	Ken Hopkins
V235LWU	Shamrock	W10CAE	Caelloi	WRN134V	Edwards Coaches	YAP104	Edwards Coaches
V236LWU	Shamrock	W82NDW	Bebb	WRN137V	Edwards Coaches	YBF681S	Berwyn
V259DCC	Silver Star	W83NDW	Bebb	WSU259	Williams	YCU961T	Arriva Cymru
V304EAK	Shamrock	W84NDW	Bebb	WSU472	Ken Hopkins	YDD133S	Mansel David
V305EAK	Shamrock	W86NDW	Bebb	WSV410	First Cymru	YDE350	Richards Bros
V307EAK	Shamrock	W87NDW	Bebb	WTA420	Thomas Rhondda	YDE679	Jones Login
V309EAK	Shamrock	W108NDE	Silcox	WTG330T	G M	YDE734	Summerdale
V418FCY	Wilkins Travel	W200ODE	Edwards Bros	WTG331T	Shamrock	YDR224	Gwyn Williams
V553ECC	Arriva Cymru	W233KDO	Lewis Whitland	WTG335T	Llynfi Coaches	YDW566T	I B T
V554ECC	Arriva Cymru	W247OCC	Clynnog & Trefor	WTG341T	Llynfi Coaches	YDW752K	Newport Transport
V556ECC	Arriva Cymru	W301MKY	Shamrock	WTG342T	Watts	YJI1309	GHA Coaches
V557ECC	Arriva Cymru	W302MKY	Shamrock	WTG344T	Llynfi Coaches	YKG53	Edwards Coaches
V571DJC	Arriva Cymru	W303MKY	Shamrock	WTG345T	Llynfi Coaches	YKS22W	GHA Coaches
V572DJC	Arriva Cymru	W351UWO	Thomas Rhondda	WTG346T	Llynfi Coaches	YLP528	GHA Coaches
V573DDE	Jones Login	W352UWO	Thomas Rhondda	WTG347T	Llynfi Coaches	YMB501W	Alpine
V573DJC	Arriva Cymru	W353UWO	Thomas Rhondda	WTG348T	Wilkins Travel	YMB502W	Bryn Melyn
V574DJC	Arriva Cymru	W354UWO	Thomas Rhondda	WTG349T	Wilkins Travel	YMB503W	Alpine
V575DJC	Arriva Cymru	W391WPX	Shamrock	WTG351T	Longs	YMB508W	GHA Coaches
V576DJC	Arriva Cymru	W392WPX	Shamrock	WTG353T	Watts	YMB509W	Eagles & Crawford
V577DJC	Arriva Cymru	W393WPX	Shamrock	WTG354T	Llynfi Coaches	YMB512W	Arriva Cymru
V578DJC	Arriva Cymru	W394WPX	Shamrock	WTG355T	Llynfi Coaches	YMB516W	Arriva Cymru
V579DJC	Arriva Cymru	W395WPX	Shamrock	WTG356T	Wilkins Travel	YMB517W	Arriva Cymru
V580DJC	Arriva Cymru	W396WPX	Shamrock	WTG361T	Wilkins Travel	YMB518W	Arriva Cymru
V581DJC	Arriva Cymru	W397WPX	Shamrock	WTG365T	Mansel David	YMB519W	Arriva Cymru
V582DJC	Arriva Cymru	W439NDE	Richards Bros	WTG367T	Longs	YPD122Y	D Jones & Son
V583DJC	Arriva Cymru	W671DDN	Shamrock	WTG369T	Longs	YPJ207Y	Arriva Cymru
V584DJC	Arriva Cymru	W672DDN	Shamrock	WTG370T	Llynfi Coaches	YSF83S	I B T
V585DJC	Arriva Cymru	W673DDN	Shamrock	WTG374T	Mansel David	YSU446	Clynnog & Trefor
V586DJC	Arriva Cymru	W674DDN	Shamrock	WTG375T	Llynfi Coaches	YSU903	Williams
V587DJC	Arriva Cymru	W675DDN	Shamrock	WTG376T	Coastal Continental	YSU939	Tanat Valley
V588DJC	Arriva Cymru	W713DAX	Glyn Williams	WTG381T	Wilkins Travel	YSU985	Thomas Rhondda
V589DJC	Arriva Cymru	W714DAX	Glyn Williams	WTG902T	Thomas Rhondda	YTH317	Midway Motors
V590DJC	Arriva Cymru	W868AAY	I B T	WTH957T	K M P	YYE273T	Shuttle
V591DJC	Arriva Cymru	W875UWO	Shamrock	WTN647H	Edwards Coaches		

SBN 1 897990 67 7

© Published by *British Bus Publishing* Ltd   Telephone 01952 255669 - Fax:- 01952 222397
The Vyne, 16 St Margarets Drive, Wellington, Telford, Shropshire, TF1 3PH
www.britishbuspublishing.co.uk